CONAMARA
CHRONICLES
TALES FROM IORRAS AITHNEACH

IRISH CULTURE, MEMORY, PLACE
Oona Frawley, Ray Cashman, Guy Beiner, *editors*

CONAMARA CHRONICLES
TALES FROM IORRAS AITHNEACH

Compiled by Seán Mac Giollarnáth

—ɯ—

Translated by
Liam Mac Con Iomaire and
Tim Robinson

INDIANA UNIVERSITY PRESS

This book is a publication of

Indiana University Press
Office of Scholarly Publishing
Herman B Wells Library 350
1320 East 10th Street
Bloomington, Indiana 47405 USA

iupress.org

Originally Published in Gaelic as Annála Beaga ó Iorrus Aithneach © 1941 Seán Mac Giollarnáth

English Translation © 2022 Indiana University Press

Manufactured in the United States of America

First printing 2022

Cataloging information is available from the Library of Congress.

ISBN 978-0-253-06351-9 (hardback)
ISBN 978-0-253-06352-6 (paperback)
ISBN 978-0-253-06353-3 (ebook)

Annála Beaga ó Iorrus Aithneach
Seán Mac Giollarnáth do bhailigh
Oifig an tSoláthair
Baile Átha Cliath
1941

In memory of:
Liam Mac Con Iomaire (1937–2019)
Máiréad Robinson (1935–2020)
Tim Robinson (1935–2020)

CONTENTS

A PERSONAL NOTE
Tim Robinson

WHERE MIGHT ONE GLIMPSE SUCH a person as Myles of the Bees, who would chase a bee for a mile over bog and rocky hillside to find out its nest, or walk from his home on the coast to a remote mountain village in a similar search for sweetness, "looking for a kiss from a young woman"? Where might one hear the howls of English soldiers tricked into landing on an offshore island and left to die there by the outlawed priest they had just arrested? Or lend a hand to a fisherman's wife walking home from Galway, a hard and hilly fifty miles, with the makings of a pair of oars, a boat's sail, and its rigging tied on her back, all in a day? Or hear the desolate croak of the raven whose eggs had been stolen, hard-boiled, and replaced, and in whose nest was found "the stone of all gifts"? These beings' sole existence in the 1930s, say, was in the fireside and turf bank talk of Iorras Aithneach, an Irish-speaking peninsula of south Connemara, and their persistence down to our own days is largely due to an amateur but gifted inquirer, Justice Seán Forde, who took down their stories from the best local *seanchaithe* or bearers of old lore. Seán Mac Giollarnáth, to give him his folkloric name, was wise enough not to try to improve or correct his sources' Irish, but recorded it in all its countryside pungency and directness. When I was making my map of

Figure 1 Seán Mac Giollarnáth (1880–1970) and Sgeolán. © Bailiúchán Mhic Giollarnáth / Ford Family Collection.

Connemara in the 1990s, and later in the writing of *Connemara: A Little Gaelic Kingdom*, I found his book *Annála Beaga ó Iorras Aithneach* such a trove of placelore that I vowed to repay my debt to it by republication, translation, and annotation. The one failing of the original is due to the fact that Mac Giollarnáth did most of his research in the bar of Mongan's Hotel in Carna, so that the location of the score of little coves, rocks, and hillocks named in it were not recorded. However, when I was exploring the area in detail, I inquired out most of them and can add that extra dimension to the matter through maps and notes.

So, here at last is the fulfilment of that promise, made possible by the labors of Liam Mac Con Iomaire, who prepared an Irish version of the original in modernized spelling, taking care to preserve the dialectal tang of Connemara Irish, which he had listened to from his zeroth birthday as it were. Then he undertook an English version, which we kicked to and fro between the two of us until it seemed to us as close to the original text as the impossible art of translation allows. We dedicate the result to the Irish talkers of Connemara. May their voices never be silenced.

But what manner of man was this predecessor whose footprints I found waiting for me in the bogs of Connemara? A vague, thrown away observation of some village historian tells us that Justice Forde had been known to impose a just fine on a brewer of poitín or netter of salmon, and then, knowing that the like of such money was not to be had in the cottages, pay the fine himself. I feel I can trust this man as a sure-footed guide on quaggy bog and razor-edged granite. He is for me a figure of justice, even of Justice with a capital J.

TR

ACKNOWLEDGMENTS

THE TRANSLATORS WISH TO GRATEFULLY acknowledge the assistance of the following:

Barbara Mhic Con Iomaire; M.; Máirín Nic Con Iomaire & Dónall Ó Braonáin; John Drever; Jennika Baines, Lesley Bolton and all at Indiana University Press; Pete Feely and team, Amnet Systems; Seosamh Ó Murchú, Eagarthóir Sinsearach, An Gúm, Foras na Gaeilge; Jonny Dillon, Cnuasach Bhéaloideas Éireann/National Folklore Collection, UCD; Aisling Keane, James Hardiman Library, NUI Galway; Nessa Cronin, Centre for Irish Studies, NUI Galway; Seathrún Ó Tuairisg, Acadamh na hOllscolaíochta Gaeilge, NUI Galway; Nuala Ford and muintir Mhic Giollarnáth, Galway; Seán Ó Mainnín Photography, An Cheathrú Rua.

NOMENCLATURE

PROPER NAMES

Significant variation can arise in certain proper names and sur-names. Within the translated text, the spelling of proper names has generally been normalized in line with the orthographical conventions of *An Caighdeán Oifigiúil* (2017), the official stan-dard for writing in Irish, e.g., Diarmuid > Diarmaid; Mícheál > Micheál; Pilip > Pilib; Séamus > Séamas; Maoilre > Maolra; Marcus > Marcas; Nápla > Nábla. Bairtle has been normalized as Beairtle. Pádhraic and Pádraigín have been normalized as Pád-raic and Pádraicín respectively. In general, historical orthography has been used in surnames such as Mac Donnchadha, Ó Dom-hnaill, Ó Donnchadha, Ó Flaithearta, Ó Geannáin, Ó Laidhe. The following normalizations have also been implemented: Ó Curraidhin > Ó Curraoin; Grialais > Griallais; Mac Con Ríogh/Raoi > Mac Con Rí; Ó Ní > Ó Nia. The surnames Ó Conaola/Ó Conghaile have been rendered as Conneely.

PLACENAMES

Placenames in Iorras Aithneach and elsewhere within the Gaeltacht are generally given in Irish. Conamara refers to traditionally Irish-speaking areas in Connemara. Established English language versions of placenames are capitalized and given in parentheses following the Irish language version. Generic English language glosses of Irish placenames are not capitalized. A number of these placenames have well-established English forms and are also used in the text, for example, An Cheathrú Rua ~ Carraroe; Garmna ~ Gorumna Island. Further information regarding the history and usage of placenames within the text can be found in Gazetteer, which accompanied Tim Robinson's map of Connemara (1990).

READING THIS VOLUME

NUMBERS IN THE TEXT, AS given below, and given in parentheses [e.g., (3)], at the beginning of thematic segments refer to the originator of the lore, as told to Seán Mac Giollarnáth. This reference methodology was used by Seán Mac Giollarnáth in other publications and is preserved here. Meet the Storytellers provides further information on the individuals below.

1. Micheál Mac Donnchadha, Roisín na Mainiach, Carna
2. Pádraic Mac Donnchadha (Liam), An Coillín, Carna
3. Pádraic Mac Con Iomaire, An Coillín, Carna
4. Seosamh Mac Donnchadha, An Aird Thiar, Carna
5. Parthalán Ó Guairim, Leitreach Ard, Carna
6. Séamas Ó Conghaile, An Aird, Carna
7. Pádraic Ó Clochartaigh, Baile na Cille, Gorumna Island
8. Parthalán Mac Donnchadha, An Aird Thiar, Carna
9. Seán Ó Briain, Loch Conaortha, Cill Chiaráin
10. Tomás Mac Con Iomaire, An Coillín, Carna
11. Seosamh Ó Mongáin, TD, Carna
12. Seán Mac Con Rí, Leitir Daimh, Roundstone
13. Máire Ní Dhomhnaill, Caladh an Chnoic, Carna

14. Tomás Ó Máille, Coill Mhíolcon
15. Liam Bairéad, An Coillín, Carna
16. Mártan Ó Málóid, County Councillor, Carna
17. Pádraic Mac Donnchadha (Éamoinn), An Aird, Carna
18. Isaac Ó Conaire, Seantalamh, Galway

CONAMARA CHRONICLES
TALES FROM IORRAS AITHNEACH

—ww—

PROLOGUE

Space, Time & Connemara

TIM ROBINSON

CONNEMARA—THE NAME DRIFTS ACROSS the mind like
cloud shadows on a mountainside, or expands and fades like cir-
cles on a lake after a trout has risen. Fittingly, there is no official
boundary to the land under the spell of this name. It is also true
that real landscapes, unlike painted ones, contain their frames,
so that each is potentially world-embracing. But such a name as
this cannot be left to dissipate its powers of evocation like a scent
unstoppered; the topographer, rather, should delight in its spar-
ing, subtle, and elusive application.

On the one hand, a modern and commercializing tendency is
to call everything west of Galway, Connemara. But the territory
so defined is best called, in modern Irish, Iar-Chonnacht, for it
is that described, with the bitter exactitude of regret, by Roderic
O'Flaherty's *West or H-Iar Connaught*, written in 1684, not long
after his clan had been dispossessed by the Cromwellians.[1] His
book traces its bounds from Lough Corrib to Slyne Head to Killary
Harbor (and embraces the Aran Islands "as in a sea-parenthesis,"
to borrow his pleasing phrase). On this classic definition, Iar-
Chonnacht includes Connemara, but exceeds it eastwards.

On the other hand, the territory of the O'Flahertys' early medieval predecessors the Conmaicne Mara (which is the historical

1

kernel of Connemara, both place and name) is too restrictive, for it lay west of the Mám Tuirc watershed and the Inbhear Mór, the "big rivermouth" near Ros Muc, and so did not contain the full essence of Connemara, a prime ingredient of which is given by the Irish-speaking granite-and-waterlands further east and south. This last area, though, is culturally continuous with Cois Fharraige, further east again, and aspires to unity of social action with it under the name of Conamara Theas or South Connemara. *Ó Bhearna go Carna*, from Bearna to Carna, is the phrase favored by Gaeilgeoirí to delimit this linguistic homeland—but most Bearna people would direct you back westwards if you enquired for Connemara there, being close enough to Galway city to share its sense of Connemara as wilderness and westernness itself.

The problem, then, is exemplary, and insoluble. Place flows into place, or holds rigidly distinct from it, according to one's mode of thought. My mode, to declare it at the outset, is that of the dis- criminating earth-worshipper. For me, Connemara, is the land that looks upon the Twelve Bens, that close-knit, mandala-like mountain range, as its stubborn and reclusive heart.

Connemara has had a degree of independent existence for about 460 million years, according to recent theories. Before that time the landmasses and ocean basins, carried on the slowly drifting plates that constitute the earth's surface, lay in configurations quite different from today's. The Atlantic did not yet exist, and an ocean the geologists call Japetus separated two continents, one comprising what was to become North America and the north- west fringe of Europe, and the other, the rest of Europe. The future Ireland was as yet in two pieces, half of it on the north side of the Japetus ocean basin, and the other half on the south. What one might call proto-Connemara lay on the coast of the northern half, two hundred miles or more west of what is now Donegal. Its rocks had largely been laid down as sediments of various sorts two hun- dred to one hundred million years earlier in the Dalradian (Later Cambrian) period, during the birth of Japetus; subsequently a three-mile-thick layer of the basic rock, gabbro, coming up molten from deep in the earth's mantle, had been forced between its strata. As the two continents now moved towards each other, squeezing Japetus out of geography, the rim of the northern one was crumpled into long ridges, the eroded remains of which are today's "Caledonide" mountains, that is, those of Norway, Scotland, the north of Ireland, Newfoundland, and Appalachia. In this upheaval proto-Connemara's rocks were repeatedly folded, faulted, and thrust to and fro, until it became completely detached and was driven eastwards by the oblique collision of the two landmasses. As the two halves of Ireland were finally rammed together, proto-Connemara was slid southwards over volcanic rocks of the southern shore of Japetus, and welded into its present position.

By then Connemara's rocks had been kneaded and baked to various degrees. A thick sandstone layer, pinched inside a complex fold running east-west across the region, was recrystallized into a quartzite of great hardness; clayey materials that ended up on the outside of the fold were metamorphosed into less resistant schists, while strata of ancient limestone were transformed into marble. Erosive eons later, the quartzite stands high, giving us the silvery, glittering peaks of the Twelve Bens and the Mám Tuirc mountains; the softer schists have been worked down to form the lowlands south of the mountains, the narrower transverse valleys north of them, and the broad corridor of the Inagh valley separating the two massifs. Connemara's famous green marble crops out here and there along the southern flank of the mountain ranges. The dark-toned hills of Cashel and Errisbeg to the south, Dúchruach and Currywongaun to the north, are forged out of the contorted layer of gabbro. In the final stages of the collision, four hundred million years ago, several great domes of molten granite were intruded from below; when exposed by erosion of the rocks above them, they proved vulnerable to weathering and now form the knobbly, sea-invaded plain of south Connemara and low-lying islands such as Omey on the west coast. In one small area known to geologists as the Delaney Dome, northwest of Errisbeg, all the original substance of Connemara has been worn away so that the underlying floor appears as through a hole in a carpet, and one can stand on rock that formed the land south of Japetus.

A few great fault lines roughly delineate the Connemara of this essay. An east-west trending fault lies offshore to the south, blanketed by the carboniferous limestone from which the Aran Islands and the Burren have been carved. To the north, the mountains of Connemara are separated from those of Mayo by the dramatic fiord of Killary Harbor, excavated by glaciers in the recent Ice Ages out of a zone of sedimentary rocks weakened by another fault. The Maam Valley, to the northeast, has been similarly enlarged by fault-guided erosion. Finally a less obvious feature, the Shannawona fault, running from near Scríb southwards across the granite regions, may explain the striking difference between Cois Fharraige to the east, with its uplands descending in orderly slopes to a straight seacoast, and the fantastic filigree of peninsula and inlets west of Ros an Mhíl; the latter region has been downthrown by over a mile relative to the former, and the more fractured upper levels of the granite brought within the erosive influence of the sea, in which they now lie half drowned.

During the last Ice Age, the snow, piling up on the shadowed lee side of the mountain peaks, congealed into glaciers; inching downhill, plucking stone out of the slopes behind them, and so excavating corries, these glaciers contributed themselves and their load of rock to a sea of ice grinding outwards over the lowlands and stripping them of their covering soils. When the ice finally melted back, from fifteen thousand to ten thousand years ago, a raw landscape was revealed of polished rock strewn with countless smooth-worn stones of all sizes. The south is particularly burdened with huge boulders, some of which are individually named landmarks today, one of the largest being forty feet high. In certain areas just south of the mountains, and further west, the glacial debris was molded by the ice flow into the streamlined mounds called drumlins; these now stand out on the brown levels of the bogs as isolated, grass-green hills, or on the western shores as islets and promontories with cliffs of boulder-studded clay.

In due course a tundra growth of least willow, soon followed by dwarf birch and crowberry heath, crept forth across this wasteland, to be followed as times mellowed by woods of birch and hazel, and then great forests of oak and pine. It seems to have been human agencies—fire and the stone axe—that put an end to these woodlands, around 2500–2200 BC, perhaps in conjunction with a deterioration in the climate. Heathers, sedges, bog asphodel, and sphagnum moss flourished, forming a blanket bog that spread and deepened, creeping down from the exposed hillsides, seeping out from waterlogged hollows, drowning the forest, pickling its roots and fallen trunks in bog water. Now, when the accumulated layers of peat are cut away for fuel, ghostly grey armies of tree stumps come to light.

For how many tides have Connemara folk gathered shellfish on the strand? It may be that some of the scattered heaps of whelk, limpet, and oyster shells, laid bare where dunes are eroding, date like similar shell middens in the Dingle peninsula from the Middle Stone Age, 6,500 years or more ago. These first stranders would also have gathered nuts and berries in the forest margins, and stalked the network of rivers and lakes after wildfowl and fish. (Their stone implements have been found at Oughterard, but not so far in Connemara proper.) It may have been another five hundred years before settled farming began. In one place that "Neolithic Revolution" has been dated with astonishing precision, thanks to the fact that Connemara's mildly acidic lake sediments and peat bogs preserve any pollen incorporated in them and so keep a diary of changes in the flora of the vicinity. A core was taken out of the bed of a little lake in Sheeauns near Cleggan in 1987, and the organic residues at various levels in it dated by the radiocarbon method. By analysis of its pollen content, the following sequence of events was reconstructed. Unbroken forest of oak and hazel surrounded the lake until about 4100 BC, when small clearings were made in which wheat was sown and weeds such as plantains sprang up. A hundred years later, this forest lost its few elms; in fact, the elm was in decline all over Europe at that time, perhaps because of a fungal epidemic like today's Dutch Elm Disease, spread by growing human traffic. At a level in the core corresponding to shortly after this elm decline of 4000 BC, tree pollens are largely replaced by those of grasses and meadow flowers; the forest had been almost totally removed and tillage superseded by cattle ranching. Finally, in about 3800 BC, the lake was deserted, and forest returned. Whether agriculture continued elsewhere nearby, having merely shifted its location, is unknown, but it seems that the shores of Lough Sheeauns lay in wilderness until the end of the Bronze Age, almost two thousand years later.

These pioneer farmers thought much about death. Successive (or perhaps contemporaneous) groups of them disagreed on the matter and set their differences down (illegibly, alas, to us) in the various styles of communal tombs, built of weighty rock slabs, that are their lasting memorials. About thirty of these megalithic tombs are known from Connemara; twenty-one of these have been identified only in the last few years, along with a spate of other discoveries that have totally undone the received idea that the region is archaeologically a virtual desert. These lapidary but opaque statements in their ruin still cause dissension. I have seen seminars of archaeologists arguing fiercely among such heaps of tumbled stones, like would-be heirs over a garbled will. An established school of thought has evolved a fourfold classification of these monuments into passage tombs, court tombs, portal tombs, and wedge tombs. The first type, best known from the stupendous round tumuli of the Boyne Valley, does not occur in Connemara. In the others, the roofed chamber or chambers in which the burials and grave goods were placed constitute a roughly rectangular gallery, covered by an elongated cairn, which is usually now much reduced. Court tombs have an open, crescentic forecourt defined by upright stones at one end of this cairn, presumably for ritual purposes. In the closely related portal tombs, the chamber is roofed by an often gigantic capstone, poised on two tall, jamb-like pillar stones in front and a smaller stone behind. Wedge tombs are so called because their lintel-roofed galleries are lower and narrower at the rear than at the front, which usually faces west. Each of the four types has its own distribution pattern, its cultural affinities and presumed origins in the wider megalithic scene of western Europe, and its allotted hour in a hypothetical account of the evolution of the Irish Neolithic. A residue of the incomprehensibly dilapidated or unaccountably odd is relegated to a non-category of "unclassified megalithic tombs." But here in Connemara, the rebellious younger archaeologists point out, court, portal, and wedge tombs crop up apparently ecumenically, while over a third of the total, including some impressive and moderately well-preserved examples, are numbered among the despised and neglected unclassifiables.[2] So these discoveries are further backing for those crying "Down with the fourfold theory! Let us have a new Neolithic, of which the cornerstones will be those rejected by our elders." It is likely that this emergent theory will assign a much earlier date to the wedge tombs than their present niche at the very end of the Neolithic and will emphasize regional and independent developments in tomb style.

Nearly all these tombs lie close to the long sea inlets of Omey and Ballynakill parishes; this northwestern area, with its comparatively widespread marble outcrops and glacial deposits, was then as it is now the most fertile and prosperous quarter of Connemara. And the distribution of monuments presumed to date from the Bronze Age—mainly standing stones, single, in pairs, or in alignments of up to six—is very similar. The impressive alignment on the crest of drumlin near Renvyle has long been known, and sufficient finds have been made recently to establish north-west Connemara as comparable with southwest Munster and mid-Ulster, the principal foci of the distribution of such monuments. Elsewhere in Connemara the most striking example is an alignment of six small boulders on the ridge of a moraine in Gleann Eidhneach, which I came across in 1986. Several of these new sites have been revealed by turf cuttings; and to see the pair of milk-white quartz boulders newly exposed in the black trench of a turf bank on a hilltop in Crocknaraw, north of Clifden, and to realize that at least half a dozen other standing stones and several other megaliths are or were visible from that point, is to be given a glimpse of a cultural landscape the meaning of which has been lost beneath the bogs.

In many parts of Ireland, the most typical monuments of the pagan Iron Age and Early Christian periods, the so-called "ring forts," are very numerous; but in Connemara they are strangely rare. The three drystone cashels and two earth-banked raths of north Connemara, the two earthen promontory forts on peninsulas of the west coast and the fragmentary stone ones in Inishbofin, probably represent Iron-Age militarism. The twenty or more crannógs or lake dwellings that have been identified with some certainty in the western and southern lowlands of Connemara may be the local equivalent of small ring forts, the circular stock-yards around the isolated huts of Iron Age or Early Christian farmers. Perhaps the growth of bog, overwhelming the hillside pastures, forced the evolution of a lake culture, or of unenclosed shoreline settlements now marked only by great shell middens. Certainly Connemara was far from deserted at this period, which pollen records from various sites show to have been a time of increase in cereal crops and their weeds.

However, it seems that the pattern of a populated coastal fringe and an empty interior, which largely obtains today, was established by the early Middle Ages. Connemara's radiating peninsulas and its islets broadcast in the ocean must have answered to the misanthropy of the sixth century, when every hermit wanted a desert to himself. Some of the many religious sites on the rim of Connemara are named from figures who seem at home in pure legend, like the fisherman's saint, Mac Dara, also known as Síothnach, a name that perhaps associates him with squalls of wind, as do several folktales told of his powers. Other foundations are attributed to personages who appear convincingly in history, such as St. Colman, who retired to Inishbofin after losing the argument between the Irish and the Roman Church over the true date of Easter at the Synod of Whitby in AD 665 (thus initiating the sequence of Celtic causes in retreat to Connemara, which continues to the present day, and of which he should be the patron saint).

The roofless late medieval chapel and ancient graveyard, still in use, that mark the location of St. Colman's monastery are idyllically sited in a valley mouth on the sheltered side of Inishbofin, between a reed-fringed lake and a sandy beach. St. Mac Dara's islet, on the other hand, is of elemental simplicity, a low dome of bare granite on which a tiny stone-roofed oratory, the structure of which imitates that of primitive cruck-built wooden chapels, sits as sedately as a winkle on a rock. For the celebrations of the saint's day, July 16, the fishing boats of the nearest harbors of south Connemara bring hundreds of people to his island, but for the rest of the year its wind-polished silence and mica-glinting emptiness are perfect luxury to the ascetic soul. But the sea sanctuary best suited to more turbulent spirits is that of High Island, two miles out into the Atlantic from the west coast of Connemara. It is only accessible on calm days when a boat can edge into a narrow cove at a point where its tall cliffs are climbable, and an Early Christian cross slab rises from the wind-trimmed sward above. The remains of a little chapel and the monks' corbelled stone huts cluster within a slight cashel wall at the farther, western end of the island, as if to get full penitential advantage of storm-driven spray. The foundation is attributed to St. Feichín, also associated with Cong and Omey Island, who is said to have died in AD 664. Formerly, the island belonged to Richard Murphy, who wrote some of his best poems out of his occasional days of retreat there.

Not long after the era of the saints, the Conmaicne Mara appear out of the shadows of prehistory as the secular rulers of the region. The Conmaicne were a people who claimed descent from Conmac, a son of the legendary Fergus Macraoi and Queen Maeve; the branch of them who lived west of the Corrib were known as the Conmaicne Mara, the Conmaicne of the sea, to distinguish them from their cousins further east. The Ó Cadhlas were their leaders; the *Annals of Inishfallen* mention a Murtagh Ó Cadhla, chief of the Conmaicne Mara, among those who fell fighting the Norsemen at Clontarf in 1014. Later they were reduced to historical footnotes by the coming of the O'Flahertys, but their name (anglicized as Keeley) still occurs in Connemara.[3]

The O'Flahertys, a powerful clan who had produced several kings of the province of Connacht in the seventh century, held the rich limestone plains east of Lough Corrib until the thirteenth century, when the de Burgos, the first of the Normans to move so far west, gradually forced them to retire to Connemara. With the O'Flahertys came dependent clans whose names occur in local history: the O'Hallorans, the O'Lees, the Duanes. The Joyces, a Welsh-Norman family, settled in what became known as the Joyce Country, around the Maam Valley, under the O'Flahertys' protection. By the sixteenth century the O'Flahertys were building tower houses on the Norman model, from which, if the oral traditions be true, they tyrannized over humbler folk. The main stronghold of the eastern branch of the O'Flahertys was at Augh-nanure near Oughterard. The western branch had castles spread out around the coastline, at Ard (near Carna), Bunowen, Doon (near Streamstown), and Renvyle, and inland at Ballynahinch on a former crannóg. Small communities of Carmelites and Dominicans were established by the O'Flahertys near this last-mentioned center of power, from which, under the Elizabethan dispensation, the old Conmaicne Mara was renamed as the barony of Ballynahinch. Mere vestiges of the Ard, Bunowen, and Doon castles survive, while the lake tower at Ballynahinch has been much altered by subsequent owners to serve variously as a prison, a brewhouse, and a picnic bower. Thus the best preserved of the Connemara tower houses is now Renvyle, which has been nearly cross-sectioned by collapse, revealing its simple structure of three square, vaulted rooms one above the other, linked by spiral stairs in a corner.[4]

The O'Flaherty chiefs ruled Connemara according to the ancient Brehon Law until Elizabeth's wily soldier-statesmen, who rarely ventured into the region, divided and seduced them. In 1585 they accepted the agreement known as the Composition of Connacht, abrogating their Gaelic rights and enregistering themselves in the feudal hierarchy. Thenceforth they were hereditary landlords rather than the elective custodians of clan territory, and the chief the Crown wished to see as head of all could call himself Sir Murrough O'Flaherty. Nevertheless to the notables of the growing merchant city of Galway, the O'Flahertys were still the atavistic lords of a hinterland rank with rebellion, smuggling, and piracy. It took the fierce political and religious crosscurrents induced in Ireland by England's Civil War to bring Galway's citizens and the O'Flahertys together even momentarily; that was in 1642 when Galway opted for the Catholic Confederation, then campaigning in the name of the King, and called in the O'Flahertys' hordes of "wild Irish" to help besiege the nearby English fort, which was manned by supporters of Parliament. But King Charles lost the war and his head, and Cromwell came to purge Ireland of its rebelliousness. By July of 1651, one of his generals was encamped before the city of Galway and his ships were in the bay. Iar-Chonnacht, and especially Inishbofin, then became crucial to the Confederation's hopes of reinforcement from the continent. A small force of mercenaries sent by the Duke of Lorraine landed in Inishbofin in October with arms for Galway, but the city had to surrender, together with the Aran Islands, by April 1652. Towards the end of that year, the Aran Islands were recaptured by a force of six or seven hundred men from Iar-Chonnacht and Inishbofin, but the Cromwellians moved several men-of-war and nineteen hundred foot soldiers, first against Aran and then against Inishbofin, which ended its forlorn resistance in February 1653.[5]

A few years later the Commonwealth Council ordered the building of a fort in Inishbofin and started to use the island as a prison camp for Catholic priests, as an alternative to transporting them to the West Indies. The priests languished there (half-starved, on an allowance of twopence a day, according to a contemporary source) until well after the restoration of Charles II in 1660. After about 1680, the fort was abandoned. It was regarrisoned by the Jacobites in the War of the Two Kings ten years later, but since then its history has been merely one of stealthy dilapidation. The cut limestone surrounds of its arches and windows have all been burnt for lime, but its curtain walls and the diamond-shaped bastions at each of its four corners still stand, in picturesque raggedness. Visitors sailing into Inishbofin pass under its dark gaze at the narrow harbor mouth, where it sprawls upon a low cliff with a menacing, crablike presence.

In the years following the victory of Cromwell's army, the old clan system was finally broken up, and it is said that Connemara was almost depopulated by famine, plague, and massacre.[6] One of the O'Flaherty chiefs who had joined the Galway citizens in 1642, Colonel Edmond, of Renvyle, was wanted for murders committed in the course of a plundering expedition he and his men had undertaken as a relief from the tedium of besieging the English fort. A band of troopers was dispatched to Renvyle to find him and was eventually led by the clamoring of ravens to a small cave in a dark wood, whence they dragged the colonel and his wife, "and truly who had seen them would have said they had rayther been ghosts than men, for pitifully looked they, pyned away from want of foode, and altogether ghastly with feare."[7] Colonel Edmond was hanged, and the other O'Flahertys expropriated as "forfeiting traitors" for their part in the rebellion. Soon Connemara was being carved up for distribution among Protestants to whom the Cromwellians had obligations and Catholics who had been dispossessed of estates elsewhere and transplanted westwards.

The main Protestant beneficiaries of England's reformation of Connemara were a Sir Thomas Merridith, one of Cromwell's commissioners, who acquired townlands here and there, including Ballynahinch, and soon cashed them in, and Trinity College, Dublin, who remained as landlords of much of the Inagh and Maam Valley areas until the end of the last century. Catholic transplanters included the Earl of Westmeath, who was given the Renvyle area but later regained his former lands and sold Renvyle to a branch of the Blakes of Galway, and the Geoghegans of Westmeath, who stayed on as landlords of Ballindoon parish until ruined by the Famine. Several of the eminent Catholic merchant families known as the "The Tribes of Galway" were granted tracts of wilderness in place of their Galway estates; the D'Arcys found themselves with the peninsulas of Omey parish and the glens of Kylemore, while the Blakes, Frenches, and Lynches shared the granite of south Connemara with the Martins, who also acquired Cleggan. Most of these grantees managed to avoid actually having to come to Connemara, and some regained parts of their old estates after the restoration of Charles II. The Martins, in the person of "Nimble Dick" the lawyer, actually put together the largest estate in the kingdom and held on to it through the Williamite period despite their Catholicism, virtually succeeding the O'Flahertys as masters of Connemara.[8]

Nimble Dick's great-grandson Richard (known as "Hairtrigger Dick" from his many duels) from time to time found it convenient to retire from cosmopolitan prodigality into the fastnesses of Connemara, where no bailiff dared pursue him. His father had made a modest house out of an inn he owned on the bridle path by the lake at Ballynahinch, and from the 1790s this became the court of a mysterious kingdom, reports of which irritated the authorities and entranced the romantic. Its endlessly devious southern coastline by nature took the part of the innumerable local smugglers against the revenue cutter, and the Martins were known to entertain with the finest of wines and brandies. Its craggy glens sheltered bands of outlaws who had fled there from the yeomanry's vengeance upon Mayo after the French-led rebellion of 1798; among those with a price on their heads was the notorious Father Myles Prendergast, whose secret ministrations to his Catholic flock were winked at by the Martins for years, although they themselves, like most landowning families, were now Protestant. Richard's tenantry would march into Galway to vote for him in its famously turbulent elections; their number was greatly augmented by the refugees from anti-Catholic pogroms in Antrim that he welcomed onto his estates in 1796. After the Act of Union in 1801, he was Galway's representative at Westminster, where he won another nickname, Humanity Dick, for his bill against cruelty to animals; at home, tenants who beat their donkeys could find themselves imprisoned in the old tower house on the lake isle of Ballynahinch. It is said that when his friend the Prince Regent boasted of the avenue at Windsor, Martin retorted that this own avenue was fifty miles long, being the road from Galway.

But his two hundred thousand acres were too poverty-stricken to fuel Humanity Dick's spacious capacity for life, and by the time he died, hiding in Boulogne from his creditors, the estate was heavily in debt. His son Thomas, known as the King of Connemara, resided more continuously at what was now called Ballynahinch Castle and tried to salvage the family fortunes through a copper mine on High Island, marble quarries in the southern foothills of the Twelve Bens, and kelp burning on the seaweed-rich shoreline. Contemporary accounts portray him as a benevolent and beloved despot, but local oral history retains less fond memories of him.[9] Maria Edgeworth was one of the visitors drawn to Connemara by the Martin legend, and in 1833 she met at Ballynahinch his daughter Mary, "one of the most extraordinary persons I ever saw."[10] This elegant and self-possessed young lady, who reminded Edgeworth of a Leonardo portrait, was prodigiously well-read in half a dozen languages ancient and modern: "Do think of a girl of seventeen, in the wilds of Connemara, intimately acquainted with the beauties of Aeschylus and Euripides, and having them as part of her daily thoughts." Indeed Miss Martin seems to have been all the imagination could require, as the Miranda of these poetic and yet slightly comic realms. She had studied engineering (at the age of thirteen or fourteen!) with the great Alexander Nimmo, then engaged in laying out the roads of Connemara, while from a former Napoleonic officer in exile at Ballynahinch she had acquired a knowledge of fortification, a passionate Bonapartism, and a barracks-room turn to her French. While showing the Edgeworth party the marble quarries, she was attended by a spontaneous aggregation of rustics, which she referred to as her "tail"; when the visitors commented on her ability to communicate with these people, she calmly replied, *"Je sais mon métier de reine."* A rather sugary version of this engaging heroine figures in Charles Lever's novel *The Martins of Cro'Martin*; a more bitter memory of her was handed down by the local people whom, it is claimed, she forbade to use the ancient burial ground near the Castle because their noisy lamentations disturbed her. The pathetic fate of the Princess of Connemara will be mentioned below.

In the early years of the nineteenth century, the idea that Connemara could be civilized and made profitable persuaded others of the old Galway families to come and live on their estates. In about 1814, John D'Arcy projected a market town and harbor at a spot called An Clochán, the stepping-stones, by the principal river mouth of the western shore, and began by building himself a Gothic castle and a grotto. Between 1822, when the government engineer Alexander Nimmo undertook both the harbor and the road from Galway to the new town, and D'Arcy's death in 1839, a Protestant and a Catholic church, 185 dwellings, most of them three-storied, two hotels, three schools, a police barracks, court-house, jail, distillery, and twenty-three public houses had accrued to its basic triangle of wide, unpaved streets. The population had grown to eleven hundred, and An Clochán had been "fashion-ably anglicized" as Clifden.[11] Merchant vessels were bringing in a wide range of necessities never felt as such before; corn, fish, kelp, and marble were being shipped out, and this place formerly "only remarkable for smuggling and illicit distillation" was now yield-ing considerable excise duties.[12] Daniel O'Connell's "Monster Meeting" at Clifden in 1843, when he spoke on Repeal of the Act of Union to a crowd said to number one hundred thousand, may be taken as marking the coming-of-age of the capital Connemara had so long lacked.

While D'Arcy was beginning this transformation of his estate, the Blakes similarly were interesting themselves in something more than the rents of Renvyle, of which they had been absentee landlords since 1680. The O'Flahertys, former lords of the land, having hung on as middlemen there for generations, found them-selves dismissed into still deeper obscurity when Henry Blake was inspired by the potentialities of a newly discovered slate bed nearby to take over their long thatched cabin, give it a slate roof, and install his family in residence. Like most formerly Catholic landowners the Blakes had by then adopted Protestantism and the ideology of progress. The family's *Letters from the Irish High-lands*, published anonymously in 1825, are full of concern for the welfare of their periodically starving tenantry and evince some interest in their culture; nevertheless the little Catholic chapel the O'Flahertys had built near the house was self-evidently ob-jectionable and had to be removed. (In one of the letters describ-ing the ensuing rumpus, Henry Blake states that it was within a hundred yards of the house, whereas in fact it was four hundred yards away; the uncharacteristic inaccuracy perhaps betrays an uneasy conscience about the matter.) Another branch of the Blakes of Galway had moved out onto their estates in southeast Connemara by this period and became the Blakes of Tully. Enlightened travelers on the coast road from Galway would notice a change in the landscape as they approached "the seat of Mr. Blake, whose improvements and clearances give an agreeable repose to the eye, wearied with the interminable succession of rock, boulder stones, cabins and loose stone enclosures."[13] The obverse of such commendations is the ogreish role these Blakes play in local folklore, as the best hated of all evictors and rack-renters.

Alexander Nimmo, having provided Connemara with a rational road network and planned the piers that were started at Leenaun, Cleggan, Roundstone, and other points as relief work during the "distress" of 1822, was himself nursing a private project during this optimistic period. At Roundstone, he states in his Coast Survey of 1836, "as the tenant of the farm on which this pier is situated was very clamorous for damages alleged to be sustained by him during the progress of the work, I ventured at my own expense to purchase up his interest in the lease, as the most likely way to settle his claim; I now hold it by lease under Mr. Thomas Martin, and expect soon to have a tolerable fishing village; several people are already settled there, and I am building a store for the purposes of the fishery."[14]

The street Nimmo created there passes above the little cliff that forms the inner wall of his characteristically boldly conceived harbor, and then climbs a hill to admire the much-painted prospect of the Twelve Bens across Roundstone Bay; we owe to him the handsomest of Connemara's villages, the decisiveness of its layout only superficially obscured by modern developments.

These crowded years of progress were tragically terminated by the Great Hunger of 1845–48, a natural disaster which a grossly malformed society could not mitigate. The peasant population of Connemara, much reduced by the want and pestilence of the 1650s, had been augmented by the Cromwellian resettlements and by refugees from Antrim in 1796 and Mayo in 1798. The biological rate of multiplication, upon this expanding base, was phenomenal. Population was rising generally in Europe throughout these two centuries, but in few places was the rise so steep as in the poorest parts of western Ireland. Even the periodic famines caused by dependence on one crop, the potato, liable to fail for various reasons, did not check the giddy compilation of short generations. The Connemara gentry, having long conformed to the Protestant church under the pressure of the penal laws that made it impossible for Catholics to pass on their estates undivided, were now almost as distinct in culture from their tenantry as were the Anglo-Irish elsewhere. The master of the Big House, being at once landlord, employer, Justice of the Peace, and fount of charity, was unchallengeable. His worthy upkeep was provided for by rents that absorbed all the output of his tenants' farming, fishing, kelp burning, and cottage industry, for happily the lower orders could live off their amazingly productive potato beds alone; their teeming marriage beds, on the other hand, threatened to overwhelm all estate-improvement schemes and had to be countered by eviction and assisted emigration. The shading and coloring lent by individual cases to the schematic figure of class relationships faded into insignificance when the potato blight struck. At that time, most Connemara people owned nothing (literally nothing, many of them; no cart or donkey, no boat or net, no chair, lamp or bed); when their sole foodstuff turned to black slime, they became paupers overnight. The limited capacities of the British government, civil service, and public to respond to, or even conceive of, the cumulative horrors of the next few years in Ireland were soon exhausted. By the autumn of 1847, in Connemara, the public roadworks upon which the stonebreaker could earn the price of a bowl of Indian meal had been closed down, overwhelmed by the crush of desperate applicants; the Clifden workhouse was bankrupt and had voided its hundreds of feverous skeletons to live or die in the open; ragged hordes were creeping into Galway to face the long nightmare of the Atlantic; what happened in the mountain valleys and the islands is recorded only by small boulders marking nameless graves.[15]

At this juncture it was revealed to the rector of Wonston in England that the Lord had chastised the Irish with a view to making them "come out from Rome," and that in Connemara in particular there was a potential winning of broken and contrite hearts not to be despised.[16] The Reverend Alexander Dallas set up his Irish Church Mission where he had the backing of the Protestant gentry; soup was provided for children attending his schools; some hungry souls "converted" and were damned for it by their parish priests; little colonies of outcasts grew up in the shadow of the rectories, and for three decades, until the venture lost conviction and faded away, the spiritual education of Connemara was the mutual abuse of bigots. One area in the northwest, Letterfrack, was for a time spared this and other post-Famine plagues through the work of a Quaker couple, James and Mary Ellis, who in 1848 were moved to settle there, to demonstrate by personal example how resident landowners could and should stand between their tenantry and the gales of misfortune. Neighboring gentry grumbled at their paying laborers eightpence rather than sixpence a day, but the Ellis's farm and its well-serviced estate village prospered while all Connemara was in decline. Sadly, after nine years of struggle, James's ill-health and the death of his wife led him to sell out to a supporter of Reverend Dallas and return to England.[17]

In secular matters too, Connemara's agony appeared as opportunity to some English eyes. The Poor Law Extension Act of 1847 had thriftily transferred the whole burden of famine relief onto the local rates, and such top-heavy estates as those of the Martins, the D'Arcys, and the O'Neills (as the Geoghegans had renamed themselves) had capsized as a result; the Encumbered

Estates Act of 1848 having removed certain legal obstacles, the creditors could now force on sales. The entail of the Martin estate had been broken by Thomas Martin in favor of his daughter, and when he was carried off (by a fever contracted in visiting his former tenants in Clifden workhouse), Mary and her newly wedded husband had fled the avalanche of debt, first to Belgium, and then to America, where she died in a New York hotel after a premature confinement on shipboard. The 192,000 acres of the Martins' former kingdom were put up for auction in 1849. The Bill of Sale stated that, since the drawing up of the list of tenants, "many changes advantageous to a Purchaser have taken place, and the same Tenants, by name and in number, will not now be found on the Lands"; but not even this sinister assurance was enough to attract bidders.[18] The mortgagees, the Law Life Assurance Society of London, then bought in the estate very cheaply and by rack-renting and evictions carried on the Famine's work until 1872, when they sold the lands, with a few small Mayo estates thrown in, for £230,000 to Richard Berridge, a London brewer.

The D'Arcy lands too had been mortgaged to English financiers, the Eyres of Bath, one of whom took over Clifden Castle as his summer residence when the estate fell into their hands. In 1862 the Blakes of Renvyle had to sell off the eastern half of their lands to the heir to a Manchester fortune, Mitchell Henry, who set about taming the wet mountain slopes and housing himself on a princely scale, employing hundreds on his model farm, extensive drainage schemes, and the elegant Gothic mansion of Kylemore Castle. Other new proprietors in the relatively encouraging northwestern quarter were residents and improvers too, and indeed it is as if an afterglow of the Ellis's Quaker sense of social responsibility has lingered there to this day.

But at the other extreme, in south Connemara, the granite itself was being stripped bare by the ever more desperate "winning" of turf for sale to Galway city and the turfless limestone areas south of Galway Bay. Here the poorest of Connemara's poor were still mercilessly harried by the Blakes of Tully and the agents of absentee landlords, including the Berridges themselves, whom the increasingly menacing words and deeds of a no longer acquiescent tenantry kept away from their new home at Ballynahinch. The Land League, originating in the equally miserable oppression of County Mayo, was beginning to organize resistance to evictions, and in the first days of 1881 a great hosting of tenants on the Kirwans' estate at An Cheathrú Rua drove off a server of eviction notices and his police escort. Although the Kirwans were still evicting there a decade later, such events as this "Battle of Carraroe" cumulatively extorted reductions in rent and improvements in security of tenure and forced upon the government a sense that the moral and economic resources of landlordism were inadequate to the needs of these shameful western backyards of the kingdom. In 1891 the Congested Districts Board was set up to further the development of regions that could not in their present state support their populations, and in Connemara it found everything to be done. Over the next thirty years harbors were improved, small fishing fleets subsidized into precarious existence, herring-curing stations built, lace-making schools opened, and, slowly but inexorably, the landlords bought out, the jumbled smallholdings on their estates rationalized, and the laborer given his own field to labor at last.

This history, for so much of its course a river of sorrows, has flowed through and at times almost swept away a singular culture—not that of the provincial gentry, but of the humble farmers and fisherfolk—a culture which conserved ancient words and ways and had its matted and tenacious roots in a sense, deeper than any economic or legal realities, of being in its own place. As the Irish language withdrew, throughout the century of famines and modernization, to its present lairs, principally in the south of the region, only a proportion of its oral lore was appropriated by English. But where Irish lives, that tradition is still so voluble in story, song, and placename that one wonders if Connemara's days and nights were longer formerly, to hear all that was said and sung in them of Connemara. Around the end of the last century, that peasant culture came to represent the true Ireland to one wing of the nationalist movement; through Patrick Pearse, who regularly returned to Ros Muc as to a well of inspiration, its values entered into the veins of the republic he declared and died for in 1916 and works in them obscurely still. Since Independence the Gaeltacht (the areas officially designated as Irish-speaking) has been treated with varying small degrees of positive discrimination by the governments of the day, and successive generations of the dedicated, through Raidió na Gaeltachta, local co-operatives, and other organizations, have insisted on Irish as a language of modern society and its arts. Despite compromises, defeats, and disappointments, despite even the numbing effect of continued emigration, the stony south is now socially more vigorous than any other part of Connemara, apart from the historically and geographically favored exception of Ballynakill in the northwest; the little turf harbor of Ros an Mhíl has become the county's major fishing port, and An Cheathrú Rua, with its industrial estates run by Údarás na Gaeltachta, the Gaeltacht Authority, has pulled itself together into a recognizable town.

Emigration, though, is the face in the windows of empty houses throughout Connemara. Youngsters go in search not only of work but the conviviality their depleted villages cannot provide. Grants from Údarás or the Industrial Development Authority help to plant occasional industrial projects in this generally unfavoring far-western ground; some survive and even flourish, while others disappear in a whiff of scandal. The traditional livelihoods of fishing and farming are still basic to Connemara. Many households, whether most of their income is from fishing or bed-and-breakfast or a factory, have a few young cattle in a few rushy fields, which they will sell on as two-year-olds to be fattened in the midlands' lusher pastures. Like cattle, sheep attract "headage" grants; the shepherds drive their battered cars out along rough tracks and sweep the hillsides with binoculars to check how their black-faced ewes, badged with fluorescent paint, are surviving the gales, the rain, and the foxes. There are Connemara ponies on the hills too, especially around Cashel and Roundstone, which will be exhibited and sold at the August show in Clifden. Most households have an allotted strip of bog from which to cut their yearly supply of turf, and in some places turf is cut by machine on a commercial scale. Fishing from the smaller harbors, other than Ros an Mhíl, is limited by the size of the boats; few of the trawlers are big enough to follow the winter shoals of herring once they have left the coast. Half-decked boats do the round of the lobster and shrimp pots and dredge for scallops in the bays, and in summer net the incoming salmon. Over the years the rafts of mussel farms and the cages of salmon and sea-trout farms have multiplied, first in the sheltered inlets of the south coast, and now, as the engineering is developed, in more exposed positions. Carna and Na hOileáin in the south are suddenly earning comparatively good money from locally, nationally, and internationally based fish-farming companies, while western villages like Roundstone have so far tended to resist the intrusion of alien technology into their pure waters. Most lucratively of all, if only for a few brief summer weeks, Connemara unites the harvest and harvest festival of tourism; restaurants and craft shops open, there are dances, deep-sea angling contests, horse races, pony shows and, best of all, the regattas to which the famous old brown-canvassed, tarry-hulled Galway hookers come sailing out of the past.

All that I have briefly told happened within view of the Twelve Bens, an elemental, constant, presence that would, if the status of the Earth had not been usurped, instill our daily ways with a certain thoughtfulness, like a great cathedral among busy streets. The free-flowing beauty of this landform has been more slighted by the material progress of the last forty years than by centuries of neglect; it is time to redress the balance. When in the 1950s the powerlines marched out across Connemara's vaporous spaces, their assertion that the remotest cottage was part of modern Europe did as much to maintain human presence there as the dole, but the landscape shrank under the lash. More recently rectangles of pine forest have reduced some of the finest mountain glens to banality, with little or no prospect of economic compensation—an ugly mistake, which should be undone by removing the worst examples and helping the blemished land tone back into harmony with the rest. Everywhere in Connemara there are potential conflicts over the sharing out of its resources: the fertilizers and silt washing down streams from forestry plantations are inimical to famous salmon rivers, the traffic to and from new industries breaks down pleasant old roads and bridges, the fencing of sheep ranges impedes the freedom of hill-walkers, the chemicals and detritus from fish-farming cages may threaten traditional shellfish beds. The present enthusiasm for mariculture could ebb, leaving a tidemark of dereliction around Connemara's shores. Prospecting licenses covering nearly all of Connemara have in the last few years been issued to Irish and international mining companies who have scented gold, and the ruthless technologies needed to extract it from huge amounts of ore could be unleashed on our hillsides. A proposal in the 1980s to site an airport in unspoiled country near Clifden focuses a contradiction between the facilitating of tourism and the conservation of what the tourists come for. Another much criticized development, the scattering of cottages and bungalows along the network of roads on the coastal plains, which appalls the city visitor who misidentifies it as suburban sprawl, perhaps deserves more sympathetic understanding than it usually receives. As a new social form, much in need of aesthetic education but full of human potentialities, its evolution is traceable from the breakup of the estates, when their clusters of hovels were replaced by isolated cottages each on its own strip of land; now those households have moved down to the roadside and acquired cars or emigrated and sold out to the holiday population that enlivens these areas for the brief summer but leaves them dark-windowed through the long winter.

All these difficulties of Connemara life can be mitigated, and perhaps the present work, that images the oneness of the place and projects the dimension of the past onto the surface of the present, may hint at the spirit in which modern life and its habitat could be reconciled. But there is much more at stake than the rationalization of land use, for Connemara is not just the sum of its resources; it stands aside from and ahead of our quarrelsome human purposes, being part of what we live for as well as what we live by. It is in fact something difficult to speak of in our present condition of civilization. How can I indicate this Connemara but as the edge of brightness that follows a cloud shadow across the mountainside or the stillness of a lake before the trout rises?[19]

NOTES

1. O'Flaherty and Hardiman 1978.
2. Gibbons 1991.
3. See Robinson 2006, 302 for further discussion.
4. See Robinson 2006, 300–306.
5. See Robinson 2006, 310.
6. See Robinson 2006, 310–311.
7. See Hardiman 1975 and Robinson 2008, 48–49.
8. See Robinson 2006, 300–361 for an extended treatment of the Martins.
9. See Robinson 2006, 330–343.
10. Edgeworth, 1833 in Butler, 1950.
11. See Robinson, 2008, 225.
12. Commissioners of Inquiry into the State of Irish Fisheries. 1836. *First Report*. Dublin.
13. Wakeman, 1852, 28.
14. See Appendix, Commissioners of Inquiry into the State of Irish Fisheries. 1836. *First Report*. Dublin.
15. See Robinson 2006, 209–215.
16. See Dallas 1872 and Robinson 2008, 230–236.

17. See Robinson 2008, 91–96.

18. See Robinson 2006, 343–352.

19. This essay was first published in *Connemara. Part 1: Introduction and Gazetteer*, Folding Landscapes, 1990 and was reprinted in *Setting Foot on the Shores of Connemara and Other Writings*, Lilliput Press, 1997. References are provided to more recent and more extensive discussion of selected topics in Tim Robinson's Connemara trilogy: *Listening to the Wind* (2006), *The Last Pool of Darkness* (2008), and *A Little Gaelic Kingdom* (2011).

—ɯ—

CONAMARA CHRONICLES

An Introductory Note

LIAM MAC CON IOMAIRE

IORRAS AITHNEACH, THE STORMY PROMONTORY, is located on an economic and geographic periphery at the edge of Europe, facing the Atlantic and weather. According to the 2016 Census, the peninsula and associated islands are home to a population of some 1,790 residents. Its land primarily consists of hillside, bog, and moor, and settlement has tended to cluster in traditional village or *clachan* habitation patterns along a 30 kilometer sea-shore fringe. Urbanization, such as it is, is confined to the main streets of Carna and Cill Chiaráin, where remaining community services such as schools, health centers and police stations are located.

The author of *Conamara Chronicles: Tales from Iorras Aith-neach*, Seán Mac Giollarnáth, offers an alternative perspective on this geography. In a fulsome and generous obituary on one of his primary collaborators, Micheál Mac Donnchadha from Roisín na Mainiach, Mac Giollarnáth maps out a different reality: "Travelling east along the road brings one to Aill na Brón where a world of lore is still to be found, and towards the west is Carna, and Coillín, the two Ard villages and Maíros. The scholar unfamiliar with the folklore of these villages is only in the beginning of his learning."[1]

This statement crystallizes not just Mac Giollarnáth's attitude
to the locality in which he worked ceaselessly as a collector and
editor of oral literature over decades but much about folklore and
ethnology in Ireland during the early to mid-twentieth century.
Romantic, rural, and pastoral visions abounded in the literature
of the cultural revival, in English and in Irish, and the collection and publication of folklore became intrinsically linked with
language revival and acquisition, nation-building, and identity.
In this respect, critical groundwork had already preceded the
foundation of the Irish Free State in late 1922.

The foundation of the Gaelic League or Conradh na Gaeilge in
1893 provided a nationwide focus for revivalist energy and organization. Publications were required to maintain communication
between branches, to assist and facilitate the acquisition of Irish
by a burgeoning number of learners, and to promote literacy in a
culture that had been at best ignored and at worst marginalized
by the National School educational system, which had been established in 1831. Literary activity in Irish during the nineteenth
century was precarious, scattered and the manuscript traditions
of earlier language periods survived due to the efforts of a few
dedicated antiquarians and scholarly societies in Belfast and
Dublin.

Such efforts were generally far removed from Gaeltacht communities located mostly in coastal areas on the southern, western, and northwestern seaboard. In Connacht and in Conamara
in particular, the prevailing economic and social conditions for
much of the nineteenth century eventually brought about the
establishment of the Congested District Board in 1891. However,
native tradition-bearers and schoolmasters such as Daniel Faherty or Dómhnall Ó Fotharta (c1834–1919), living in Caladh
between Roundstone and Ballyconneely, just west of Iorras Aithneach, brought out a compilation of traditional lore in 1892, *Siamsa an Gheimhridh* (wintertide entertainment).

Scholars and learned travelers such as Jeremiah (1835–1906) and Alma Cardell Curtin (1847–1938) also came to Ireland from the United States between 1887 and 1893 and actively sought out myths, stories, and folklore in Irish-speaking districts across the country. The Aran Islands, West Kerry, and the Blasket Islands were also the subject of much international interest. The Curtins traveled widely and visited Cill Chiaráin in Iorras Aithneach to collect oral literature from several informants, with the assistance of the parish clerk. One of the Curtin's informants—Seán Éadbhaird Ó Briain—would later collaborate with Seán Mac Giollarnáth and had a highly regarded repertoire of traditional hero tales.[2]

The compiler of *Conamara Chronicles: Tales from Iorras Aithneach* originated in east Co. Galway. Seán Forde or Mac Giollarnáth (1880–1970) was born on September 13, 1880 at Gorteen, Ballymacward, some nine miles from Athenry, being the eldest son of Patrick Forde (1837–1912) and Bridget Curley (1854–1936). The Fordes ran a shop and a small farm holding and raised eight other children. Seán was educated locally, and having received extra tuition from an uncle who was a schoolteacher, he obtained a position with the Inland Revenue of the British Civil Service and commenced work in Somerset House in London in 1902. Mac Giollarnáth joined the Gaelic League while in London and came to know significant literary figures in the Gaelic revival such as Micheál Breathnach (1881–1908) and Pádraic Ó Conaire (1882–1928). He also associated with luminaries of the Irish Literary Society Stephen Gwynn (1864–1950) and Robert Lynd (1879–1949) and began to take an active part in nationalist politics joining the Irish Republican Brotherhood.[3]

Returning to Ireland in 1908, his interest in matters literary saw him take the post of editor with a short-lived monthly journal, *An Connachtach*. The preeminent Gaelic publication of that era, *An Claidheamh Soluis*, was edited by Patrick Pearse (1879–1916), with a weekly circulation that reached seven thousand copies at times. Mac Giollarnáth succeeded Pearse as editor in 1909, supported by the Galway branch of the Gaelic League, an editorial tenure that lasted from November 1909 until September 1917. He was in fact the longest serving editor of that publication and the discourse arguing for the development of a vision for modern Gaelic literature can be traced throughout this era.[4] Publication of *An Claidheamh Soluis* continued during the tumultuous year of 1916, with a noticeable lacuna between April 29 and May 27, 1916 primarily due to events in Dublin.

Although a member of the Irish Volunteers, it appears that Mac Giollarnáth took no active part in the Easter Rising itself. Folklore and rural customs did form part of the staple provision in *An Claidheamh Soluis*, but Mac Giollarnáth's column and editorials also demonstrated an open intelligence and curiosity regarding international developments in drama and modern narrative. However, the political fallout within the Gaelic League following the 1916 rising brought sustained infighting within the League and the pages of *An Claidheamh Soluis* became a battleground for various factions within the organization. Mac Giollarnáth tendered his resignation as editor in light of several petitions and motions to the League's annual conference or Ard-Fheis calling for editorial reform. Mac Giollarnáth was succeeded as editor of *An Claidheamh Soluis* by Piaras Béaslaí (1881–1965).

Mac Giollarnáth's other contributions to periodical journalism during these years included insightful pamphlets on Patrick Pearse and James Connolly (1868–1916), both published under pen names (Cóilín, Gerald O'Connor) in 1916 and 1917 respectively.[5] The precarious nature of such a livelihood at a time of considerable political unrest may have prompted his application to study as a solicitor with the Incorporated Law Society in 1916. Qualifying as a solicitor in 1920, Mac Giollarnáth established a legal practice in Athenry, close to his native district. Rural unrest, land disputes and the necessity for arbitration brought about the

Republican Courts, established by Dáil Éireann. From June 29, 1920, Dáil courts were established with civil and criminal functions, and with differing jurisdictions—parish, district, or supreme—and offered an effective and widely accepted alternative to British judicial institutions until the outbreak of civil war in June 1922.

Seán Mac Giollarnáth was nominated to the bench of the Dáil District Court by Austin Stack (1879–1929), and following the Anglo-Irish Treaty and the establishment of Saorstát Éireann, the Irish Free State, a J. M. Forde is named as a solicitor recognized as a District Justice under the District Justices (Temporary Provisions) Act of 1923. On the advice of writer and cultural activist Pádhraic Ó Domhnalláin (1884–1960), Mac Giollarnáth was assigned to dispense justice across west Co. Galway with direct responsibility for the Irish-speaking districts of Conamara. Such a post allowed Mac Giollarnáth to travel widely across several communities and would have afforded him opportunities to identify potential collaborators in several districts in Conamara, including Doire an Fhéich, An Mám, but particularly in Carna and Iorras Aithneach.

The stability associated with his appointment to the bench facilitated a marked increase in literary output. The 1920s saw the development of Mac Giollarnáth as a skillful translator, and the newly formed government established a dedicated Irish language imprint—An Gúm—with the aim of providing accessible, idiomatic reading material for adults and children alike. *Saoghal Éanacha* (1925) is an early example of Mac Giollarnáth's personal interests in nature, the outdoor life, and specifically the life of birds finding their way into print. This ornithological interest would go on to yield further publications, *Ríoghacht na nÉan* (1935), a translation of Oliver G. Pike's *Birdland* series from the 1920s and *Féilire na nÉan* (1940).

The publications branch, An Gúm, was situated within the offices of the Department of Education and was regarded as both a boon and a curse by creative writers in Irish, providing translation piecework for future literary giants such as Máirtín Ó Cadhain (1906–1970), Séamus Ó Grianna (1889–1969), and the latter's brother, Seosamh Mac Grianna (1900–1990) and also subjecting them to bureaucratic discipline, which was often a bone of contention.[6]

During the 1920s, literary and cultural periodicals began to give way to published compilations of lore, local history, traditional hero tales, and other materials due to the new state supports and publishing infrastructure. Tomás Ó Máille (1880–1938), anthologist, linguist, Irish Volunteer, and Professor of Modern Irish at University College Galway, had also served as editor of a periodical, *An Stoc*, between 1917–1920 that specialized in oral literature and traditional lore from Connacht. Folklore and oral literature were being slowly and surely institutionalized in the service of the identity building of the new state.[7] There was a constant demand for anthologies of traditional songs, for example.

Publications such as Tomás Ó Máille's *An Ghaoth Aniar* (1920) (Westerly wind), *Bruth fá Thír* (1923) (Flotsam and jetsam) by Pádhraic Ó Domhnalláin and Tomás Ó Raghallaigh (1883–1966), and *Sgéalaidhe Leitir Mealláin* (1926) (The Lettermullen Storyteller) by Peadar Ó Direáin were closely followed by Fr. Tomás Ó Ceallaigh's seminal work *Ceol na nOileán* (1931) (Island music). Tomás Ó Máille produced an excellent edition of traditional poetry that focused on the output of poets associated with North Conamara, *Micheál Mac Suibhne agus filidh an tSléibhe* (1934) (Micheál Mac Suibhne and the mountain poets). He also edited *An Béal Beo* (1936) (The living mouth), a compilation of idiomatic phrases and colloquialisms in Connacht Irish. From Iorras Aithneach, Séamas Mac Con Iomaire's (1891–1967) treatise on sea and marine life *Cladaí Chonamara* (Conamara seashores) was well-received on publication in 1938.

Traditional lore, songs, and tales are being cultivated, collected, edited, and shared with new and growing audiences throughout the 1920s and 30s.[8] It is in the context of such publishing ventures that Mac Giollarnáth's systematic approach to the compilation and publication of traditional lore in Iorras Aithneach should be assessed. Towards the end of the 1920s, material from Mac Giollarnáth's hand finds its way onto the pages of *Béaloideas*, the academic journal of folklore established by the Folklore Society of Ireland in 1927.[9] Initially, Mac Giollarnáth highlights the lore of Peadar Mac Thuathaláin (c1865–1930), a native of Indreabhán in Cois Fharraige, who lives in Galway city, beside the Small Crane market on Sea Road. Professor Tomás Ó Máille had made the introductions between them.

Their collaboration resulted in a posthumous book-form collection *Peadar Cois Fhairrge* (1934), but occasional folktales from Iorras Aithneach, related by Micheál Mac Donnchadha from Roisín na Mainiach, were published in 1930 and 1932. These individual tales preceded the first significant corpus from Iorras Aithneach published in *Béaloideas*, "Tiachóg ó Iorrus Aintheach" (A collection from Iorras Aithneach) (1932), a collection of 45 segments, edited by Mac Giollarnáth.[10] Séamus Ó Duilearga (1899–1980) provided references to folkloristic literature and goes on to comment, "The miscellany of West Galway folklore material here published is one of the best and most interesting collections of folklore ever contributed to this or [any] other Irish periodical."[11]

The miscellany was noteworthy in that it didn't contain *Fiannaíocht* or hero tales, traditionally regarded as the prestige genre of oral literature. However, working with many of the same collaborators in Iorras Aithneach, Mac Giollarnáth went on to edit a compendium of hero tales, *Loinnir Mac Leabhar agus Sgéalta Gaisgidh Eile* (1936), along with biographies of the storytellers and photographic plates of each of them individually. The publication was of a very high production standard and was issued under the imprint of An Gúm.

Working with largely the same informants—Micheál Mac Donnchadha, Pádraic (Liam) Mac Donnchadha, Pádraic Mac

Con Iomaire, Seán Ó Briain, Tomás Mac Con Iomaire, Seosamh
Mac Donnchadha, Beairtle Mac Donnchadha, Beairtle Guairim,
Marcas Ó Maoilchiaráin, Seán Mac Con Rí, Tomás Ó Nia—Mac
Giollarnáth continued to collect and collate material from Iorras Aithneach. A second compendium of lore and local history
relating to Iorras Aithneach was published as "An Dara Tiachóg
as Iorrus Aithneach" in *Béaloideas* in 1940, which ran to seventy-
two segments over one hundred pages or so.

The methodology of redaction was well established by this stage
with thematic arrangement of segments, credited to individual
contributors and presented in a normalized orthography. *Annála
Beaga ó Iorrus Aithneach* appears shortly afterwards in 1941.
Conamara Chronicles: Tales of Iorras Aithneach contains 251 short
episodic tales sourced from 18 named collaborators.[12] It is worth
noting that two of the named contributors (Seán Ó Briain and
Séamas Ó Conghaile) cannot be associated with particular tales
within the collection although Seán Ó Briain was a significant
contributor to *Loinnir Mac Leabhair agus Sgéulta Gaisgidh Eile*
(1936) and "An Dara Tiachóg as Iorras Aithneach" (1940).

The compilation is arranged in fourteen thematic chapters
and offers deep insight into regionalized folk history and lore.
The subjects of these *Conamara Chronicles* were conceived and
contributed in the spirit of a living community narrative, a stark
counterpoint to the documentary approach of institutions and
officialdom. It is apparent that hagiography was not confined to
medieval manuscripts when the volume of lore concerning saints
and their locations is considered. There is much to interest the
social historian in the chapters concerning the uprising of 1798,
vigilantism, and agrarian unrest. Insight into community charac-
ters—"Big Men"—may focus on one gender only and are indica-
tive of the general approach to folklore collection and informant
selection in the 1930s. Trade, particularly by sea, ensured that
Iorras Aithneach constantly looked to the wider world and established national and international connections, which facilitated
fishing, trade, and smuggling. It is hardly surprising that feats

of seamanship were the subject of tale and song. *Conamara Chronicles* is a mine of information regarding placenames and topographical lore and has been used extensively by Tim Robinson in his several works on Aran and Conamara. Equally, as tradition bearers acutely conscious of the prestige of their verbal art, there is valuable information within the tales regarding education, learning, and literacy. The final chapter—"Custodians of Traditional Lore and Storytellers"—may not present much in the way of hard biographical fact in terms of Mac Giollarnáth's collaborators, but it speaks strongly to the character of the contributors and their worldview. A clear relationship of esteem between compiler and contributor also emerges in these final segments. If color and atmosphere are stronger in Mac Giollarnáth's characterizations of his collaborators than analysis and argument, his informants were well served by his comparatively speedy redaction of their lore. Ironically, working at a remove from the Folklore Commission may have allowed him greater freedom and scope to publish the material. That being said, the publication of several folktales and the seminal collections "Tiachóg ó Iorrus Aintheach" (1932) and "An Dara Tiachóg as Iorrus Aithneach" (1940) in the journal *Béaloideas* did much to enhance the emerging status of folklore as an academic discipline and arguably broadened the readership of the journal at a critical phase in its development.

All considered, Mac Giollarnáth is responsible for a remarkable feat of collection, redaction, and publication when it is considered that only some 10 percent of *Conamara Chronicles*'s material—specifically twenty-six segments—appeared previously in "Tiachóg ó Iorrus Aintheach" in 1932. Mac Giollarnáth's long-form contributions to *Béaloideas* and the monograph collections *Loinnir Mac Leabhair agus Sgéulta Gaisgidh Eile* (1936) and *Annála Beaga ó Iorrus Aithneach* (1941) are remarkable monuments to the richness and diversity of traditional lore within a relatively limited geographic area. Modern folklore scholars such as Peadar Ó Ceannabháin, Angela Bourke, Sean Williams, Lillis Ó Laoire, Róisín Nic Dhonncha, and particularly Ríonach uí Ógáin continue to explore aspects of the diverse oral literature tradition of Iorras Aithneach.[13]

When the totality of folklore collection within the region is considered, Iorras Aithneach must be considered exceptional. At either extremity of the peninsula, other folklore collectors worked assiduously with other collaborators to contribute enormously to the National Folklore Collection. Séamus Ennis (1919–1982) collected lore and tales from Colm Ó Caodháin (1893–1975) in Glinsce, but well over two hundred traditional songs were also recorded as a result of their partnership.[14] Liam Mac Coisdeala (1906–1996) worked with Éamon Liam a' Búrc (1886–1942) in Aill na Brón and Cill Chiaráin, who contributed over two hundred discrete items to the National Folklore Collection including a tale of some thirty thousand words in length, *Eochair Mac Rí in Éirinn* (O'Nolan, 1982). The various collectors also did not work in isolation from each other, often overcoming logistical and technical difficulties together. Liam Mac Coisdeala reports of a trip made in the company of Éamon Liam a' Búrc to the other extremity of the parish, "He came with me once to Coillín to the house of Patrick Mac an Iomaire, a man who matched him as an authority on the folklore of the district, and between them they gave us a fine night of storytelling (20/2/1936)." (A Búrc, Mac Coisdeala, and O'Nolan 1982, 27)

Séamus Ennis's field diaries also contain references to Seán Mac Giollarnáth and describe a visit both men made to Colm Ó Caodháin in Glinsce in July 1946: "We had a great night talking at Colm's fireside. [. . .] He said he would very much like to spend time with Colm and write material from him." (uí Ógáin 2009, 352)

The publication and availability of such a corpus of speech-generated material also excited the interest of linguists, philologists, and especially dialectologists of Irish. The language of Iorras Aithneach, and the neighboring district of Ros Muc, could reasonably lay claim to being the most completely described dialects of Irish in light of their investigation in studies by Tomás Ó

Máille, Heinrich Wagner, Tomás S. Ó Máille, Tomás de Bhaldraithe, Nollaig Mac Congáil, Hans Hartmann, Arndt Wigger, Séamas Ó Murchú, and, latterly, Brian Ó Curnáin.[15]

Following the publication of *Annála Beaga ó Iorrus Aithneach*, Seán Mac Giollarnáth published traditional lore from Micheál Breathnach (1864–1943), a noted tradition bearer living in Mám in Co. Galway, and interesting collections of material from his home ground of East Galway, which have been translated and edited by Diarmuid Ó Cearbhaill (1929–2012) whose father Domhnall Ó Cearbhaill (1891–1963) also collected tales in Iorras Aithneach from Pádraic Mac Con Iomaire, An Coillín.[16]

Domhnall Ó Cearbhaill was a journalist, broadcaster, and educationalist who had received training in folklore methodologies in Denmark and Sweden. A committee member of the Folklore Society of Ireland between 1936 and 1961, Domhnall Ó Cearbhaill had married Treasa Nic Giollarnáth in 1928, a sister of Seán Mac Giollarnáth. Domhnall Ó Cearbhaill visited Iorras Aithneach regularly throughout the 1930s with his family and stayed in Maíros. He met and came to know both Pádraic Mac Con Iomaire from An Coillín and Pádraic Mac Donnchadha (Liam). Ó Cearbhaill wrote extensively for the *Irish Weekly Independent, Sunday Independent,* and *Evening Herald* while working as a national school teacher and published many articles based on Pádraic Mac Con Iomaire's lore between 1934 and 1942. He served on the committee of the Folklore Society of Ireland between 1931 and 1961, roughly contemporaneously with Seán Mac Giollarnáth's own term on the same committee between 1935 and March 1964, when he stepped down due to ill-health.

Mac Giollarnáth returned to further literary work of his own in the late 1940s with a translation of *The Seashore* by J. H. Kelman and Rev. T. Wood, rendered as *Cladach na Fairrge* in 1947. The culmination of his own creative efforts in Irish was to come in 1949 when he was awarded Duais an Chraoibhín (The Hyde Literary Prize) for *Mo Dhúthaigh Fhiáin* (My wild district), a reflective and intimate collection of stories, tales, and descriptive prose set very much in the Conamara hinterland. As Philip O'Leary has noted: "*Mo Dhúthaigh Fhiáin* has genuine charm and remains worth reading to this day."[17]

Having retired from the bench in 1950, Mac Giollarnáth resumed private practice as a solicitor but found time to write a short monograph in English for the Cultural Relations Committee of Ireland, *Conamara* (1954). With special emphasis on Conamara's unique culture, environment, and wildlife, the style of the short work is rather romantic. In the absence of any discursive writing by Mac Giollarnáth regarding folkloristics, the work perhaps provides some indirect perspectives on Mac Giollarnáth's understanding of ethnography and folklore in general. The National University of Ireland conferred an honorary doctorate (LLD) on Seán Mac Giollarnáth in 1959, in recognition of his contribution to folklore, on the recommendation of Séamus Ó Duilearga.

Mac Giollarnáth was married to Tríona Fearon from Magherfelt, Co. Derry, who was a member of Cumann na mBan and Conradh na Gaeilge, according to her obituary published in the Irish Press on June 14, 1968. Having qualified as a medical doctor in UCD, Tríona went on to serve as resident surgeon in the Prospect Hill Hospital in Galway, the precursor to the Galway Regional Hospital. She predeceased Seán Mac Giollarnáth who died on February 28, 1970 in Galway.

Seán Mac Giollarnáth's enduring legacy can be quantified in terms of the scope and quality of his compilations, the editorial standards which he espoused, and his apparent determination to share the fruit of his and his collaborators' considerable labors with as wide a public as possible. *Conamara Chronicles: Tales from Iorras Aithneach* preserves the life, lore, and character of Iorras Aithneach for new generations of readers to enjoy.

LMCI
April 2019

NOTES

1. See Mac Giollarnáth 1941b, 149.
2. See Bourke 2009, 2019.
3. See Mac Giollarnáth and Ó Cearbhaill 2012, 107.
4. See Uí Chollatáin 2004, 40.
5. See Mac Giollarnáth and Ó Cearbhaill 2005, 2006.
6. See Uí Laighléis 2017, 74, 119.
7. See Ó Giolláin 2000, 76–77; Ó Crualaoich and Ó Giolláin 1988, 73–74; Briody 2007, 73–100 in particular for compelling analysis.
8. See O'Leary's 2004, 113 detailed discussion.
9. See Briody 2007, 77.
10. The spelling of the placename was initially "Iorrus Aintheach" reflecting strong initial vocalic nasalization, then "Iorrus Aithneach," and the modern norm is "Iorras Aithneach."
11. See Ó Duilearga 1932, 500.
12. Specific detail regarding individual informants is contained in "Meet the Storytellers," and photographs of four of Mac Giollarnáth's long-established collaborators are also published with the kind permission of the National Folklore Collection, University College Dublin.
13. See Ní Fhlathartaigh 1976; A Búrc, Mac Coisdeala, and O'Nolan 1982; Ó Ceannabháin 1983; Bourke 2003, 2009, 2016, 2019; Partridge 1980–81, 1983; uí Ógáin 1996–97, 2009, 2017; Nic Dhonncha 2004; Mac Con Iomaire 2007; and Williams and Ó Laoire 2011 for studies of subjects relating to the area.
14. A perceptive full-length study of Colm Ó Caodháin by uí Ógáin was published in 2021.
15. See Ó hUiginn 1997, 1992–93; Wagner 1958, 1966; de Bhaldraithe 1985; McGonagle and Wagner 1995; de Bhaldraithe, Hartmann, and Ó hUiginn 1996; Ó Murchú 1998; Wigger 2004; Ó Curnáin 1999, 2007, 2016.
16. See reissue of this collection, with an introductory essay by Máire Uí Chuinneáin, in Mac Congáil 2009.
17. See O'Leary 2011, 67.

ONE

—〰—

THE HOLY MEN AND THE ISLANDS

ST. PATRICK AT MÁM ÉAN (3)

When Patrick was at Mám Éan[1] he had a manservant. There was a bed there where St. Patrick used to sleep. One day he stood up above the bed on the side of the mountain, stretched out his arms, and looked down over the land to the south by the sea because he knew he wasn't to come any closer to it, and he asked of God that the land to the south be twice as productive as the land he had traveled.

When night fell and he was settling down to sleep, he told his servant: "While I am sleeping I want you to stay awake." He fell asleep, and after a while he began to speak. He was dreaming, and, in a loud voice, he put a curse on Ireland. "On the foam of the river!" said the servant. In a short while he put a curse on Ireland again, and the servant ordered the curse to be on the tips of the rushes. The tips of the rushes are withered ever since.

The third time Patrick cursed Ireland, the servant ordered it onto the top of the bracken. St. Patrick woke up with a start, and he asked the servant if he was asleep. "I'm not," said the servant, "which was very lucky for you."

"What have I said?" asked St. Patrick. He told him. "That's the reason I told you not to fall asleep. I knew I was saying it, but at the same time I couldn't stop myself saying it. The third time I said it I awoke. I knew I had done some bad work if you weren't awake to order the curse onto something else."

ST. PATRICK AND CROM DUBH (3)

On Crom Dubh Sunday, the pilgrimage to Croagh Patrick takes place. It is the last Sunday in July. At the time of St. Patrick, Crom Dubh was a pagan. He was living somewhere near Croagh Patrick. St. Patrick and himself were friends, but at the same time he wasn't willing to become a Christian. One day when he had slaughtered an ox, he sent his servant with a quarter of beef as a present to St. Patrick.

"Deo Gratias!" said St. Patrick when the servant said, "This is a quarter of beef my master has sent you." When the servant returned, Crom Dubh asked him what thanks St. Patrick gave him for the quarter of beef he was given as a gift. "He only said 'Deo Gratias,'" said the servant, "and I don't know what that word means."

"Here's another quarter we'll present him with," said Crom Dubh, "till we see what thanks he'll give for it."

The servant brought the second quarter to him. "Here's another quarter that my master presents you with," said the servant. "Deo Gratias!" said St. Patrick.

The servant went back. Crom Dubh asked him what thanks St. Patrick gave for the second quarter.

"He didn't give any thanks except 'Deo Gratias,' the same as he said with the first quarter."

"I'm sending him a third quarter," said Crom Dubh, "till I see if he gives any more thanks than that to me."

The servant came to St. Patrick with the third quarter. "This is another quarter," said the servant, "that my master sent as a present to you."

"Deo Gratias!" said St. Patrick.

The servant went back to his master. "Well, what thanks did he give you now for the third quarter?"

"He didn't give me any thanks except to say 'Deo Gratias,' the same as he said with the other two quarters."

"He should give me more thanks than that," said Crom Dubh, "for sending him my three quarters of beef as a present. Go back to him now and tell him to come here to me immediately, without delay, or else I will go to him."

The servant went back and told him that his master wanted him to come to his house and to make no delay in going there. "I'll be with you to his house now," St. Patrick said.

He came with the servant to Crom Dubh's house.

"What sort of thanks is this you showed me, Patrick, for the three quarters of beef I sent you as a present?" said Crom Dubh.

"I showed you great thanks," said Patrick. "Do you have three quarters of beef as fine as the three quarters you presented me with?"

"Yes," said Crom Dubh. "I have three quarters as fine as them."

"Place them on the scales now," said Patrick.

He did so. Patrick wrote "Deo Gratias" three times on a piece of paper and placed it on the opposite scale against the three quarters of beef, and the paper with "Deo Gratias" written three times on it lifted the three quarters of beef.

"Oh! Holy Patrick," he said, "I'm the one who is out of order with you. Baptize myself and my family. I'm going to become a Christian with you, and all the people under my command will have to become Christians."

He converted that day and he was baptized that same day, the day that's named after him ever since, Crom Dubh Sunday, the day of the pilgrimage to Croagh Patrick.

ST. BRIGID (1)

Brigid's father had two wives. The other woman began to fight with Brigid's mother, who didn't want to be fighting. She went and told the bishop about it. She was expecting Brigid at the time.

"I'll bless the child in your womb," said the bishop, "seeing as you have been driven out. You can go earning, and when your child is born you can give her to another woman to rear, and give that woman half of what you'll earn."

She went to work for a strong farmer like the man she had been married to, a big milch farmer. She used to look after the milk and make the butter, and she was in charge of all that work. When her child was born, she sent her to be fostered and continued working herself. When the child was a year old, another child died near the woman who was fostering Brigid. This woman went to the house where the dead child was, and she brought Brigid with her in her arms. When she bent down to look at the body, Brigid placed her hand on the dead child and the child came back to life again. They knew then that Brigid was blessed.

Brigid's mother became ill after some time, and Brigid went to work in her place. There wasn't a poor person who came to her that she didn't give some of the milk to, and after all that she had seven times as much milk left as her mother used to have. God was increasing it for her when He saw she was generous with it.

When the mother came back to work, Brigid could go out walking. She met this man called Ladhraic Mac Luirc. This man had horse's ears, and he would kill anybody who told him so. He asked Brigid what sort of ears he had. Brigid placed her hand on him.

"Ears like everyone else," said Brigid.

"Arrah, indeed I have not," he said. "I have horse's ears."

"Put up your hands," said Brigid. He put up his hands, and he had ears like everyone else.

"I'll give you anything you want," said he to Brigid.

"All I want," she said, "is the width of my cloak of land for a cow."

He said she could have that. She spread out the cloak, and it was getting wider and wider until a woman who saw it said it was going to cover all of Ireland. The cloak stopped then. All of the Curragh of Kildare was covered by the cloak by then, and Brigid owned the Curragh. It was Brigid's Cloak that won the Curragh.

Then there was a church where there were two bishops. Brigid came into the church where they were. When she came in, there wasn't a candle in the church that didn't light.

"The Virgin Mary is in the church," said one of the bishops.

"She's not," said the other bishop. "That is blessed Brigid whom I blessed in her mother's womb." They made a nun of her then, and she was the first nun ever in Ireland.

ST. COLMCILLE (1)

When Colmcille was dying, he ordered that he was to be put in a coffin of stone and cast into the sea. The stone came ashore near where Brigid and Patrick were buried.

Colmcille's well is in Leitreach Ard.[2] The ninth of June is his feast day. There isn't a man in the townland who'll do any work that day.

There's a Colmcille's well in Aird Thiar[3] too. There's a flagstone shaped like the lid of a pot-oven over the well. I lifted it one day while walking by the shore when there was a great ebb. The reason I lifted it was that a man had told me that if it was thrown into the sea, even as far out as beyond Sceirde,[4] it would return to the same place again. I threw it from a cliff top where the water was twelve feet deep even at the lowest ebb tide there ever was. I threw it out as far as I possibly could. I said I'd find out if this man had been telling me the truth. I came by again in two weeks' time, and it was back in the same place in the well. That's the truth as sure as you're writing it down. I saw it proven. There's a deep channel between the two townlands, Ard West and Ard East. There's a stony ridge in the channel, and the well is in a corner of the ridge, in the side of a rock, at the edge of the tide. Every tide flows into it, and it dries with every ebb tide.

MAC DUACH (1)

A tree named after a saint was able to tell people what they should do. People prayed to the saint after whom the tree was named, and the tree would tell them what to do.

A tree was named after Mac Duach, Mac Duach's Tree, and people were cured by it. A man who wanted to be rich cut strips of an old boat and went around selling them, telling people that they were strips of Mac Duach's Tree. He came to a man who had the adversary in his belly,[5] and that man bought the strips of wood the salesman had cut off the old boat. He placed his trust in God and in St. Mac Duach, and he prayed to them. He placed the strips of wood in a vessel and poured water around them. At the very moment he drank of the water, "the old boy" left his belly.

"I wouldn't mind being driven out by anything," said the adversary afterwards, "but by the bones of the old boat!"

The person who put all his trust in God and in Mac Duach did well. People in times gone by were keen to get the bones of Mac Duach, and people were selling them. They were the bones of a tree named after Mac Duach. People have great belief in Mac Duach.

SAINT CÁILLÍN'S ISLAND (5)

If some clay from Cáillín's Island near Slyne Head was scattered on a stack of corn, the mice wouldn't go near the corn. There's another island near Westport, Inis Cré, and if some of its clay was scattered on the corn, you would see the mice going off screeching. There used to be a pilgrimage to Cáillín's well on the island until another well was dedicated to him on the mainland in Baile na Léime. The thirteenth of November is the feast day, and the sea used to be rough for those going to the island.

A cripple from Munster made the pilgrimage to Cáillín's well on crutches once. He managed to get as far as the stone wall near

the well but was unable to get over the wall. That was when he
appealed to Cáillín:

"I cry out to you, Cáillín," he said,
"High King of Leinster's son,
My body is deformed
And the wall has me undone."

He was cured instantly. Cáillín has four wells; one of them
is on the Red Strand and another in Aran. Sianach Stream is in
Maíros,[6] to the west of us. There is a well there dedicated to Sianach, and people go there every Sunday.

SIANACH[7]

The Leitreach Ard people were gathering red seaweed on the
strand on the feast of Sianach. There wasn't a cock of seaweed left
on the strand that wasn't swept away, and a man who had a creel
of seaweed on his back was thrown head first and the seaweed
thrown out of the creel. The Leitreach Ard people haven't worked
on the holiday—the Feast of Sianach—ever since.

MAC DARA (2)

Mac Dara was a saint. He came from County Down; they think
he was from there. There were seven of them there in all: Mac
Dara, Mac Duach, Caolann, Cáillín, Enda, Flannán, and Feichín.

MAC DARA'S ISLAND (2)

There's nobody living on Mac Dara's Island now. There used to
be a man called Páidín Rua living on the island, himself and his
family. They stayed on there until one of his family married there.
Páidín Rua had half a holding on Oileán Máisean (Mason Island). He gave it to the son who got married, and the other son
stayed with Páidín on Mac Dara's Island.

At that time there was hardly a man in Iorras Aithneach who had more than two cows, but Páidín Rua had seventeen milch cows on Mac Dara's Island. That was because so much money could be made on the island. A ton of kelp was worth seven pounds at the time, and there wasn't a day that he didn't work two ebb tides during the seaweed season. Whichever way the wind blew, there was always shelter on some side of the island for a man to work. There wasn't a year that Páidín Rua wasn't able to earn three score or four score pounds on the kelp. He could hold on to the cattle for a few years or, if that didn't suit him, he could sell one or two of them whenever he wanted to.

In the end, the family decided it was no longer a suitable place to live and that living on an island in the sea was like being in prison. A small farm was up for sale in Cill Chiaráin, and they bought it. They abandoned Cruach na Cara, and from the day they left till the day they died—and that wasn't so many years later—they were falling back in every way. Their health failed in the end, and they died. The mainland didn't agree with them once they'd left their good luck behind them on Mac Dara's Island. The old folk used to say that too much pride is a bad thing. It's an old saying. Since they left the island, nobody has lived there. James Mongan took it over after they left. He bought the island and got a dozen years out of it. He used to have three score cattle on the island for a month at a time. He wouldn't leave them there for more than a month. He sold the seaweed rights for two pounds ten shillings a year for four men sharing. The island lay fallow for two years. The Congested Districts Board took it over, and the grazing rights were given to the townland of Más (Mace), the nearest to the island, and the seaweed rights to the townland of Aird Thiar. The grazing was divided into eleven holdings and the seaweed into seventeen holdings. Muiríleach Island is to the south of Mac Dara's Island—a small, low island. This is where the most seaweed comes ashore, hundreds of pounds' worth of seaweed. Each of the seventeen men has entitlement to the small island and the big island. An old woman who was talking to Josie Mongan's mother about the seaweed said that Mac Dara's Island had a lace of gold with the wealth of seaweed coming ashore there.

MAC DARA'S PILGRIMAGE (2)

The sixteenth of July is Mac Dara's feast day. People come from near and far on that day to make the pilgrimage to Mac Dara's Island. The well, Mac Dara's well, is to the north of the chapel. The pilgrimage is begun at the altar to the south of the chapel by going seven times round the altar and saying the Ave Maria and the Creed, then going to the chapel and doing the same thing again, then going to the graveyard and doing the same again, then to the well. Most people then come back to Mac Dara's bed and say some prayers there at the end. They have finished the pilgrimage then. The bed is at the eastern gable of the chapel, between the flagstone and the chapel gable. That's where the saint is buried.

When a person is making the pilgrimage, it is the custom to take seven pebbles in one's hand. As each round is made, he throws away one of the pebbles and so on till he has finished the seven rounds at each station. I have seen, some years, when it was like a wood there, with all the masts of the sailing boats, not to mention the rowing boats. No man ever met with an accident there until the pilgrimage was moved to Maínis.[8] The people were ordered to come to Maínis, and eight were drowned on the day of the pilgrimage. The pilgrimage was brought back to Mac Dara's Island, and that's where it is since.

It is a part of the pilgrimage to drink a drop of the water from the well, a spoonful, and to rub a drop of the water on any part of the body where there's a pain.

—⁓—

People coming to Mac Dara's Island on pilgrimage day would berth their boats at Aill na hIomluchta (ferry rock). When too many boats were berthed at Aill na hIomluchta they would go to An Aill Bhuí (yellow rock) if the weather was settled. There was never a day or night that there wasn't shelter to be had on some side of Mac Dara's Island. St. Mac Dara was promised that there would always be shelter on some side of the island. People come from all directions to make the pilgrimage, from Iorras Mór to the west,[9] Leitir Mealláin to the east,[10] and from Árainn,[11] and in olden times they came from County Clare and from Joyce Country beyond Mám Éan. People come to make the pilgrimage from Slyne Head to the west, and from Roundstone and Cashel. If the day turns bad, the woman will be worried if her husband or son is out at sea. She promises to make a pilgrimage to Mac Dara's Island if God guides the husband or the son safely home, or she promises that the husband himself will make the pilgrimage when the feast day comes round.

If a person is suddenly taken ill, a man or a woman will immediately go out and face Mac Dara's Island, imploring the saint to ask God to make that person well again and recover full health. A pilgrimage will be promised for the feast day, whatever the weather. A person can have many reasons for making a pilgrimage. In the past many people came to the island who didn't make the pilgrimage at all but were there to be part of the gathering. In years gone by there was food and drink and confectionery available. There were boat races and foot races for the young men. It's a long time now since that came to an end. Mass is celebrated there now. Not many go, apart from those who attend the Mass and take Holy Communion and then make the pilgrimage.

THE CHAPEL ON MAC DARA'S ISLAND (1)

A vessel came in to Mac Dara's Island. It was probably driven in by bad weather. It spent a few nights there, and the crew of the vessel killed the bull that was on the island and the ram that was with the sheep. The vessel sailed out at night, but they found themselves moored in the very same place the following day. That happened three nights in a row. The crew then said to themselves that the island must belong to some saint, that they had no right to kill the beasts, and that they must show some respect to the saint. They built a chapel in his honor, and Mac Dara's chapel is there since.

The cattle were then left without a bull and the sheep without a ram. There was a bull and a ram in Cruach Chaolainn,[12] and they abandoned it. The bull came in on the northwestern side of Mac Dara's Island. It swam ashore and came up through a hole in a flat rock. The hole is only the width of the bull. When the sea is wild, the water spouts up through the hole and high into the air. This is a blowhole. It's called Spout an Tairbh (the bull's spout). The ram came ashore by leaping onto a flat rock where it left the imprint of its knees in the rock. I saw the imprint myself. The ram cleared the narrow channel between the rocky foreshore and Mac Dara's Island.

BOWING TO THE ISLAND (2)

When boatmen are sailing past Muiríleach Island, on the southern side of Mac Dara's Island, they slacken their sails, lower them three times, and hoist them again three times in honor of Mac Dara, and they say a prayer at the same time. A man in a currach would take his cap off and say a prayer while passing by the island. I never heard of any man being drowned around Mac Dara's Island.

A SHIPWRECK ON SAINT MAC DARA'S ISLAND

Máirtín Shíomóin Ó Maoilchiaráin and Maitias Mac Craith were sailing home from An Chorainn[13] after selling a load of seaweed there. Fog and mist came down around them and night fell, and after they passed Ceann Gólaim (Golam head) on their journey west, they didn't see anything of the mainland that they could make sense of. They kept on sailing with a south-southeasterly wind, and they didn't notice anything till they saw the white surf breaking about four yards from the bow. Máirtín tried to turn the boat, and it took him longer than he expected, as it was running headlong before the wind. Before the boat came round, it struck the rock. It was holed, and it filled with water.

"Up the mast with us," said Máirtín.

One of them went up the mast as far as he could go, and the other man went up after him till he was just below him. The breaker came and lifted the boat out of the shallows into the deep. The tide was up to the waist of the man below. The surge was increasing, and the boat was being thrown ashore until they were cast onto the foreshore where they had no difficulty in walking onto dry land, although they didn't know where they were. They walked up from the shore and saw something like a house in the distance. When they drew closer, they saw that it was Mac Dara's chapel. They recognized the chapel. They stayed there by the gable end of the chapel till morning. They then went to look at the boat. The tide had gone out, and the boat was nearly dry. There was no damage done underneath except that a board about six inches long was smashed by the sharp point of a rock. One of the men stuffed his homespun woolen jacket into the hole, tore a scraw off a flat rock, and placed a stone on top of the scraw for weight. With the incoming tide, the fog had cleared, and the day was fine. They sailed up home to Inis Ní (Inishnee).

They had sailed in between Muiríleach Island and Mac Dara's Island in the fog. There's an inlet between the two islands that is sheltered from all winds except the southeasterly wind. The wind was southeasterly that night. The breaker was as high as a ship's mast, and that's what cast the boat ashore. If it had been the southwesterly wind the boat could have been smashed to bits, as the wind could have run over her.

The two boatmen survived unharmed that night. One of them, Máirtín Shíomóin, was drowned long afterwards, together with three others, near Maidhm an Urláir (floor wave) east of Oileán na Cruaiche, while on their way to Roundstone one day to pay the rent.

MICE ON THE ISLAND (2)

There was a man burning kelp on the sand dunes on Cruach na Cara (Saint Mac Dara's Island) one night. He lit a fire near the kiln to roast some potatoes. He left the potatoes and a bit of fish to cool on the sand dunes, and when he went back for them, the mice were eating them. He lifted the potatoes in his hands up as high as his chest, and the mice were coming up his legs.

The people of the townlands had so much respect for Mac Dara's Island that they never took any sand off it as they did off the other islands.

BIRDS ON MAC DARA'S ISLAND (2)

There are oystercatchers on Mac Dara's Island, as well as cliff birds, shags, cormorants, and redshanks. Wild geese come there in winter. There are seagulls and curlews, and there are *siúinicíní* in the sea around it—birds with a red beak; I never saw them on the island. I see sand martins going round in the sea there. Wild duck often rest on the island, and they generally hatch their brood there. I heard the cuckoo on the island, and the grey heron is there. I saw the faoille mhór[14] near the island. It's a great bird to eat. It's even better than the cormorant. Its down is so dense that gunshot slides off it unless you shoot against the down. I saw the robin there and the large wren, the lark and the stonechat.

There's a glen at the top of the island, Log na gCadhan (brent hollow). It's there the brent geese come in to land in cold weather. The brent geese come to the islands when there's frost and snow, and so does the wild goose. The brent goose can be distinguished from the wild goose. The brent goose makes a sound like a whistle, but the wild goose has more of a harsh screech. Frost and snow don't settle on the sea islands as they are warmer on account of the sea winds.

CLIFFS, COVES, AND HOLLOWS (2)

Aill na hIomlachta (ferry rock) is on the south side of the island near Oileán Muiríleach (Strawbeach Island). It was so called because people used it for ferrying cattle to and from the island, and it is also where the boats were berthed or moored on pilgrimage day.

Aill na mBroigheall (cormorant rock) is on the southeastern-most point of Muiríleach Island. The cormorants dry themselves on the rock, as do the shags. There could be ten of them there, sometimes twenty.

An Aill Bhuí (yellow rock) is on the eastern shore of Mac Dara's Island. Boats come to anchor there on the feast of Mac Dara and on other days.

An Fhuaigh Mhór (the great cove) is on the north side of the island, a deep cove between two rocks. This cove is wide enough for a five-ton boat. People are put ashore there.

An Geamaire (the poser) is on the northern shore. Red seaweed comes ashore there. An Geamaire is a high place, a high level rock. There's a streamlet trickling down from above An Geamaire.

An Fhuaigh Leanúnach (the sticking or catching cove) is behind An Geamaire. It's wide, but it's dangerous. Unless the sea is very calm, you can't put a person ashore there. There are rocky edges down in the cove, and a person fishing there usually loses his fishing line because the place is so rugged. When the line gets snagged, it sticks and is usually lost. That's why it's called An Fhuaigh Leanúnach.

An Fhuaigh Bheag (the small cove) is on the northeast of the island. It's a great place for fishing for rockfish. Red seaweed is washed in there, and the rockfish follow the red seaweed. People traditionally fished with rods in An Fhuaigh Bheag until the trammel nets were introduced. Not many people fish there now.

Mullán na bhFathach (the giants' boulder) is on the south-west of Mac Dara's Island, resting on a flagstone five or six footsteps down from the grass edge. It's thought that a strong man, or maybe two, moved it down there to clear the land. They were called giants on account of their strength. The fishing ground in front of Mullán na bhFathach can't be beaten for rockfish. The fisherman likes to cast his sinker in front of the rock. A good fishing ground is a place where fish are plentiful and there is a rocky bottom with seaweed and sea-rods growing on it.

An Leac Dhearg (the red flagstone) is a level rock on which *creathnach* (tiny-shelled dulse) is growing. It's just to the south of Mac Dara's Island. *Creathnach* has always been picked there, and every time it was picked the people feared the weather would break. *Creathnach* is shorter and sweeter than *duileasc* (large-shelled dulse). *Duileasc* grows on seaweed (*cosa dubha*, maiden-hair) and *míoránach* (serrated wrack); and *creathnach* grows on the rock without any seaweed. *Creathnach* grows on the mussel, and the mussel is stuck to the rock. *Creathnach* was usually boiled and eaten with potatoes. With a drop of milk it made a fine sauce. Shore-dwelling women used to pick *creathnach* and go into the hills to exchange it for wool. They would have a bag of *creathnach* on their way in, and a bag of wool coming home. Then they would spin the wool into thread and send it to the weaver to be woven into tweed. They had a warp frame to warp the thread for the weaver.

Carraig Mánus Mór (Mánus Mór rock) is to the southeast of Muiríleach Island, and it's a great rock for strapwrack. There's a hundred boatloads of *coirleach* (strapwrack) around it. There's no better place round the island to get a lobster. This rock is open to the ocean and the sea around it is rough, unless the weather is fine. It's a great spot for line fishing on a fine day.

Mullán an Iascaigh (the fishing rock) is to the southeast of Muiríleach Island. That's where the fishermen went when they had favorable northwesterly wind. It has always been a great fishing ground for rockfish.

Leac Mhadaín (Madden's flagstone) is a hundred yards from the fishing rock. The surrounding area is a good fishing ground for rockfish.

Tobar an Gheamaire (the poser's well) is a little distance inland from the poser, on the side of the island. It's a spring-well, and it never ran dry. Only for this well, no cattle would ever be put onto the island.

Tobar Mhic Dara (Mac Dara's well) is close to the chapel. It's embedded in the flat stone on top of the highest hillock on the island. It's a small, narrow well.

An Reilig (the graveyard) is to the east of the chapel. Most of those buried there are holy people. I haven't heard of anybody else ever being buried there. Limestone flags are placed on some of the graves, and they have sunk into the ground.

Ballaí an Díthreabhaigh (the hermit's ruins) are on the north side of the chapel. They are the old walls of a round house.

DONNCHA MÓR AND HIS WIFE (1)

Donncha had a brother. Macán was his name. He was a bad person; he was rich, and he was hard on Donncha. Donncha was poor. He had nothing but one black sheep. One of the brothers was holy, and the other was evil. He sent out a dinner invitation in Donncha's name, trying to shame Donncha on account of owning only a black sheep. The same day a spirit appeared to Donncha, and a long, low boat appeared, laden down with all the very best that could be served to a king or a prince. The ground opened as far as Donncha's house, and the long, low boat came up there. The place is called Portach Dhonncha (Donncha's bog) ever since, not far from Béal an Chloga.[15] The gentry came and everything was

served up to them, including the black sheep boiled. The poet was
there among them, and when they had finished the feast he said:

> A pity one doesn't have sense
> And control one's voice and mood
> And when generosity came
> The black sheep made good food.
> The spirit spoke to Donncha:
> "A verse in your song, Donncha."
> "Where in the song?" said Donncha.
> "Oh, he who has the calling
> Will have the verse,
> And he who has the verse will have the song." (The Song of
> Heaven).

"You can have any request you want now," said the spirit.
"What do you want?"

"I want nine nines of my relations to be inside in Heaven with
me," said Donncha.

"Oh, Donncha Mór (great Donncha) of the small heart, you
could have asked for the whole world as easy as ask for that much,
because you could have it," said the spirit.

When Donncha Mór died he went to Heaven, together with
every one of the relations he had asked for, when they died. His
wife was not a relation, and she didn't manage to get in with the
rest. When she was at Heaven's door, the Son of God wouldn't let
her in on account of the swearwords she had been using. When
a person would come and ask her for something, she'd say: "May
my eyes not see God if I have it," and she had that as a byword.
That was when Donncha's wife made the poem, and the Son of
God was listening to her recite it at Heaven's door:

> That passion down below has pained me
> Son of gentle Virgin Mary
> With noisy rabble's condemnation.
> In linen cloth they bound him fast
> In shirt of horsehair after that

A long spear with sharpened edges
Your raw flesh they cut in wedges
The hair of your head they tore in tresses
The blood from your side in a wild stream gushes.
How sad that people go mad and raging
And fail to follow the advice He gave them.
There was the body of their dead Savior
Standing there by the edge of a gravestone.
On Your white shoulders the cross You carried,
The crown of thorns upon Your forehead.
Full of nails and they all scattered
Driven to death by blows of a hammer
And, to my grief, their deed they accomplished.
You weren't lying on a feather bed
With colored bedclothes about your head
But in that color your love was harnessed
Glory be to You, You rose up from them.
The door of heaven was opened for you
You brought out multitudes to follow,
Workers, servants and laboring classes
Plunder and prey and no confessing
And the sabbath day in our hearts neglected
Confessed some sins and the rest forgot them
I never served you in proper fashion
But telling lies and much trespassing
Or else denying my own baptism
Or deserting my bed companion
Or breaking long-term Lenten fasting.
It is God who ripens the ears of corn
He brings the fish where You watch them spawn
He brings the light to moon and sun
The chicken in the egg and out again
He parts each woman from her child
The lamb, the calf, and the foal besides
A Protective Father I have in heaven
Powerful lord of the gentle sermons
And the lady of the snow-white breasts likewise
It was she who tied—it was she who untied

And many a long road with him she traveled
Of your store and treasure I implore protection
I feel wretched now for having You offended.

She would have been fine then, but she said: "And remember
that I am Eilís Ní Bhaltair." When she reminded the Son of God
of who she was, He wouldn't let her in. Donncha was inside at
the gate:
"One half of me in and one half out," said Donncha
"And I put it to you, Son of God,
That it's easy to put someone out
When a house of his own he hasn't got."
"It's true for you, Donncha," said the Son of God.
"She can come in now," He said, "but I'll make her blind. She'll
never get sight of me." She was allowed in then, but she is blind
ever since on account of the swearwords she used when she was
alive.

DONNCHA'S PRAYERS (5)

Donncha Mór was a holy man. He was married to a gruff, quarrelsome woman. Donncha would spend a good part of the morning
with his prayers, praying to God. His wife would be in and out of
the house, doing odd jobs and looking at people nearby and beyond. She would quarrel with Donncha and wouldn't allow him
to say his prayers properly. One day he went out and built himself
a cairn of stones on a hillock, and every morning thereafter he'd
go out and say his prayers at the cairn. At harvest time he was
saying his prayers there one morning while everyone else in the
village was busy binding the corn, as the day was threatening to
rain. His wife came out, and she said:

Oh, Donncha Mór of the long rosary beads,
The raven's cry is loud and clear:
Everyone in the village binding corn

And you there praying into God's ear.
Donncha paid no heed to her till he had finished his prayers, and
    then he said:
"Don't heed the scald crow, don't heed the raven,
Don't heed a woman's aggressive voice;
Whether the sun rises late or early
The weather that day will be God's choice.

Donncha arose and went binding his corn. When Donncha
began binding, all the rest of the men had to scurry home from
the rain, but not a drop fell on Donncha till he had finished binding his corn.

MASS HOLLOWS (2)

There's a place in Maínis (Mweenish) they call Aill Chaladh an
Aifrinn (cliff of the Mass landing place) to the north of Inis Srathrach[16] (straddle island). It's a big, high cliff, the height of the gable
end of a house, with shelter beneath it from the northwest wind.
The cliff is only a short distance up from the foreshore. I've heard
some of the old folk say that Mass was sometimes said there in
the old days.

There's a glen to the south of Cnoc an Choillín (hill of the small
wood) they call Gleann an Tobair (glen of the well). There's an
ancient cairn there, and there is a small well beneath the cairn.
People go there on pilgrimage. There's a flagstone over the mound
for the priest to rest his missal on. I heard that Mass was read
there, and that Fr. Muiltheach said Mass there, the priest who
left Seán na Sagart on Cruach na Caoile. He was arrested here in
Gleann an Tobair (glen of the well). This same priest said Mass
in the old field in Coillín (small wood), on the north side of the
hill. He spent some time in Tír an Fhia (Teeranea: land of the
deer) in Gorumna.

There's a green glen in Glionnán (small glen), north of Dúleitir
(Dooletter, black rough slope), and there's a big rock there, Aill

Mhór Ghlionnáin (big rock of Glionnán). I've heard that Mass was said under this rock.

I heard that Mass was often said on Tamhnach Dhúleitir[17] on the north side. People lived there. It's a lonely, remote place. There was no road this side of Cashel at the time.

There was a priest living in Maíros (Moyrus). The people's Mass used to be said in the Graveyard church there. There were nuns there too, in the old days. When the church was being built, the workmen's pay was a penny a day and you could buy a fine fat sheep for sixpence at the time. I heard that Mass used to be said in a glen to the north of Cnoc an Chaisil (Cashel Hill). Mass used to be said on Cnoc na gCorrmhíol (hill of the midges) in Iorras Beag (Errisbeg, small peninsula). Masses were said in lonely places then, as priests had been banished and had to wander and roam.

WELLS

Tobar Ciaráin (Saint Ciarán's well) in Cill Chiaráin, the ninth of September.

Tobar Colmcille (Saint Colmcille's well) on Fínis (Feenish Island: wood island) and another in Maínis in Meall Rua (red hummock). I heard there's another well, named after Colmcille on Bior.[18]

Tobar Mhic Dara (Saint Mac Dara's well) on Oileán Mhic Dara, the sixteenth of July.

There's a well dedicated to Mac Dara in Gleann an Tobair in Coillín.

There's a well by Sruthán Sianach, where the cairns are, called Tobar Sianach.

Tobar Muire (Our Lady's well) in Roisín na Mainiach, where there's a pilgrimage on the Feast of Our Lady. There's a holy well in Leitreach Ard.

Every well on the foreshore, I'm told, is named after Colmcille.

OUR LADY'S WELL (1)

There was a woman in Roisín na Mainiach long ago. Her family got the fever, and she didn't have the proper provisions for them when they got the fever. She saw a beautiful woman where Tobar Muire is now. She went to where the beautiful woman was. There was a well there, and it was full of milk, and the well remained full of milk until the family had recovered. She was able to give them milk from the well every day until they had regained their strength.

When they were strong again, the milk disappeared and the well filled up with water. The water is there ever since. The well is in a hole in a flagstone. This woman who saw the beautiful woman thought it was the Virgin Mary, and the well was called Tobar Muire. There are pilgrimages at the well on the Little Feast of Our Lady in Autumn, on the Major Feast of Our Lady, the eighth day of September, the Feast of our Lady at Christmas, the Feast of Our Lady of Candlemas after Saint Brigid's Day, and the Feast of Our Lady near Saint Patrick's Day.

NOTES

1. *"Mountain pass of the birds,"* near Recess. The "bed" is a shallow hollow in an almost vertical mountainside.
2. *Leitreach*: wet slope; *ard*: elevated.
3. *Aird Thiar*: Ard West, a subdivision of the village of Aird.
4. *Sceirde*: a bleak island with an abundance of seaweed.
5. *Adversary*: euphemism for the devil.
6. *Maíros*: from *máigh*, plain, and *iorras*, peninsula.
7. *Sianach* and *Mac Dara* are thought to be the same person.
8. *Maínis*: *máigh-inis*, Plain Island.
9. Errismore.
10. Lettermullen.
11. *Árainn*: Aran Islands, more particularly the largest of the three islands.
12. *Cruach Chaolainn*: Caolann's Stack.

13. *An Chorainn*: The Weir, near Kilcolgan in County Galway.

14. *Faoille mhór*: the great northern diver. Oystercatchers have red beaks. The white fronted greenland goose comes there.

15. *Béal an Chloga*: Bell Harbor, near Ballyvaughan in Co. Clare.

16. *Srathar*: A wooden saddle for a horse or donkey, from which turf creels can be suspended on both sides.

17. *Tamhnach*: arable place in mountain.

18. *Bior:* Spike—as in Spike Island, Cork. There's *Bior Mór* (Big Bior) and *Bior Beag* (Small Bior). Two families left Bior Mór for the mainland c.1930, leaving the islands uninhabited since.

TWO

—ᴍ—

TROUBLED TIMES

ARD CASTLE AND MAD TADHG (15)

Caisleán na hAirde (castle of the headland) stood at the head of a small creek that's a part of Cuan na hAirde (bay of the headland). The castle was in Aird Thoir (Ard East, east headland) and known as Aird an Chaisleáin (ard castle). There's a stream between Aird Thoir and Aird Thiar (Ard West, west headland). It runs down at the back of the castle.

A walled enclosure surrounded the castle completely, without door or stairway on the landward side. There was an archway on the sea side of the enclosure, with the sea flowing under the archway through which a boat could come and go. There was a device for keeping enough water in the enclosure to float the boat. There was a fairly big patch of land within the enclosure, and the castle stood in the center. The walls of the enclosure were as high as the roof of the building. The roof was made of slates, big heavy slates about half an inch thick. Pieces of the slates are still to be found. The slates were rough, heavy, and thick, mostly the same as came from County Clare.

The stones in the castle and the walls of the enclosure were not cut stones but stones that had been shaped with a sledge hammer.

The corner stones were good, but the rest of the walls were made of small stones. These small stones were stuck together with very hard mortar. Some of the stones are still stuck together. You'd still come across a large lump of mortar and the small stones—spalls—stuck in it. The mortar ran through the whole wall. Not as much as the space of a nailhead was left unfilled. The mortar is as hard today as it was the first day. You couldn't but notice it. (They say that in the old days the blood of slaughtered oxen was mixed in with the sand to make the mortar harder.) There's the odd seashell in the mortar; maybe seashore sand was used to make it. Oyster shells were often used to make lime, and it was the whitest lime of all. Seashore sand needs a lot of lime, much more than lake sand or land sand. There's no limestone to be seen in the old walls. There was no trace of iron there. The stones look as if they were collected on the surface.

There was a street or pathway between the enclosure wall and the castle. That's where Tadhg na Buile (mad Tadhg) is buried, at the foot of the castle wall. The man who killed him threw him out the window, and he was buried where he fell. There was a small dock inside the archway below, and a stairway going up inside the walled enclosure. An enemy couldn't get in unseen. The well of spring water was outside the enclosure; the well is still there, forty yards from the wall between the Ó Cathasaigh's house and Pádraic Mac Con Rí's house. The servant girl who fetched the spring water would come out in a small boat under the archway and come back in again the same way. The night Tadhg was killed, she had gone out for water and she met the sailor, the man who killed him. He asked her if she'd let him in when Tadhg would have gone to bed. She said she wouldn't, that Tadhg would kill her. "Don't worry," he said, "he won't." When Tadhg had gone to bed, the servant girl pushed out the small boat to the sailor, and he went in under the archway in the boat. She showed him the room where Tadhg and his wife were asleep. He went in and killed him with a knife.

"Throw the dirty thing out," the wife said, "before he destroys the bed." The man who had stabbed him threw him out.

It's not been that long since the castle was demolished. The stones were carried off for building dwelling houses. It's not been that long since the slates were still on the castle. When Thomas Martin (who died in 1846 or 1847) was in Baile na hInse (Ballynahinch castle), a man in Ard took slates off the castle. Thomas Martin sent for him and was about to send him to prison until the man promised he wouldn't go near the castle again.

Tadhg had a big boat with a crew of maybe six oarsmen whenever he went to sea. Those men were armed, just like soldiers or guards.

Tadhg na Buile wouldn't allow anybody to cut turf anywhere near the castle. He made the Ard people go east to An Aird Mhór to cut turf, and the signs are there still; the whole hillside is laid bare down to the flagstones.

The O'Flahertys charged rent for the land. They only demanded what was their due. If they didn't get that, they would seize a beast and a crock of butter.

—⚹—

Seosamh Mac Donnchadha (4) had this to say about Tadhg na Buile:

Tadhg na Buile was not an outlaw. He was demanding his rights according to Irish law. The tenants were not willing to pay him rent. Then he began to seize booty (cattle, sheep, etc.). He had a big boat and had a dock built in a creek under the castle—Cuainín na hAirde (the little bay of Ard)—which is the border between the two villages. He had a sluice gate in the dock so that there was always water for the boat. He had a large crew in the boat, a rowing boat that he used for going to Árainn (Aran) and to County Clare.

He had a wife called Síle Ní Fheilpín. It was said that he had kidnapped her. This is how he was killed. A widow's son from Inis Leacan, off Roundstone, had been away at sea for a long time. Tadhg was not in Ard when he left. He came home, and his mother laid some food in front of him. "I have no sauce," she said. "There's a crock of butter there for Tadhg na Buile (mad Tadhg), and if I don't have that for him, he'll take away the cow."

"What sort of man is Tadhg na Buile?" said the son.

She told him.

"Hand me down the butter," he said, "and leave matters between me and Tadhg."

I suppose Tadhg na Buile seized the cow. The widow's son came over at night and spoke to Tadhg's servant girl. She let him in. He went up to where Tadhg was asleep and stabbed him in the bed. His wife, Síle, was in the bed. "Get rid of him," says she, "before he destroys the bed."

It is said that it was a man of the Mac Donnchadha clan who killed Tadhg na Buile. Some of the *seanchaithe* (custodians of oral tradition) say the man who killed him was from Iorras Mór (Errismore).

O'FLAHERTY OF AUGHNANURE (18)

A poor widow lived near Aughnanure Castle.[1] Two sheep of hers strayed onto O'Flaherty's land. O'Flaherty sheared the two sheep and kept the wool in exchange for the grass the sheep had eaten.

The widow had a son. He was overseas in a foreign country as a soldier or an army officer. The mother didn't know where he was as she hadn't heard from him since he left. Shortly after the two sheep were shorn, the son came home. He came to his mother's house but didn't tell her who he was. He asked her for board and lodging. He was given that. He began to ask her how things were in the country and what the local landlord was like. She told him about the hard life she had herself and what O'Flaherty had done to the sheep. The son said nothing, but the following morning he got up before break of day and went and hid near O'Flaherty's castle. He stayed in hiding until O'Flaherty came out to go for a walk in the wood, and he killed him in the wood. That O'Flaherty was called Marcas of Aughnanure Castle.

The morning Marcas was killed, a carter was on his way over to Athenry (in East Galway) with a hogshead of wine. He met Dónall O'Flaherty in Oranmore.

"Have you any news?" Dónall asked the carter.

"O'Flaherty of Aughnanure was killed last night," said the carter.

"Don't go any further," said Dónall.

The second carter came along, and he had the same story.

"Wait a while till the third carter comes," said Dónall to him.

The third carter came, and he had the same story.

"It's a true story if three people have it," said Dónall.

Dónall then told the man with the wine to tap the hogshead and to give everybody a drink. "No matter who drinks it, it's Dónall will pay for it," says he.

O'Flaherty's ghost used to be seen in the wood. He appeared as a ghost to the basket maker there. When the man who was making a little basket lifted his head, he recognised it was O'Flaherty. He asked him what was the matter with him or what made his feet so thin—O'Flaherty's feet were wasted away. The ghost answered him:

> Every cruel law I made,
> Every plunder I committed,
> To God's house I didn't go;
>
> I left the workers to sweat
> And the poor without care,
> But the grass of the two sheep
> Left my feet thin and bare.
>
> I spend a night in the burn,
> A night in the stream,
> A night wandering the hills.
>
> Wet and cold is my bed,
> With rain and cold wind.

Atonement now is what my task is—
While yours is your little basket.

The basket maker glanced down at the little basket. When he glanced up again, the ghost was gone.

Marcas O'Flaherty was in Aughnanure; Dónall was in Oranmore; Caolán was in Cnoc an Dúin (the hill of the fort, west of Clifden). Murcha na Putóige (Murcha of the Intestine) seized and plundered from Slyne Head to Oranmore. This Murcha seized butter in lieu of rent from the poor.

BALLYCONNEELY

There's a village in Iorras Mór (Errismore) called Ballyconneely (Baile Conaola: settlement of the Conneelys). Nobody other than the Conneely clan lived there while the O'Flahertys were lords of Conamara. O'Flaherty lorded it over the Conneely clan. The Conneelys weren't as submissive as he would have liked in serving him as he demanded. There were so many of them that they considered themsleves independent of him and indifferent to him. O'Flaherty didn't like this. He turned against them completely. He ordered his gang of men to go and set the village on fire one night. They committed the treacherous act. They set the village on fire, and those who weren't burnt in their houses were killed, all but one woman who was pregnant. She went on the run unknown to them. She had a son. She reared him until he was twenty-one years old. When he reached the age of reason, he got his mother talking and asked her for her stories about his father and his people; were there any of them still to be seen or was there any news of them, and how he himself came to be there. His mother told him that the O'Flahertys burnt the village where his people lived and killed all those who weren't burnt to death.

"If that's the way," he said, "I'll avenge my people on the O'Flahertys, either that or they'll kill me."

At that time O'Flaherty was living on a lake island with a narrow channel of water between it and the mainland. When the young man came to the lake bank, he was afraid he wouldn't be able to leap over to where O'Flaherty lived. He went and cut six long rods, tied them together, and laid them out over the water to measure the distance. He brought them with him then and laid them on level ground and went to try if he could clear them in one long jump. He then took a run, and he cleared the rods. He knew then that he could jump onto the island. He went onto the island that same night. He killed O'Flaherty and his son and his wife that night. O'Flaherty had a young woman of a daughter. He didn't kill the young woman. People used to say that himself and the young woman got married and that his mother returned with him to Ballyconneely.

It is said that the kith and kin of that man who killed the O'Flahertys are still alive in the country. Feichín Thomáis Ó Conaola is one of them. There was nobody stronger or more ablebodied than them. The night of the storm off Cleggan (1926), Feichín Thomáis was on the sea. He came ashore, himself and a man from Inis Bó Finne (Inishbofin, island of the white cow).

The young man who killed old O'Flaherty was the son of a son of An Ceardaí Rua, (the red-haired craftsman).

The Red-Haired Craftsman Ó Conaola and his son were killed together. The young man wasn't born at the time.

THE LITTLE BAY OF THE SHANTY (3)

Cuainín na Bothóige (the little bay of the shanty) is in Leathmhás (Halfmace). When a priest used to live in Maíros (Moyrus), he had a servant boy and a servant girl. The boy went fowling one day, through the townland of Dumhaigh Ithir and on to Leathmhás.[2] I think there was no dwelling house in Leathmhás at the time. He saw a little shanty that he hadn't seen before, built at the head of the little bay. He looked in the door of the shanty, and he thought he saw two women inside. They appeared to him to be in dire need of food and clothes. They looked thin and agitated and very poorly clad. He turned back. When he got home, he told the priest what he saw, that they seemed to be in dire need of food and clothes and that they should be helped. The priest told the girl to put so much bread and meat and some clothing together and to bring it to them. The girl got herself ready. She brought a parcel of bread and meat and some clothing to them.

It seemed to the priest and the boy that the girl was a long time gone, and as it was now getting late, the priest told the boy to go looking for her. He didn't see any sign of her returning till he had reached the shanty once more. When he looked in at the door of the shanty, the girl lay dead on the floor. They were boiling a piece of her body over the fire. The boy had a loaded gun in his hand, and when he saw what they had done to the girl, he shot the two of them.

The pair in the shanty were two men from some foreign kingdom who came off a ship wrecked off the foreshore there. They built the shanty they were trying to live in. The place is called Cuainín na Bothóige ever since (the little bay of the shanty).

I heard that much from Marcas Ó Laidhe, my mother's father.

THE STONY BEACH OF THE SPANIARDS (4)

In the time of the Armada, a Spanish vessel was shipwrecked on the foreshore off Leathmhás in a place they call Duirling na Spáinneach (stony beach of the Spaniards). The men who made it to shore alive were badly treated. There was one youth who survived and took refuge in a wood on the north side of Cnoc an Choillín. A man from Dumhaigh Ithir who was looking for cattle in the wood met the half dead youth. He brought him home with him and gave him the very best of care until he recovered. He reared him the very same as he reared his own family. The young Spaniard's name was Fernandez. When he became a young man, he said it was time for him to go home. He got his passage on a boat to Galway, and it was very easy for him to get a boat from Galway to Spain as there was a lot of sea traffic between Galway and Spain at the time.

Years later a vessel came to anchor at the spot where the other vessel had been shipwrecked, at Poll Gorm (blue pool), in the shelter of Oileán Mhic Dara. Boats came out from the mainland to the vessel, and every man who went aboard was ordered down below the hatches. I suppose that when this man who reared the Spanish youth went on board, he thought he half recognized one of the Spaniards on the vessel, and he spoke the name Fernandez a few times. The Spaniard walked over to him and asked him why did he mention that name. He said it was the name of a Spanish youth he had reared.

"Are you the man who reared me?" said the Spaniard.

"I am," said the man from Dumhaigh Ithir.

"If you are, you are pardoned, and so are all the others with you," and I suppose they were lucky—because "treachery brings its own punishment."

The Spaniards were intent on revenge. The Spaniard who returned had brought the report back to Spain about the ill-treatment meted out to those who had made it ashore in Leathmhás.

MOOR OF THE FOREIGNERS (12)

A priest from the land of Ulster came on the run to Cnoc an Choillín in Iorras Aithneach. He had been fighting against the army for a long time in Ulster, and he had to go on the run. There was another priest called Ciarán who used to accompany him. They (the army) caught up with Ciarán. If they could find out where Fr. Dónall was, they would spare Fr. Ciarán's life. They were more angry with Dónall than with the other priest. Ciarán said that he'd find him. They came down from the north till they reached Conamara, and they found him in Iorras Aithneach, in a townland called Coillín (little wood). Ciarán recognized him, as did some of the others. They said that he'd pay now for all the trouble he had caused them.

The priest said he wasn't the least bit afraid of dying, that he was as happy to be on the other side as to be in this life. "But if I'm to die," he told them, "my mind is greatly troubled on account of a bag of gold I had, and I have buried it in the ground on that island out there, Cruach Chaolainn, and nobody can find it but myself."

"If there's a lot of gold there, you won't die at all. We won't kill you at all if there's enough there to do us," said the officer in charge of the soldiers.

"I'm willing to give you the gold and then to die," said Fr. Dónall.

"How will we get to the island?" said the officer.

"I'll get a boat," said the priest, "and we won't tell anybody where we're going."

The priest got the boat, and he sailed out to the island with them. They came ashore on the lee side of the island, and he got out himself and got a grip on the boat. He held the boat till they all had come ashore. When they were all out and walking up the island, he gave the boat a push out again, jumped into it himself, and lay down on the bottom of the boat. The wind was with him, and he got the boat out. They began to shoot at the boat, but they couldn't see him as he was on the bottom of the boat. When he was far enough out, he hoisted the sail and sailed back home again. He sent a message throughout Iorras Aithneach, Iorras Beag, and Iorras Mór that no boat was to rescue them. During the following seven or eight days, the people of the mainland could hear one of the men calling and shouting. He was standing on a high hillock on the island. He had a powerful voice. (There are a few people in the world who can project their voices, and it's unbelievable how far; there were such people long ago.) The priest himself heard him. After fourteen or fifteen days, he wasn't to be heard, and the priest said: "No shout will be heard from Seán from Caorán na nGall any more."

A week after that, a boat went out and found them all dead. They were all together there dead on the hillock, and they were buried together, and the place is called Caorán na nGall (moor of the Englishmen) from that day till this.

This priest was a high-ranking priest. Fr. Ciarán went up to him and confessed to having informed on him.

"You were out of order," said the priest. "You shouldn't have done it."

"I was overcome by cowardice," said Ciarán, "and for fear of death, I told them."

"I have settled with them now, and I'll forgive you," said Fr. Dónall.

THE KERNS (4)

A kern was a middleman between the landlord and the tenants. The first group of Seosamh Mac Donnchadha's kinsmen came to Iorras Aithneach as kerns. The tenant would pay rent and would give so many days' work as well—the rent wasn't enough. (The tenants' wives would weave for the kern's family. See "Marcas Ó Cualáin" under "Smugglers.")

A KERN OF THE MAC DONNCHADHA CLAN (4)

The Mac Donnchadha Clan came to Iar-Chonnacht from Céis in County Sligo. I heard that they first came as followers of the O'Flahertys. They were great fighters, and I believe they followed that trade. They spread out from Iar-Chonnacht all over Conamara. They were very powerful in Conamara once, and there was scarcely a townland in this parish (Carna) without one of them as kern. One of them was a kern in Leitreach Ard, another in Maíros, one in Dumhaigh Ithir, one in Leathmhás, and one in Maínis.

The Más kern was going to Galway one day in the company of a rich Galway merchant he used to have dealings with. This merchant had a strongman who was very able-bodied, and the merchant boasted that this strongman of his was the most able-bodied man in the town of Galway. The Mac Donnchadha man told him he had six sons and that he'd wager any bet with him that any one of the six was better than the merchant's strongman. The merchant replied that his own strongman was better than any of his six sons. They placed the bet. Mac Donnchadha didn't know which one of the six sons was best, but the merchant ordered that the six be brought to Galway and that his strongman would try the best of them. A messenger was sent off to Conamara on a gelding, and the kern's six sons were ordered down to Galway as soon as they could.

They were all equally able-bodied, and it was decided in Galway that the first man of the six who would step off the boat on the quay wall in Galway would be the man who would try the strongman. One of the six was known as Aodh Buí (Yellow Hugh). He was very strong, but he wasn't as steady on his feet as some of the others, and the kern was rather worried that the lot would fall on him. A sharp lookout was kept for the boat, to see them coming, and as soon as they were seen, the kern and the rich Galway merchant were on the quay wall before them. When the boat reached the wall, who would be the first man to jump out of it but Aodh Buí!

"You weren't often in such a hurry, Aodh Buí of the stumble, you rascal," said the kern. "You have put my big bet in danger."

The kern's family didn't know till then what business they had in Galway, and Aodh Buí asked his father what the bet was about. The father told him then.

"If that's the case," said Aodh, "you needn't worry."

They were rigged out and went onto the field for the wrestling.

They stripped off and grabbed one another, and it wasn't long till the strongman was laid low with a broken leg. The kern had won the bet.

NINE YEARS DRUNK (4)

Aodh Buí had a brother who was an awful drunkard. He and another brother were in Westport one day with a sloop. The drunkard was drinking till he was drunk, and the steady brother was so mad with him that he went to sea in another vessel that was sailing out of Westport. Nine years later, to the very day, he returned to Westport in a trading vessel. The brother was there before him, and he was drunk. "That's the longest drunkenness I've ever heard of," said the sailor.

THE BATTLE OF THE PILLOW (3)

Maolra Dubh Mac Donnchadha was the kern in Dumhaigh Ithir. He had nine sons. One of them went to sea and was a long time gone. When he came home, nobody recognized him and he didn't tell them who he was. He had to share a bed with the youngest son, and they only had one pillow. The little fellow had the pillow, and the seaman tried to take it off him. The little fellow kept a grip on it while they left the bed, went all over the house, and out onto the street. The big fellow swung the little fellow around him and threw him and the pillow ten yards away.

PROINSIAS MHAOLRA ÓIG (4)

Proinnsias Mhaolra Óig Mac Donnchadha was from Gorumna. He was in Catherine of Russia's fleet, Catherine the Great. They had laid seige to a certain town. The town's defenses were pillars in the sea, with chains strung between them. The vessels had spent a year outside and had failed to break through. Everybody was frustrated, and Proinnsias said that if he could have charge of the fleet for one day, he would seize the town. The request reached Catherine, and she said that he could have it if he thought he could do the business. He said he could, if he got a favorable day. When a day that suited him came, he ordered the vessels to hoist their sails, and they all came together under full sail against the chains and burst their way in through them. They seized the port town.

Proinnsias Mhaolra Óig was made an admiral that same day. He was a private seaman in the morning and an admiral that evening. He got the admiral's badge to wear on his uniform, but he was advised not to wear it in the town as it would be too noticeable. He didn't take the advice, however. He was so delighted with it that he wore the badge on his coat. The people they were fighting against recognized him, and they killed him before the end of the second day. (The storyteller told me he heard this little tale from a man who spent a while in Galway Prison and who had read it in a book he was given in the prison.)

PLACING YOUNG MAOLRA (7)

Maolra Óg Mac Donnchadha lived in Tír an Fhia (land of the deer) on Gorumna Island. His people owned Tír an Fhia and An Trá Bháin (Trabane: the white strand). The name Maolra is still common among his people. They built walls in the middle of the graveyard in Trá Bháin for their dead to be buried within. They are still being buried there—it is their heritage.

MAC DONNCHADHA OF THE FOURPENNY BIT (16)

The Mac Donnchadha clan of the Fourpenny Bit had three estates: Iorras Fhlannáin (Errislannan, Flannán's peninsula), Baile Conaola (Ballyconneely), and Iorras Aithneach. They had tenants, and they laid a fourpenny charge on every house with smoke in its chimney. The reason they laid the fourpenny charge on the houses was to have a fund to help any tenant who was in need, so that he didn't have to emigrate.

The Mac Donnchadhas of the Fourpenny Bit had a house in Leitreach Ard in Iorras Aithneach known as the Demesne. The walls of the house still stand. Maolra Mac Donnchadha lived in the Demesne.

—∿∿—

"I belong to the Mac Donnchadha Clan of Céis myself," said Pádraic Mac Donnchadha (2), as do all of the Mac Donnchadha Clan in Aird Thiar. The first of them came from Gleann Iar-Chonnacht (Glen of West Connacht). There were two other groups of the Mac Donnchadhas in this community, but each group was unrelated to the Mac Donnchadhas of Céis and also unrelated to one another.

There was a group of the Mac Donnchadhas who had a mark on the pot, and there was another group known as the Mac Donnchadhas of the Fourpenny Bit. One of them sold his son for fourpence. (This doesn't tally with the account of the Mac Donnchadha of the Fourpenny Bit given by Mártan Ó Málóid. As regards the group who had a mark on the pot, they were so generous with those who visited them that they never let anybody out without the night's lodging, but they'd never overdo their generosity, and even if the king himself visited them he would only get what they laid out. They would never go beyond the mark on the pot.)

THE FIRST MAN OF THE MARTINS

The first man of the Martins who came to Conamara was a merchant from Galway, and he bought Conamara for twenty pounds. When the O'Flahertys were dispossessed, their land was given to a British soldier. He came to see and to walk the ground, and he came as far as Gort Mór (Gortmore, big field, Ros Muc). He stood on the hill in Gort Mór and looked to the west, and all he could see were lakes and bogs and swamps. He wasn't encouraged by what he saw any more than he was with what he had seen from Oughterard westwards. "Devil a bit of me will go any further," says he, and he turned back again. He met the Martin man from Galway in Oughterard, and they had a drink together. He sold the estate to the Galway man, and twenty pounds is what he got for it.

THE MARTIN MAN LEVYING RENTS

There was a Conneely man in Ardach (Ardagh, height, near Clifden) at the time the Martins came to Ballynahinch after the O'Flahertys were driven out. This man was under oath not to tell anybody what benefit the O'Flahertys got out of Ardach. The Martin man approached him and offered him Ardach for three pinches of pepper if he'd tell him the benefits of Ardach.

The Conneely man stuck his walking stick in the ground and placed his hat on the stick. He then spoke to both the stick and the Martin man:

"It's to you, hat, I am telling this. The wool that made the blanket that was over this gentleman last night grew in Ardach. The flax that made the sheet that was underneath him grew in Ardach. The sea trout and the netted eel are to be had in Ardach, as is the salmon. It can produce wheat and oats, potatoes and barley, and it is a fine spot to live in."

He had then told the benefits of Ardach, but he couldn't find three pinches of pepper anywhere in the land, and he had to pay the Martin man rent like everyone else.

NOTES

1. *Achadh na nIúr*: field of the yews, near Oughterard, Co. Galway.
2. *Dumhaigh Ithir*: *dumhach*, sand dune; *ithir*: soil.

THREE

THE YEAR OF THE FRENCH (1798)

FATHER MYLES PRENDERGAST (4)

Traditional lore (seanchas) about the Year of the French (1798) is to be found all over the Galway Gaeltacht (Irish speaking area). There is a lot of lore in Iorras Aithneach about Fr. Myles Prendergast, a priest who came on the run to Conamara after escaping from Castlebar jail (in Co. Mayo). This is what Seosamh Mac Donnchadha (4) had to say.

The people of Ard saw the French vessels sailing west in the Year of the French. While fishing around Sceirde (bleak island), they saw the warships sailing west. There's no counting the number of people who came in to Iorras Aithneach on the run at the end of the war and the years immediately after.

A Commins man came on the run from Leinster to Béal an Átha Fada, and he had a gun.[1] A long time later, when troubles broke out again, his gun was taken off him. Things settled down again then, and the guns were returned to their owners. When Commins got his own gun back, in Clifden, he took it aside with him and kissed it: "My poor comrade that I had at Vinegar Hill," he said to the gun.

Liam Barry was the first person to set up shop in Carna. He sold salt and other goods that fishermen needed, ropes, tar, oakum, and nails. There were great catches of herring every winter in those days—winter herrings. The herring fishing failed the odd year, and it failed completely one year when Liam Barry had more salt in store than ever before, and he didn't sell the salt. He used to say to himself: "Barry's salt will have its day," and the catchphrase is to be heard here ever since. A person is often told, "Your day will come, as did Barry's salt."

Liam Barry was a stranger. He was a bailiff for the Martins, and he had a stillhouse going at the same time and a wild gang helping him. Every man who came in to him was given a hornful of poteen. The poteen was for nothing if the person drank it. If he didn't drink the poteen, it wasn't for free, because Barry's servants would beat him up. That was Carna law, as they used to say.

Liam Barry was in Carna before the Year of the French (1798) and later. When Fr. Myles Prendergast was on the run, he was in Barry's house one night, himself and Liam Ó Flaithearta from Roisín an Chalaidh.[2] They began to quarrel, and Fr. Myles was seized and tied up in Barry's cellar. Liam Ó Flaithearta sent for the Yeomen to Ballynahinch. Ó Flaithearta himself was bailiff for the Ffrenches (landlords) in Roisín an Chalaidh and in Maínis. There was a man in Carna, Séamas Mac Donnchadha (Séamas Nábla), and when he heard the Yeomen were coming he went down and set the priest free. The priest escaped eastward through Roisín na Mainiach and Caladh Mháinse. When the Yeomen arrived, they followed him. An Ó Fatharta (Faherty) man was burning kelp in a kiln in Aird Mhór; Fr. Myles gave him his coat, and this man ran ahead of the Yeomen and the Yeomen after him. Fr. Myles ran through the smoke till he reached the sea. A man of the Cooke clan in Aill na Brón gave him a boat that brought him to Leitir Calaidh on the east side of the bay.[3]

He was never captured. He had a little house in Béal an Átha Buí (Ballinaboy), and that's where he lived in his latter years.[4] He died of old age. May God have mercy on his soul and on all the souls of the dead; he suffered life.

It was Colonel Richard Martin who was in Ballynahinch when Fr. Myles was captured. The priest was from County Mayo, and he was in jail in Castlebar together with two of his brother's sons, Alfie Gibbons and Seán. Their own relations were supplying them with food, and they sent a key in to them, hidden in a herring's belly. They escaped out as far as the main gate, where the sentry was slumped over his gun and fast asleep. They caught hold of the sentry, but neither of the two Gibbonses had the courage to knock him out, and Fr. Myles had to do it. He hit him with a piece of metal, and the three of them escaped.

The Séamas Mac Donnchadha who cut the ropes and released Fr. Myles in Liam Barry's cellar was the grandfather (on his father's side) of Micheál Mac Donnchadha (Micilín Pháidín Shéamais), the storyteller who lives in Roisín na Mainiach. The nickname "the priest" came down to Séamas's son and to his grandsons. There is one of them still alive called "Colm an tSagairt" (Colm the priest).

The Ó Fatharta man who wore the priest's coat and ran ahead of the Yeomen to lead them astray was the grandfather of Seán an Chóta, who was the biggest man in this community for a long time.

—w—

Pádraic Mac Donnchadha's (2) account of Fr. Myles's escape from jail is the same, nearly word for word, as Seosamh Mac Donnchadha's account.

When Fr. Myles was in prison, the Gibbonses and himself cast hidden lots to see which of them would have to knock the gate-keeper out. The lot fell on Fr. Myles, but he didn't intend to kill him. The gatekeeper was asleep. The only implement they had was a sledgehammer, and he hit him on the head with it, not intending to kill him but to knock him out. But it happened that he killed him with the blow. They took the key off him, they opened the lock, and the three escaped.

—⚋—

Parthalán Mac Donnchadha (8), a neighbor of Seosamh Mac Donnchadha in Aird Thiar has this account of Fr. Myles.

Fr. Myles came on the run here from County Mayo. He settled down in Crón Aidhle, near Aill na gCuil (cliff of the flies), Tuaim Beola (Beola's tomb).[5] He was made very welcome there, and the people treated him well. Colonel Martin had the army in Ballynahinch, and Crón Aidhle was too close to Ballynahinch. He left Crón Aidhle and came to Glinsce, and he came to a good place. The people of Glinsce treated him decently and generously, and they would have done so forever if he had stayed among them. He left Glinsce after a while, and he came to Barry's in Carna. It was not a friendly house he came to when he came to Carna. Barry had a shop of all kinds. He sold salt and drink and fish. He had a stillhouse, and the still was not idle. Barry was generous to Fr. Myles for a while, but in the end he tried to earn some money on him because there was a price on Fr. Myles's head, dead or alive. The day the army was sent for, Barry seemed in a generous mood toward the priest. He locked the door of Fr. Myles's room. It has been said that he had taken some drink and that they sent for the army when they found him drunk.

There was a servant girl there who heard that the messenger had gone to Ballynahinch. She told Séamas Nábla Mac Donnchadha, and Séamas Nábla released Fr. Myles from the room; he broke the window and let him out. He told him a messenger had gone to Ballynahinch for the army and that the army was on its way. By then, the army was at the bridge between the two lakes between Carna and Cloch an Mhíle (the milestone).

He escaped downhill to the east. Two big boats were drawn up on dry land at the mouth of the river. The anchor of one of the boats tore the calf of the priest's leg, and it was badly cut. Nevertheless he kept on walking—he had to—till he came to a kiln where kelp was being burnt in Roisín na Mainiach. The man who was burning the kelp was called Ó Fatharta (Faherty), and I've an idea he was the great-grandfather of the Sergeant in Gort Mór (Ros Muc).

The priest told the Ó Fatharta man of the danger he was in, that the army was looking for him. The Ó Fatharta man had actually seen the army approaching. He told the priest to take off his coat and his caroline (hat) and that he would put them on himself and make the army walk some more. "You'll stay here and the strapwrack (seaweed) will cover you," he said.

Fr. Myles stripped off and hid himself under the strapwrack. The Faherty man put on the priest's coat and hat, and off he went over the moor in the direction of Cill Chiaráin. He kept going till he reached Ros Dugáin (Duggan's point) on the seashore in Coill Sáile (wood of the salt water). He went into a house there and told them he was on the run instead of the priest and that he was in great peril. The man of the house told him to take off the coat and hat and that he would hide them for him.

There was a *ciseog* (shallow basket) of potatoes on the floor, and they were about to eat a meal. He was told to sit at the basket with the rest of them and that nobody would know but that he was one of the household. It wasn't long till the army arrived. They came to the house and asked if they had seen a man in black passing by. The man of the house told them they had, that he had gone out in the boat that had just sailed out from the shore, and that he had heard the stranger calling out to the people in the boat, asking them to take him on board and bring him to Béal an Daingin[6] just across the bay. The army kept going east as far as Inbhear (Inver, river mouth) in Ros Muc, but they failed to get a boat that would follow the boat that had put to sea, and they didn't hear any more about Fr. Myles.

Fr. Myles stayed around here in this community till the wound in his leg had healed. I have an idea that he later lived on this side of Clifden, in Ardach (Ardagh) or in Ballinaboy. He lived in Mongach for a while. The Ó Fatharta man moved house and went to live in Cois Fharraige. This Faherty man's daughter married Seán Ó Caola in Aird Thiar. She was the mother of Seán an Chóta Ó Caola.

—∽—

The fourth of January, 1937. Seosamh Mac Donnchadha, Beairtle Mac Donnchadha, and Seosamh Ó Mongáin (Joseph or Josie Mongan) are with me here in the hotel in Carna. Having read to them all the lore about Fr. Myles that Beairtle gave me last year, we heard some more.

The following is Seosamh Mac Donnchadha's (4) account.

Fr. Myles was staying one night with an Ó Mainnín man in Gleann Chóchan (Glencoaghan). He was asleep in his room early in the morning. There was a young woman in the house, and she went out for a pailful of water. When she came in, she said there were men coming down to the house with caps she had never seen the like of on anybody. When Fr. Myles heard her, he was up like a shot. These men were running in one door as he was going out the other. They followed him a long way over the moor till he came to the bank of a river. He cleared the river in one leap and not one of the Yeomen was able to clear it. There was frost on the ground, and Fr. Myles stumbled on it after clearing the river. An icicle pierced his knee and wounded him. He said that if the Yeomen had been able to jump the river as he had done himself that he'd be in a fix, as he was lame. I think that was the time he was sent to Iorras Aithneach.

It was said that the Martin man was trying to get a pardon for him. He sent Fr. Myles an invitation to meet him, and he came. The pardon had a condition that Fr. Myles would not accept, and when he wouldn't, the Martin man said, "I can't help it, but you had better be off down to Iorras Aithneach."

The following is Beairtle Mac Donnchadha's (8) account.

The reason Fr. Myles didn't accept the pardon was that his two companions, the two Gibbonses, Aibhistín (Austin) and Seán, were not to be set free as well as himself. Joseph (Josie) Mongan (11) said: "Fr. Myles lived for a while in the house where Máirtín Aodha Mac Craith is now. Micheál Dhiarmuid Liam Ó hUaithnín (Greene) told me that; he's dead for the past sixteen years. He was three score and ten years at the time. He also said that he was a Prendergast."

Beairtle Mac Donnchadha again.

It has been said that Fr. Myles went east across the bay to the islands the time he was reported, the day he gave his coat and his hat to the Ó Fatharta man at the kelp kiln. It's thought he didn't stay long over there till he went back west again. He went to live in Imleach Mór or in Béal an Átha Buí. There used to be a big fair in Béal an Átha Buí at the time. A man was killed at the fair one day, and Fr. Myles was sent for. The priest came as the man was at death's door. Nevertheless he reached him in time and anointed him. He then said he thought he had done his last service for God. He was a great age by then.

Seosamh Mac Donnchadha again.

I heard an old man say Fr. Myles was a Prendergast. There wasn't a man who came in to Conamara (on the run) who didn't change his surname.

He stayed with Seán Locard in Glinsce (Glinsk) for a while. When he was leaving, Seán gave him some advice. He told him to avoid the big shots and to trust and care for the ordinary people. Seán Locard was a stranger in the place. He had a little house of his own in the end, and the neighbors were helping him. He wrote Leabhra Eoin (John's Books) for people who came looking for them.[7] This "book" was from the gospel of Saint John, and people used to wear it around their neck.

Fr. Myles must have got his college education overseas because he had no respect for the new priests coming out of Maynooth.

—⁓—

MORE ABOUT FATHER MYLES

Seán Mac Con Rí (12) Is The Storyteller

I knew an old woman who used to bring food to Fr. Myles when he was hiding in Gleann Chóchan (Glencoaghan). She was a young girl at the time. She was born in Aird Thiar. Her mother died, and her father remarried. She left home and went to relatives in Gleann Chóchan. They were of the Mac Con Rí clan. They used to send food to the priest, and the young girl was the one who brought it out to him.

Séamas Mac Con Rí was the one who was in Gleann Chóchan in the Year of the French. My own people were related to him. Séamas had a son called Maolra (Myles) who went to live in Barr na nÓrán (Barnanoraun). Maolra had a son called Micheál, and Micheál's son is now there, another Maolra. The boys who were on the run from the Black and Tans used to be in Maolra's house in Barr na nÓrán. The Black and Tans came to the house one night, but Maolra's wife heard them coming. She got up and hid the money in her armpit and went back to bed again, beside her husband. When the Tans came in, they began to search the chest.

"Are you getting anything?" one of the men asked the man who was searching.

"Nothing but receipts," said the other man.

They left again without getting any money.

Micheál Mac Suibhne used to be on the run with Fr. Myles.[8] That's what he was talking about when he said,

"What caused my downfall was not battle or tax
But playing my part for Ireland."

Three other men were on the run together with Fr. Myles, a
Mac Con Rí man, a Mac Conaola man, and an Ó Máille. These
three men and the priest were arrested once and were thrown
into Galway jail. They broke out one night, and in the morning
when a washerwoman came to the river with her washing, she
saw four men under the bridge. She went home and told her husband about the four men under the bridge and that they couldn't
come out on account of the flood.

"Did you tell anybody?" he asked.

"I didn't," she said.

"That's all right," said the husband, and he locked his wife and
the children in a room, for fear she'd utter a word, until he'd have
time to get the men away. He went to the bridge and got a rope
in to them and brought them onto dry land. He brought them
to some house where they got food, and then they walked out of
Galway, one at a time. Each of them took a different road, and
they met up again in Conamara.

One night when Fr. Myles was being pursued, a spy put water
on his pistols. When he found them wet, he said that he was never
made a duck's nest of until that night.

There was an aunt of my mother's that I knew, a Mulkerrins
woman, who was married to a Conneely man in Iorras Fhlannáin
(Errislannan), and she often saw Fr. Myles. Lord Mayo, one of the
Burkes, got a pardon for him, and he went to live in the middle
of the moor to the east of Béal an Átha Buí (Ballinaboy), to the
east of Marconi's place.[9] He had a shanty of his own there, and
my grandaunt often saw him. One day he was caught in a hail-
storm, and he took off his hat to let the hailstones hit his head.
My mother's aunt saw that.

Addendum

There isn't a place that Fr. Myles spent some time in that there isn't
some lore still about how he was hunted by the English. When
he first came in to Conamara from County Mayo, he lived for a

while in a house in Maoileann (Mweelin, flat-topped hill), across
the lake from Kylemore. He was there until two strangers came
round who raised a lot of suspicion. The two used to pretend to
be fishing, but as soon as Fr. Myles heard about them he took to
the hills and went as far as Moyard. Thomas Conroy who lives in
Kylemore says there is a cleft in a rock on Binn Bán (white peak),
the highest peak of the Twelve Pins, called Fr. Myles's Cleft, and
I suppose he spent some time in hiding there. There's a place
on the way from Moyard to Gleann Chóchan where he spent
some time until the pursuit caught up with him again, as told by
Seosamh Mac Donnchadha and Seán Mac Con Rí. He always
headed south. He went to Crón Aidhle and from there to Inis Ní
and to Glinsce in Iorras Aithneach after that. He was pursued
into Iorras Aithneach even. He escaped to Leitir Calaidh (Lettercallow) from Iorras Aithneach, but he didn't spend much time
in the islands. He went to the far west of Conamara then.

There's a cave near Clifden called Fr. Myles's Cave. There's a
quarry in Leitir Dín (Letterdeen) where he hid from the Yeomen.
He was going the road on horseback one day when he heard the
sound of cavalry behind him. He turned the horse into a quarry,
and the soldiers passed him by to the west without seeing him.

He is still remembered in Doire Bhrón near Clifden where he
lived in a hut of his own at the end of his life.[10] The walls of the hut
are still there. There is a Mass rock there that's called Fr. Myles's
Rock now. It's said he used to say Mass there, with the rock for an
altar. There's a well near the rock, Fr. Myles's Well. It was in Doire
Bhrón that he shot the spy who followed him from County Mayo.

The priest often slept in the house where Pádraic Mac Con
Rí and his sister now live. Their grandfather, Micheál Mac Con
Rí, was living in Tuar an Sceichín (Tooraskeheen) in the priest's
time. The priest used to stay in his house. One black, dark night
a stranger came the way, and he came into the house. He saw Fr.
Myles. The priest didn't trust him, and he wouldn't stay in the

house that night. Micheál Mac Con Rí had to escort him to Barr na nÓrán in the middle of the night.

The house nearest the bridge in Gabhlán (Gowlaun, small fork), on the south side, that's where Fr. Myles died. There are people living in the house still. A Mac Con Rí woman was there at the time, and it was she who laid him out. He knew he was dying, and he had given her instructions about how he was to be laid out and buried. It is believed he is buried in the old cemetery in Clifden. The blessings of God on his soul. As for the two Gibbonses who escaped from prison with Fr. Myles, the two of them came to Conamara. Aife (Austin) was killed in a fight in Inishbofin, and his lament is in print.[11]

The cleft where Seán Mac Giobúin used to hide is on the eastern shoulder of Dúchruach (black peak) the mountain above Kylemore. He spent a long time in the area. He walked the hills and was fond of swimming in the lakes. He said that Loch na gCat (lake of the cats) was the cleanest lake he ever swam in. He returned to County Mayo to a wedding. He was arrested, and Denis Browne hanged him in Westport. Browne was his godfather.

PEOPLE ON THE RUN (3)

Tadhg Ó hAnainn came to Coillín, himself and his wife and two children. They came on the run from Sligo after the Year of the French. They had a sod hut in Coillín. Tadhg used to be called Tadhg Mór, and there's a field behind my house called Garraí Thaidhg Mhóir (Tadhg Mór's field). There's a kiln in the field used for hardening grain before sending it to the mill to be ground. There was a mill there at the time.

There was a man called Ó Cearbhaill living in Roisín an tSamha, who came west across the Shannon. He was a weaver, a linen weaver and a wool weaver. He was able to do every sort of weaving.

There was a man of the Mac Con Buí clan in Roisín na Mainiach who came west across the Shannon after running from a battle.

RENT (17)

When the last of the Martins, Thomas Martin, left, the tenants' rent was trebled. Más (Mace) was paying £32 rent, with Cnoc Buí (Knockboy, yellow hill) thrown in for pasture. When Law Life came in, they levied £106 on the townland and took Knockboy off the tenants.[12] The Más people were living off the sea, suffering misery to earn rent for the landlord.

THE PEDLAR OF GREEN HOLLOW (1)

There was a wandering pedlar, and he had a wife. He had picked out certain houses to stay in, in his comings and goings. He used to come to this part of the country. He left his wife behind him once when he didn't want to bring her with him to wherever he was going. He left her in a house where there was a shop, and off he went to where he was going himself. When he was coming back, it was nighttime as he was approaching the house where his wife was. He met up with two men on the road, and the three of them were walking together until daybreak. These were troubled times, and there were guards on the roads. When the three men met the guards, the guards arrested them. They took them away with them—they were tied up and made to walk ahead of the guards. They were walking till they came to a house.

Anybody caught out late during these troubled times was to be shot. When they came as far as the house, the first person they put up against the door to be shot was the pedlar. One of the guards stood out in front of him to shoot him, but the gun misfired three times. They threw him aside from the door after these three failures, and another man was put against the door and was shot. The gun did not misfire and the bullet killed him. The third man was then shot and killed. It was said that the pedlar couldn't have been doing anything wrong, for if he were, he'd have been killed on the first attempt. He was set free.

The pedlar came to where his wife was, and the following night the guards came to the shop where they were staying. It was announced that the guards were coming. Any man wearing a blue coat was to be killed. The pedlar's wife immediately told her man to make a *cruipidín* (a makeshift stool) of himself and that she would sit on him. He bent his head down between his legs and she sat on him and draped her long petticoat down around him. There wasn't a bit of him to be seen.

The guards came in, and there wasn't a man in the house they didn't stab with their lances. They didn't go near any woman. The only man to escape with his life was the Pedlar of Poll Bán.

NOTES

1. *Béal an Átha Fada*: mouth of the long ford, near Ballynahinch.
2. *Roisín an Chalaidh*: little headland of the landing place.
3. *Aill na Brón*: rock of the millstone.
4. *Béal an Átha Buí*: mouth of the yellow ford.
5. *Beola's tomb*: he is said to have been a giant or a chieftain, from whom Na Beanna Beola / Beola's peaks (the Twelve Bens) are also named.
6. *Béal an Daingin*: Bealadangan, mouth of the stronghold.
7. *Leabhar Eoin (John's Book)* consists of the opening words of the poetic prologue to St. John's Gospel, folded and wrapped in scapular form about the neck, or concealed in clothing, and came to be used in Christian devotion throughout the Middle Ages as a protective and healing charm.
8. *Micheál Mac Suibhne* (1760–1820) was an Irish language poet, born near Cong, then part of County Galway and now in County Mayo. He spent most of his life in Conamara. Tomás Ó Máille published nine of his best poems in *Micheál Mac Suibhne agus filidh an tSléibhe*, 1934.
9. *Guglielmo Marconi* (1874–1937) was an Italian-Irish electrical engineer, generally credited as the inventor of radio communications, and

he invented his historic "Wireless Telegraphy" Patent No. 12,039 of 2 June 1896. In 1905 a high-powered station was set up by Marconi in Clifden, Co. Galway, which from October 1907 provided the first reliable transatlantic telegraphy service.

10. *Doire Bhrón:* wood of the millstone.

11. Ó Máille 1934, 61

12. *The Law Life Assurance Society*: At one time, this company based in London held up to 165,000 acres in County Galway through the disposal of property by the Encumbered Estates Court following the Great Famine of the 1840s. (Robinson 2008, 130, 150; 2011, 39)

—ᵐ—

THE TORIES/VIGILANTES

TORIES IN IORRAS AITHNEACH (1, 2)

THERE WAS A GANG OF people here long ago, called the Tories, to defend the rights of any poor person who suffered injustice. The way they worked was to go out in secret by night, and to any man who had done something wrong they would punish him or worse.

There was a man named Breathnach (Walsh) in a certain town who kept raising the price of food on all the markets, having bought and stored a lot of the food himself. When the poor people tried to buy the food from him, he would have raised the price. Then he was warned not to raise the price on the poor, but he didn't heed the warning. He was given a second warning, but he didn't heed that either. They only gave him the two warnings. A man accosted him on the road and shot him. (That was all Seosamh Mac Donnchadha told about the Tories or Vigilantes.)

It is said that a Loideán (Lydon) man from Maíros was in charge of the Tories in Iorras Aithneach. A boatman from Conamara was in his boat in Galway harbor one day, or in An Chorainn, when an Englishman was killed in County Clare.[1] A man who had the appearance of a gentleman came to the pierhead and asked if there was any man from Conamara in the boat. The boatman said he was from Conamara. The man on the pier put his hand in his pocket, took out a watch, handed it to the Iorras Aithneach man, and told him to bring it to Séamas Ó Loideáin in Maíros and that he would have to deliver it to him or that there would be trouble. He gave the watch to Séamas Ó Loideáin. The watch was a signal.

Tomás Pheadair Mac Donnchadha of Aird Thiar (Ard West) was in the Tories at that time. A man approached him one day, as he was sowing potatoes in his field, with a message asking him to go to a certain place that night with the Tories. His wife saw the stranger talking to her husband. She knew that her husband was active in the Tories and that this man had come for that purpose because he had come some distance, from Cashel maybe or even further away. She stole up behind the stone wall to listen to them, and she found out that they were going to do something wrong. The stranger saw her leaving and knew she had overheard everything.

"I'm afraid," he said to Tomás, "that your wife has only till tonight to live, when these men gather together."

"I can't help that," said Tomás, "but whatever death is chosen for her, I can't say a word against it."

She herself knew the hatchet of death was hanging over her, and she left the house. She went into a cave in the foreshore for shelter. She stayed there, and when the Tories gathered that night, they found out that she had heard what they were about to do. Every man said she had to be killed, and Tomás Pheadair, her husband, had to say the same thing. The house was searched, and they failed to find her there. They searched all around it outside, and they didn't find her there. They then told Tomás to make her swear she'd never say a word of what she had heard.

She stayed where she was till the tide began to flow into the cave. She said she might as well be killed as drowned, and she left the cave halfway between life and death. She went into another cave that seemed safer, and she stayed around there till the sun had risen the following morning. When she reluctantly returned home, Tomás had just got up. He asked her where she had been, and she told him.

"You are the luckiest woman of your race," he said. "You would have been killed if you had been caught in the house, and I wasn't able to help you. You'll have to swear now that you'll never mention a word of what you've heard!"

She promised she wouldn't, of course, and she didn't as long as any of those who were alive then were still alive. She lived till she was a good old age, and she told everything in the end.

—⁓—

I read the lore about Tomás Pheadair Mac Donnchadha and about his wife being condemned to be shot by the Tories to Beairtle Mac Donnchadha (8) and to Seosamh (4). Beairtle confirmed it.

Pat Bhile told you the truth. Tomás Pheadair and his wife, Nuala Seoighe (Joyce) were my grandfather and grandmother. It was Brian Ó Laidhe (O'Lee), the son of "The Doctor," who sent her a message to leave the house the night the Tories were to come.[2] Brian himself was a Tory, and he heard what they had planned. Her husband didn't tell her at all, and no one was harder on her than her sister's husband. When she got the message from Liam Ó Laidhe, she left the house and brought her son Pádraic with her. He was six years old at the time. Pádraic was my uncle. He was a year and a half or two years older than my father, and my father is nine years dead. He was ninety-six when he died. He was four years old when his mother, Nuala Seoighe had that narrow escape, which means it's a hundred and one years since she spent the night in the seashore cave, 1835 or 1836. My father was born in the second month of Autumn 1831. I heard him say that. (January 4, 1937)

TORIES IN ERRISMORE (2)

There was a gang of Tories in Iorras Mór.[3] The man who was their captain was the man who swore against them. Seven or eight of them were arrested, convicted, and deported, for whatever their terms were. Others went on the run and saved themselves. The man who informed on them was taken into the barracks to be sent to England when the court case was over, and he was in the barracks for two weeks without putting his nose outside during all that time. The rest of them put their heads together and decided to draw hidden lots to see which of them was to shoot him. The lot fell on a married man, who had a wife and five children, to keep watch on the captain. He was given a firearm and was sworn not to tell his secret to any man, no matter who, and if any man pushed him too far, to shoot him. The rest of the Tories walked around near the barracks at night to see if he was doing the job properly.

When a certain young man grew impatient, he came out at the dead of night and went to the man who was watching for a chance to kill the captain. He didn't let anything on, but asked him what he was doing there.

"Mind your own business!" said the watchman. "It's none of your business to be asking me questions."

"You'll have to tell me," said the young man.

The watchman put his hand into his armpit pocket to get his firearm, and the young man caught him by the two hands.

"Good man yourself!" he said. "Only for you were about to do that to me, I would have done it to you. Go home now," he said, "and I'll take your place and see what I'm about to do."

The married man went home, and there wasn't a happier man on earth. The young man came home, and the household were asleep. He took a cock belonging to his mother and cut the head off it as he was approaching the barracks again. He spilled every drop of the blood over his head, face, and clothes. He came up to the barracks and knocked at the door. The guard opened the door and saw this young man lying outside, who seemed to be very weak and barely able to speak. The guard asked him what happened to him, and he said three men had killed him on the road outside. The guard woke everyone in the barracks and told them there was a dead man here. They asked the young man which road his three attackers took, and he told them. They ran to see if they could catch them till they had gone two or three miles. When the guard who remained in the barracks thought they were a long time gone, he went outside to see if there was anybody stirring. The captain who swore against the men was stretched on a stool beside the fire. When he heard the talk about the man who was attacked, he straightened up. The young man immediately put his hand in his armpit pocket, took aim, and didn't leave a drop (of blood) in him. Then he ran off by a different road. When the police came back, they found the informer shot dead, and nobody knew who did it. The young man was never captured.

I seem to remember hearing that the young man who shot the informer was a Conaola (Conneely) man.

SEOIRSE Ó GRÉACHÁIN (2)

It was a County Clare man who first introduced the Tories to this part of the country. There was no Tory here till the Clareman came. He came while on the run, and his name was Seoirse Ó Gréacháin (Grayhan/Grehan). He settled down in Maíros in Seán Ó Loideáin's house, where there were men of action and valor. Seán Ó Loideáin himself was old at the time, but the young men were active, as were most of the young men in the country, I believe. It's a little over a hundred years now since the Tories were here.

Seoirse Ó Gréacháin died of a sudden ailment in Maíros early one summer. Maolra Seoighe (Myles Joyce) in Glinsce heard he was ill and came to see him. He was dead when he got there.

When he came in, he asked the people of the house if he was alive. They said he wasn't, that he was dead for the past few hours or so.

"Was he searched?" he asked.

They said he wasn't. Maolra Seoighe searched him and found a book in his pocket with the names of a few hundred men in it from as far west as Clifden and from Cashel to the north. He immediately placed the book at the back of the fire and burned it. The army was within a mile of the house by the time the book was burned. They had heard that Seoirse Ó Gréacháin was in Maíros, and they were coming to arrest him for something he had done in County Clare. He was dead before they came.

The Maolra Seoighe who burned Seoirse Ó Gréacháin's book was a weaver, a piper, and a schoolmaster, and he was very good at each of those trades. He was able to read, write, and teach Irish and English. There was no schoolhouse, but he went from house to house. He would spend a fortnight or a month in some house in the townland, and all the young men from the neighboring townlands would come to him. He spent a good while in An Aird and did great teaching there. It was he who taught Paitsín Eoin Mac Con Rí who was a top class scholar.

They used to call Maolra "The Yellow Piper" on account of being a musician. He had four sons: Uáitéar, Stiofán, Maolra, and Pádraic, and a daughter whose name was Úna.

Uáitéar was a weaver, the same as his father, but he wasn't a patch on his father. The father was so good at his trade that he could weave a picture into the cloth. Uáitéar lived in Más, but he died in Inis Ní (Inishnee). He had a daughter, Bríd. She married a Kelly, Paits Ó Ceallaigh. They had a son called Máirtín. It was for Máirtín, when he was a youngster, that his grandmother made the song they call "An Ceallacháin Fionn" Nóra Mháirtín Nic Taidhg was the name of the grandmother who began composing "An Ceallacháin Fionn." (The Little Fair-Haired Kelly). She had a sister who was known as Bairbre Mháirtín. Bairbre's own daughter had a son called Tomás Ó hUaithnín (Greene), and she began replying to her sister about Tomás, each of them praising her own daughter's son and disparaging the other daughter's boy.

It was Seosamh Mac Donnchadha who added that much to what Beairtle Mac Donnchadha had said. And Pádraic Mac Donnchadha had this addendum: Uáitéar (Walter) never wore a shoe. The soles of his feet were so hard that he used to break the whelk shells when he walked on them.

NOTES

1. *An Chorainn*: The Weir, near Kilcolgan, County Galway.
2. The mythical island of Beag-Árainn is thought to have been found west of the Aran Islands and south of Na Sceirde, a cluster of rocks west of Iorras Aithneach. Beag-Árainn corresponds with Hy-Brasil (Uí Bhreasaíl) and Árainn Bheag (Ó Con Cheanainn 2002).
3. *Iorras Mór*: Errismore, big peninsula.

FIVE

BIG MEN

BIG SEÁN Ó MAOILCHIARÁIN (MULKERRIN) (4)

There was a man living on Oileán Máisean (Mason Island). He was called Seán Mhic Dhónaill Dorcha (dark). He was a big, strong man, a boatman and fisherman. He went around with Raghnall Mac Donnchadha's family from Dumhaigh Ithir. It was he who tied and carried the colt in his arms out from Cruach na Caoile (Deer Island) and placed it in the boat. One day he was one of a crew who were killing basking sharks. When the shark was speared, it ran with the rope, and the man who was letting the coil run free got his foot entangled in the spear rope. Seán Mór grabbed the rope and held the shark while the other man got his foot out of the tangle. Only for Seán Mór the shark would have pulled the other man out of the boat. But the shark brought the boat under, and the crew were thrown into the deep. Another boat rescued them, but their own boat had disappeared with the shark.

Seán Mór used to sail around the coast killing basking sharks. They used to sell the livers in Westport. He was in a pub in Westport one night. The woman of the house had a daughter, and she offered the daughter to Seán Mór. "I'm not good enough for your daughter," said Seán Mór. "I'm a poor man, I have no wealth. I wouldn't be suitable for her." But he married a woman in Bun Dorcha (Bundorragha, dark end) on Killary Harbor later, and that's where he spent the rest of his life. Síomón Bhriartaigh Dhónaill Ó Maoilchiaráin, Pádraic Mac Donnchadha Liam's grandfather, told me he was of the same stock as Seán Mór.

Fishing for the basking shark has long since ended, and the kerns have long since left Dumhaigh Ithir, but Seán Mór was there at the time. Maolra Mac Donnchadha's family were at war with the Seoighigh (Joyces). Maolra used to put a suit of clothes on Seán Mór and bring him along as one of his own sons. When Seán Mór shook hands with one of the Seoighigh, he'd squeeze so hard that he'd leave the man impaired.

In those times, they would travel far from home and they were known far and wide. When they were stormbound, they would spend a week or two in Inishbofin, in Westport, or in Killary Harbor. A man often married far from home, as Seán Mór did in Bun Dorcha. Seán's people are a long time here. It's impossible to say how long.

Marcas Ó Maoilchiaráin, who is here with us, is of that same stock. He was born in Aird Thiar. His father came from Más. Marcas's father was a great storyteller. Tomás Mac Con Rí in Inis Ní was good, but he came from Aird. Máirtín Réamoinn Mac Donnchadha used to be storytelling in Marcas's house. Marcas was related to Máirtín's wife. This Máirtín Réamoinn was Micil Pháidín's grandfather on the mother's side.

THE Ó MAOILCHIARÁIN CLAN (2)

The Ó Maoilchiaráin Clan lived on Oileán Máisean (Mason Island). They were very big men. One of those big men was known as Leanbh Mhanannáin[1] (Manannán's child). Aill na Croise (rock of the cross) cemetery is in the sand on the easternmost point of the island. A spring tide uncovered the bones. There was a thighbone that was nearly as long as the blade of an oar. The only one of them left now is Pádraic Aindriú Ó Curraoin, and his mother was a Maoilchiaráin. (There's hardly a seanchaí or story-teller in Iorras Aithneach who isn't related to the Maoilchiaráin clan. They are deeply rooted in these parts, and it's nearly certain that they are all steeped in traditional lore and literature. What-ever anyone says, there isn't another community in Conamara with as much traditional lore and oral literature as the Carna community in Iorras Aithneach.)

SEÁN OF THE FROCK COAT (2)

Seán Ó Caola who lived in Aird Thiar was Seán an Chóta's father. He was married to a Faherty woman, and it was thought to be from her that Seán an Chóta got his strength and his size. It is said she was from Cois Fharraige.[2] She was a big, strong woman. She was able to walk to Galway and back, and no other woman was able to do it faster. She carried the makings of a mainsail of canvas on her back from Galway once together with the makings of a pair of oars.

She had three sons, Seán an Chóta Ó Caola, Pádraic Ó Caola, and Micheál Ó Caola. Micheál married and went to Damhros (Dawros, ox peninsula) in Leitreach Ard (Letterard, high rough slope). Seán married in Aird, and Pádraic didn't marry at all. Seán wore a frock coat till he was a grown man. That's why he was called Seán an Chóta. He was six feet four inches tall in his bare feet when he was fully grown, and he was broad and strong as well. He said he was always afraid to lay a fist on a man for fear it would kill him.

He worked on the land, but he mostly worked in boats, ferry-ing seaweed to An Chorainn (The Weir) or Kinvara nearby. He used to fish and occasionally fished for lobsters when they were in season. His handiwork is to be seen anywhere he built a stone wall. The big stones he put in a wall would test the strength of four men nowadays. But strong and all as he was, there was a stronger man in Ard. One day Seán had a boat in the quay at Poll an Ghlasoileáin. The boat was empty, but he was to load it with seaweed to bring to Kinvara. He overslept that morning, and when he reached the boat the tide had gone out. He untied the ropes and got ready to push the boat out. He tried his best but it failed him. The tide was still going out. He tied the ropes again and went home. There was a Maoilchiaráin house quite near the quay, and there was a big, strong young man there standing in the doorway watching Seán. He would have gone to help him only for they weren't friends. When he saw that Seán had gone home, he went down to the boat himself, untied the ropes, put his back to the boat, and pushed it out. Every man who heard it said he was a better man than Seán an Chóta. His name was Tomás Shéamais Ó Maoilchiaráin. They used to say that Tomás was twice as strong as him because the tide had gone out a lot further since Seán an Chóta tried to push the boat out. A man's strength of the tide had ebbed from the boat.

Pádraic and Seán an Chóta were living in the one house, but in the end each of them was making out for himself, and each had his own fields. They went as partners to cut a load of seaweed—strapwrack, for fertiliser—to Carraig Dháimhiú one day. They cut a big load. They had a creel in the boat, and when they reached land again, Seán said he'd bring a creel of the seaweed up to his field. When Pádraic saw the amount of seaweed, Seán brought in his creel he said he'd bring a creel himself. They each took every second creel, and they carried the whole load in four creels each, but Pádraic's four creels weren't quite as big as Seán's four creels. Seán an Chóta was as straight as a reed. Even though he was very big, he was a quiet, friendly man. He had the longest two arms you ever saw. He was barely eighty-eight when he died. He used to sow a lot of potatoes and sell them—he was a great man for the potatoes. There was a secret society at the time trying to keep all prices down. They were called Tories. They heard he was selling potatoes, and they ordered him to part with them for so much per stone weight. He charged a halfpenny more than they had ordered. They came to his house at night and knocked at the door. Seán an Chóta got up and opened the door to see who was there. A stone was thrown at him and hit him on the head, and he was knocked out on the spot. He spent the best part of a month and a half in bed before he was able to go out. There were men from his own townland in the Tories. They were there from far and near, I think. If they couldn't cause enough annoyance to any man who challenged them, they might take the man's boat and place it on top of Coillín Hill. A boat was often carried off and left in the middle of the village.

Seán an Chóta married Anna Nic Con Rí from Aird Thoir (Aird an Chaisleáin). They had a family, three sons and four daughters. Pádraic Sheosaimh Phatsaigh Mhóir Mac Donnchadha in Aird Thiar was Seán's daughter's son. Seán's sister was the grandmother of Micheál Ó Gaora (Geary) and Seán Ó Gaora in Carna. Seán Ó Gaora is the man who won £10,000 in the Sweepstake. When the Carna children were playing rounders, they'd ask for the ball to be thrown "three times the height of Seán an Chóta" in order to complete the short run known as "the hen's run."

SEÁN AN CHÓTA AND SÉAMAS MÓR (4)

Tomás Shéamais Mhóir Ó Maoilchiaráin, the man who pushed out the boat that Seán an Chóta failed to move, as Pádraic Mac Donnchadha told us, was a bigger man than Seán an Chóta. He had a bigger frame and was better built than Seán, and he looked healthier. Those big men were very quiet; they'd fight only if they had to, and then only with their hands. Those two men were very gentle and very quiet. There was a big man in Aran, and he was very like Tomás Shéamais Mhóir.

Ó Maoilchiaráin challenged Seán an Chóta to a fight. Seán an Chóta came to fight him on Caorán na hAirde (Ard moor). Seán

approached a man called Seán Mac Donnchadha who was burning kelp in a kiln. This man was known to have been very able-
bodied himself, but he was a good age by then. Seán an Chóta
told him he wanted him to see that he got fair play in the fight.

"Very well," said Seán Mac Donnchadha, "but I'll have to get
somebody to keep the kiln going till I come back." He sent a
young son of his to get someone to mind the kiln, and then they
headed off. A young son of Seán Mac Donnchadha's followed
them, and it was he who recounted it later.

Off they went and Ó Maoilchiaráin and his own man were on
Caorán na hAirde before them and a large number of people who
had come to watch the battle. The two men stripped to the waist
and fought for a long time, and you couldn't tell which of them
was the better man. So many of Ó Maoilchiaráin's people had
gathered that Mac Donnchadha thought Seán an Chóta would
be afraid to get the better of the other man or that his friends
wouldn't be pleased if he did. He told Seán an Chóta: "I can't
ensure you'll get fair play any longer, and you'd better walk away."

Seán an Chóta left and that was the end of that fight, but nobody knew which of them would have been the victor if they had
fought it out. There were no relations of Seán among the crowd
who were watching the fight. They all belonged to the Maoilchiaráin's side. Seán Mac Donnchadha was my grandfather, and his
young son who followed him to Caorán na hAirde to see the fight
was my father.

SEÁN AN CHÓTA AND A STRONG MUNSTERMAN (4)

A man called Slattery was on the run in this part of the country.
Seán an Chóta and himself were handbarrowing stones one day
from Caisleán na hAirde over the stream to Aird Thiar. They
were taking the stones out of the castle. They had a very heavy
stone on the barrow one time. Slattery was wearing slippery shoes
without nails, and he slipped and stumbled. He had to lay down

the barrow. Seán an Chóta laughed. I suppose he thought the stone was too heavy for Slattery. When Slattery heard the laugh, he went over to the heap of stones and lifted the heaviest stone he could take between his two hands. He laid it on the barrow with the other stone.

"Now," he said to Seán, "maybe this will get another laugh out of you." They lifted the barrow and brought it to the house, but there was no laugh out of Seán this time.

NOTES

1. Manannán mac Lir is a sea deity in Gaelic tradition. Several supernatural powers are ascribed to Manannán, including a capacity to shroud himself in mist, thus making him invisible to his foes, and a crane bag (corr bolg) that contained all precious and powerful items in his possession. Cf. (Vendryes 1953–54, 239–54).

2. *Cois Fharraige*: Literally, beside the sea. Generally refers to the northern coast of Galway Bay, encompassing Bearna, just west of the city and stretching as far west as Ros an Mhíl.

SIX

—⚋—

ROBBERS AND TREASURES

THE FAIR ON THE GREEN (1)

There was a man of the Uaithnín (Greene) clan, Cóilín Aindriú, living in Coillín. He happened to be in Galway long ago when he was a young man on a Fair Day on the Green. He thought he had never in all his life seen so many people and cattle. There were big heavy jobbers there (men buying and selling farm animals) from every part of Ireland, and maybe from England. When the fair was in its prime around twelve o' clock, two youths began to fight one another. One of them was stronger than the other. The strong youth hit the other with his fist and knocked him down and began to kick him. Every scream out of the one who was down would make a Turk take pity on him. The trading stopped and everybody rushed to where the fight was going on, trying to make the peace before the youth was killed. After a while the fighting stopped all of a sudden, and what had happened was that a jobber had been robbed of seven or eight hundred pounds he had in his pocket.

"BOLG" ("BELLY") (1)

There was a notorious robber in Galway, and I don't know what his name was, but his nickname was "Bolg." There wasn't a man in Galway who could lay a glove on him. Everything "Bolg" did was worse than the last; the man who's bad will be bad in every way. "Bolg" wasn't afraid of any man. There was a boatman from Conamara who had a big sailing boat. Séamas Mac Griallais (Grealish) was his name. The Grealishes were great men. There wasn't a Griallais man drowned in living memory. He was in Galway this day with his boat moored and waiting to be loaded. It was a fine day, and he went out to the top of Céibh Nimmo (Nimmo's quay) and went out for a swim. "Bolg" spotted Séamas Mac Griallais and swam out after him to drown him. There were people on the pier shouting at Séamas that "Bolg" would drown him, and he slowed down until he let the other man come near him. He kept watching him over his shoulder, and when he saw "Bolg" was near him, he dived like a cormorant and let the other man pass above him. When "Bolg" had gone ahead, Séamas came up behind him, forced him under, and kept him underwater till he really made a *bolg* of him. "Bolg" barely made it ashore. He wasn't able to get out of the water till people helped him. They barely managed to lift him out. Séamas Mac Griallais quietened "Bolg." From then till the day he died, he wasn't as active as he used to be. Séamas taught him that he had to look out for himself in future. Séamas got great praise from the people of Galway for the drowning he gave "Bolg." He thought no one could fetter him but Séamas Mac Griallais fettered him.

ÉAMONN HANLY AND LARRY SCULLY (1)

There were two robbers in Galway, Éamonn Ó hAinligh (Hanly) and Larry Scully. I don't know which of them came there first, but they attacked one another and neither of them was gaining on the other.

"Be off with you," said one of them.

"You be off with you," said the other.

"I thought," said Éamonn Ó hAinligh, "that no man could get the better of me unless I met Larry Scully."

"Musha, I thought," said the other man, "that no man could get the better of me unless I met Éamonn Ó hAinligh. I'm Larry Scully."

"I'm Éamonn Ó hAinligh," said the other man.

They shook hands then and went into partnership, helping one another. There was nothing that could be protected from them then, in Galway or anywhere near Galway.

They were on the bridge every night so that everything going in or out was theirs. There were two brothers from Conamara, Séamas Ó Geannáin and Seán Ó Geannáin (Gannon), who were bringing a herd of bullocks to the fair in Béal dhá Éan to the east of Galway. When they came onto the big bridge, the two jumped out at them, Éamonn Ó hAinligh and Larry Scully.

"Be off with you," they said to to the Gannons.

"You be off with you," said the Gannons.

The four of them attacked one another, two against two, man-to-man. The Gannons were well able for them and had half thrown the other two over the bridge on the north side to drown them, when the watchmen arrived. The robbers were badly beaten up. The watchmen arrested them and put them in jail. The Gannons were unhurt and were allowed to go their way.

THE ROBBER ON THE BRIDGE (1)

There was a husband and wife, and they were very poor. They didn't even have a night's supper. The man told the woman that he'd stand on the bridge and wait for the first person to come by, and then he'd kill him with a blow of a spade handle. He took the handle out of the spade and stood on the bridge with it. He soon heard the sound of a man on horseback approaching. When the horseman reached him, he said "Halt!" The horseman halted.

"What do you want?" said the horseman.

"I want money," said the man.

"Why do you want it?"

"I'll kill you with the spade handle if you don't give me money," he said.

"Do you have anything to protect yourself but that spade handle?" asked the horseman.

"No," said the robber.

The horseman pulled a pistol out of his pocket.

"Do you see that pistol?" said the horseman. "There are nine bullets in it; any one of them will kill you, but I believe you're a poor man and that you have nothing."

He put his hand in his pocket and gave him five pounds.

The robber took the money, and the horseman put the pistol back in his pocket. But what did the robber do then but lift the spade handle and hit the horseman on the top of the head and knock him off the horse. He thought he had killed him. He mounted the horse himself and brought it home with him. When he came home, he took off the saddle and threw it up on the loft. Then he took the horse with him to a place where there was a fair, and he sold the horse.

When he had spent the price of the horse, as well as the five pounds the horseman gave him, himself and his wife had nothing again. They were as poor as they ever were. All they could do was shut the two doors and take to the roads, not knowing where they were going. They kept on walking for a whole week until one evening they happened into a public house. Like all public houses, there was a snug. There were three men sitting in the snug having a conversation, each of them boasting of how good a man he was.

"I was always a good man," said one of the men, "till I had a little mishap due to my own lack of gumption."

"Musha, how did it happen to you," asked another one of them.

"I was going the road," he said, "and I had a horse that I wouldn't part with for a thousand pounds. I came to a bridge, and there was a man there who had a spade handle. He told me to hand over. I asked him if he had anything to protect himself with but the spade handle. He told me he didn't."

"And are you going to rob me with the spade handle?" I asked him.

"I am," said he.

"I put my hand in my pocket and gave him five pounds, and I put the pistol I had in my hand back in my pocket. And what did he do then but swing the spade handle and hit me on top of the head and brought me down off the horse. He went off with the horse then and left me there, not knowing whether I was dead or alive, after my giving him five pounds. There was two hundred pounds in one of the saddle pockets and a pair of pistols in the other. I was as sad to lose the money as the pistols."

The very moment the man in the shop heard all this, he beckoned his wife to leave.

The three men talking in the snug in the public house were three robbers. While they were drinking, the spade handle man found out that the man he had robbed was himself a robber. The man and his wife went home and found the two hundred pounds and the pistols in the saddle that had been thrown up on the loft.

RED LIAM AND SEÁN OF THE CANS (1)

There were two robbers from Clifden. Liam Dearg (Red Liam) was a Mannion man and Seán na gCannaí (Seán of the Cans) was a Lavery man. There was another man, a Conneely man, living near them who was a son-in-law of Seán na gCannaí. This Conneely man had a daughter, a young girl. One night Liam Dearg and Seán na gCannaí had a big sum of money on the table. The little girl, Conneely's girl, was in the room, but they took no notice of her. When Liam Dearg had laid out a big pile of money and Seán na gCannaí had laid out another big pile of money, Seán na gCannaí stood up from the table and got a wooden washing bat. He came up behind Liam Dearg and killed him with one blow of the bat. He then hid him under the bed, Seán na gCannaí and his wife, and they buried him at night.

The little girl came home to her father and mother's house. She stayed at home that night. The following day a priest was coming to hear confessions.

"I won't go there again," said the little girl, "till I go to confession to the priest."

The little girl went to confession to the priest, and she told the priest all she had seen and that her parents were trying to send her back to Seán na gCannaí's house. When the Mass was over, the priest spoke to the Conneely man and told him not to send his daughter to Seán na gCannaí's house any more. She didn't go there any more.

Liam Dearg was poor. Seán na gCannaí was rich. Those two robbers lived near Loch an Ghadaí (thief's lake). "You're as bad as Liam Dearg," is a byword people have for somebody who's dangerous. I've always heard a contrary person being compared to Liam Dearg.

THE THIEF'S LAKE (3)

Loch an Ghadaí is near the road, on this (east) side of Béal an Átha (mouth of the ford) to the west of the Creaga Móra (great crags). The Half Way House is near by. There's a little island in the lake overgrown by holly and osier. This island is where Liam Dearg (Red Liam), the thief, lived, and he had a boat for going in and out. He used to watch the road to see people coming or going to Clifden on their own. If he failed to catch them on the way there, he'd catch them on the way back, and he'd take their money or whatever they had bought. At that time no woman was willing to travel that road without two or three escorts for fear of Liam Dearg.

POWERS' WALL (3)

There's a lake in Caladh an Chnoic called Loch na bPaorach (Powers' lake).[1] At the western end of the lake, there is an old ruin surrounded by a little garden. The ruin is called Balla na bPaorach (Powers' wall). There was a house there long ago that belonged to four men of that surname who came in from somewhere outside. They were stealing sheep and cattle. They kept on thieving for a long time as nobody had the courage to stand up to them till they had plundered everyone's livestock. People said the only thing to do was to creep up on them at night and kill them inside in the house. The local people got together one night and killed every last one of them inside in the house. No Power has lived in these parts since.

THIEVES AND MOBS (3)

There were mobs of men long ago roaming around in partnership. Anything they wanted they had to get it or else they'd take it by force. They would take a crock of butter from a house, and pigs and cattle. They'd go to a certain house then where they'd eat what they had stolen. There was very little law at the time; this is over a hundred years ago.

Groups of men were plundering, stealing cattle, and selling them elsewhere. The people were afraid of the mobs. Unless you had a friend in the mob, you had no protection. "A friend in court is better than a coin in your purse."

TORIES (1) (CATTLE STEALERS)

A man who was a drover, buying and selling cattle, was at a fair buying and selling, and he had a dog with him. He wouldn't part with that dog for anything; he was that good. When he was coming home, he must have gone into some house, and when he came out, the dog wasn't there. He searched high and low for it but failed to find it.

Five years later, he was at a fair where he bought a big herd of cattle and drove them to where there was going to be another fair the following day. When it was nearly nightfall, he turned the cattle off the main road into a byroad, and he went into this house. The only person in the house was a woman. He asked her if he could have the night's lodging, and she said he could. He told her he had cattle, and she told him there was a field beside the house where he could keep his cattle till morning, when he'd be bringing them out again.

He put the cattle into the field and came back inside. When he had eaten his meal, the woman said, "There's a bed up there, and you can go up and sleep in it."

When he went into the room to go to bed, a dog he hadn't seen till then came up behind him, and with every garment he took off, the dog would catch him by the calves of his legs and try to drag him out of the room again. When he had undressed down to his shirt and was about to go to bed, the dog jumped onto the bed. The bed turned upside down, and there was no knowing how deep it was underneath or the deadly contraption beneath it.

He came back out of the room when he had dressed himself.

"Why," he asked the woman, "did you set that trap for me?"

"I had to do it," she said. "This is a tory house. I am a long time here. They have played that trick on a lot of people," she said, "people like you who come with cattle. They kill the people, and they have the cattle for themselves in the morning. They'd have your cattle too, and they'd have yourself somewhere you couldn't be found. But you're just as badly off now because they'll kill you, and they'll kill me too when they won't find you dead when they come back."

"Have you any fire arm in the house?" he said.

"I have," she said, "and many."

She gave him some sort of fire arm, and she kept one herself. He said he would kill the first man to come in the door himself, and he asked her to help him. They would take one each of the other two, as there were three men in all.

When she let the first man in the door he shot him, and she shot the man who came in after him just as fast. The last one of them received two bullets. They richly deserved it as they had killed many a person themselves.

They had abducted the woman from her parents to be their servant girl. The drover gave himself up, and he spent seven years being sent from prison to prison before being released. He got off somehow. It was the dog he lost at the fair five years before that saved his life.

STOCKING MERCHANTS (4)

There were no shops in Conamara long ago, but stocking merchants came in from outside. Those merchants sold all sorts of clothing, white handkerchiefs, and small light wares that were easy to carry. They would sell these to the local people and buy stockings from them in return. They would sell the stockings in Limerick and in Dublin.

Many the merchant was treated unjustly. There were robbers in the area. They used to take their money off them and might even kill them. A merchant was killed on Cnoc Buí (Knockboy, yellow hill) and was thrown into Loch an Duine (lake of the person). He had been followed from Doire Iorrais.[2] Three men were seen following him. I suppose he wouldn't part with his bag as long as he was alive. There was a hut on the green patch by Loch an Duine where people booleying cattle would spend the night. When the merchant saw the hut, he thought there might be people there. He made for it, with the robbers after him, but he didn't come out alive.

They killed him and threw him into this lake and went off with his bag. Bailiffs working for Réamonn Óg Mac Donnchadha in Maínis found his body some days later, and they buried him in the ground.

There was a merchant in my grandfather's house one night. He was eating at the table when a traveling woman came in. When she saw the merchant, she fainted. They helped her to her feet and asked her what was wrong. She told them she hadn't seen the merchant who was at the table since the day he killed her husband. They asked the merchant was that true, and he said he'd rather have it said that he killed a man than have it said that a man killed him.

Life was rough at the time, and there was no end to the crimes being committed. The robberies took place around Cnoc na hÁb-haí.[3] That's the way people came into Iorras Aithneach, along by Cill Chiaráin Bay. There were no bridges on the rivers then, and I remember myself the time the bridge was built over Crompán Choill Sáile.[4]

The stocking merchants were respectable people, but the wares they had for sale were limited to what they could carry on their back. They had safe houses to stay in when they came around. There were no means of shopping in Conamara.

BURIED TREASURES: THE DREAM (1)

The buried treasures found in Ireland were hidden by people who were afraid that others would have their money when they were gone. People who bury treasures like that don't rest easy after their death till the treasure is found. They become cats or eels guarding the treasure until a way of recovering it is found. They set people dreaming of how to recover the treasure and where to find it. We know for certain that there are many people who were set dreaming like that by a spirit. They shouldn't tell anybody if they hoped to find any of the treasure, and they shouldn't attempt to uncover it till they had all the directions correct themselves and till they have had the dream three times. The third time, the spirit will tell them how to unearth the treasure, as the spirit told Tomás Buí Úraid.

PÁDRAIC Ó GEANNÁIN (1)

Pádraic Ó Geannáin in Caladh Mhaínse (Callowfeenish, harbor of Feenish) was visited by a spirit two nights in a row. He was told that there was a treasure under such and such a rock down in Leitir Caisil (hillside of the cashel). The following day he took his spade, went to Leitir Caisil, and began digging underneath the rock. He had hardly dug more than a sod or two when he heard a voice beside him, and the voice spoke and told him to listen to him.

"Why didn't you bide your time?" said the voice to him. "If you had bided your time you'd have some benefit," he said.

Then the spirit disappeared.

Pádraic was driven from the spot because he didn't wait for the right directions. He was given no more information, and he never found the treasure. He shouldn't have moved or spoken about it till he had received the third message.

TWO KEGS OF GOLD (2)

There were two kegs of gold in a lake in the north of Ireland. Lots of people had seen the kegs in the lake with an eel coiled around them. Everybody who saw them was afraid to touch them until this particular man came along. When he saw them, he knew for certain there was a treasure in the two kegs.

He brought a hen out on the lake with him to give to the eel while he'd be taking up the treasure. The eel showed no interest in the hen, and it didn't move while he was taking up the first keg. He took up the second keg then, and the eel didn't hinder him.

When he had brought in the two kegs, the eel turned into a man and followed him ashore.

"You're a great man," the eel man told him, "you are rich forever now and my term is up." That was the end of his term there.

When he opened the two kegs, they were full of gold. The eel became a man as soon as he lifted the kegs. His term didn't end until a man came along with enough courage to bring up the kegs.

MAITIÚ Ó CORBÁIN'S TREASURE (2)

Maitiú Ó Corbáin lived in Aird Thiar. He was married to Máire na gCnoc (Mary of the mountains), a daughter of Micil Shéamais Thiobóid Mac Con Rí from Barr na nÓrán.[5] Living with Maitiú was his sister's son, whose father was dead. The sister's son had a dream that there was a treasure hidden in a stony ridge in Roisín na Long[6] in Aird Thiar. He told his uncle Maitiú on each of three mornings that he had been dreaming that night. He told Maitiú that he had been ordered to bring Maitiú and Liaimín with him and to search for the treasure and that the three had to be together.

"That's all nonsense," said Maitiú. "Don't tell anybody or they'll just make fun of you."

Maitiú then went to work on his own in search of the treasure and found it, and nobody knows how much money he found.

The sister's son told another man, and himself and the man went to the spot. He saw the place dug up and looking as if the pot had been lifted. The imprint of the pot was left in the flagstone. That's all the sister's son saw of it, but from then on Maitiú looked as if he had seen some of the treasure.

THE DEAD MAN'S TREASURE (2)

A man called Síomón Bhriartach, an Ó Maoilchiaráin man from Leitreach Ard (Letterard), was coming over the mountain to

Carna on a summer's morning. He saw a man on the top of a hillock drying pieces of gold on his overcoat. The overcoat was spread out on the top of the hillock, and gold pieces heaped high on top of it. There were so many pieces that there wasn't room for them on the coat. The man didn't notice Síomón Bhriartach till he was nearly beside him. When he noticed him, he tucked the tails of the coat in on all sides to cover it. Síomón didn't want to look too closely at him because he recognized the man who had been dead for fifty years. He went on his way and left him there. He didn't know what became of him after that. He was handling the gold and mixing it up as if he was letting the sun in at it.

It was on Loch na Scinnín ridge in the townland of Maíros that Síomón saw the man with the gold. It is said that Maolra Dubh Mac Donnchadha, a middleman who lived in Dumhaigh Ithir (Dooyeher), left a hidden treasure in Maíros. He had hidden the treasure on the north side of the temple. A group of people came over from England to Maíros looking for the treasure and brought implements with them. They dug up a great amount of stones there. They found a drain that ran underground there, but they didn't find any of the treasure. That's about two score years ago.

On hearing this, Seosamh Ó Mongáin said, "I remember my father getting a letter from Spain telling him there was a treasure hidden in Maíros. It was one of the Mac Con Rí clan who wrote to him. My father gave the letter to Annraí Conneely's father in Clifden, and the attorney took the letter away with him. I remember it well. It was written in the letter that the treasure belonged to the Mac Con Rí clan."

TREASURE HOLE FIELD (2)

It's said there's a treasure hidden in Garraí Phoill an Chiste (treasure hole field) on Cnoc an Choillín (hill of the small wood). Micil Mháirtín Chaitlín searched for the treasure and went as near it as to see the pot, but an ugly serpent was entwined round the pot and Micil took fright. He covered the pot again. Micil Ó Cualáin was the man's name.

A TREASURE IN ERRISBEG (2)

There was a man out on Iorras Beag hill (Errisbeg, small promontory) one day looking for sheep. He saw in a vein in the cliff a vast amount of gold pieces. Pieces of gold were lying on top of one another from the top of the cliff to the bottom. He had no means of carrying them except to take off the cap that was on his head. He was picking the pieces of gold and putting them into the cap till he had filled it to the brim. He brought the pieces of gold to Mac Con Uladh, a nailsmith in Roundstone; he thought the smith might buy them off him. Mac Con Uladh crossed himself when he saw the man with the cap full of gold pieces.

"I found them up in a cliff on Iorras Beag hill, and there are so many of them as would make everybody in the community rich, if they're worth anything," said the man.

Mac Con Uladh promised him twenty-five pounds for the capful, and gave him a bag and told him to go to the same place and bring all he could back with him. When he came to the same place, it looked no different than the rest of the cliff. No gold or silver was to be seen, or any sign of it. He was the sorry man, and had good reason to be, for not having taken enough of the gold with him when he came upon it.

THE PRIEST'S GOLD IN THE LAKE (1)

A brother and sister were living in the one house. When the father and mother died, the brother shared the house with her. Then the sister got married and left him alone. The brother began to drink and fight till he drank all he had. All he had saved he drank it, except for the house and land. He then left the house and went back to his sister, and she had very little welcome for him. She knew about all he had done. Her husband was very kind to him though, and he had no objection to his coming to his house empty-handed. There was a lake near the in-law's house, and there was a keg full of gold in the middle of the lake that could be seen by all the men and women in Ireland. If anybody should covet the treasure and would begin to go out into the lake, an eel in the lake would rise up and churn the lake into a whirlpool for fear somebody should take away the keg of gold.

The brother was there one day when the in-law was out. The sister was talking to him.

"You've made a right mess of your life," she said, "spending your money foolishly. You are now the way you are. It's many a man in your predicament would go out to the keg in the lake," she said, "and would try and get hold of it."

"Arrah, wouldn't the eel devour me," he said.

"I believe nothing would make any difference to you," says she—and that's what really angered him.

He went to the lake. When he came to the edge of the lake, the eel didn't stir. He went out as far as the keg, and the eel didn't stir until he had brought the keg onto dry land. That's when he got the fright with all the noise the eel made, and he commanded it if it was a baptized member of the Church, to appear in the form he held when he left this life.

At that very moment a priest was standing at his shoulder.

"You're a great man," said the priest. "You have plenty now," he said. "During the time I was on earth, I was amassing that money and putting it in the keg for fear anybody else would have it. My heart and soul was in it," he said, "and I had no thoughts for my soul. When I died then, I was placed as a serpent keeping watch over it and fated never to leave it till I got a courageous man like you who would ask me a question. You have plenty now, and you'll have plenty for the rest of your life. You'll offer up Mass for my soul," he said, "till I go into Heaven, and you'll give up your carousing for as long as you live."

The priest disappered then. He laid the keg to one side. On the following day himself and the brother-in-law went for a stroll together.

"Is there any patch of land for sale around here?" he asked the brother-in-law.

"Upon my soul there is, and good land," said the brother-in-law.

"We should go and see it," he said.

"We won't go today, we'll wait till tomorrow," said the brother-in-law. He thought he was going light in the head.

When they went to bed that night, the brother-in-law began telling his wife what her brother was saying, that he was asking if there was a patch of land for sale in the locality.

"Gone in the head he is," said the wife, "and it's no wonder, any man who has spent all he had and spent the most of it foolishly, but let you go along with him till you see what happens."

He went along with him till they met the man who was selling the land. When he had walked the land, he said he'd give him a hundred pounds for it, and the man accepted that. He counted out a hundred pounds to him.

When they came home, the sister asked, "Did you buy the land?"

"We did," they said.

"I thought you already had land," she said to the brother.

"It wasn't for myself I bought it," he said, "but for this decent husband of yours who found no fault with me for being poor any more than if I were rich. I have land of my own when I attend to it."

He went home. He attended to the land. He bought stock, worked the land, married a woman, and didn't drink or carouse again for the rest of his life.

THE OLD WOMAN IN ATHENRY

There was an old woman in Athenry (in east Galway). She had a son married in the house with her. They had a servant girl. When the girl went to morning Mass, they (the married couple) went to twelve o'clock Mass, and when the couple went to morning Mass, the girl would go to twelve o'clock Mass. When they had left the house one Sunday, the old woman asked the girl if the son was long gone. The girl said, "They're not at the chapel yet."

"Will you give me the saucepan so, asthore," said the old woman.

"I will," said the girl.

"And will you give me paper and thread?"

When she had brought them, the old woman soon called her again.

"Now," said the old woman, "you'll place this saucepan on the fire."

"I will," said the girl.

The paper was placed over the top of the saucepan, and the thread tied around the paper.

The girl felt the saucepan was heavy and knew there was money inside it. She spread out a sheet, took the paper off the saucepan, spilled the money onto the sheet, and she had two hundred guineas.

She then went and filled the saucepan with old yellow butter, tied the paper around the top again, and placed it on the fire. It wasn't long till the old woman spoke.

"Do you think that's boiling yet?" she said.

"I know it's not," said the girl.

"When it's boiling, you'll let me know," said the old woman.

"I will," said the girl.

When it began to boil, the girl went and told her.

"It's boiling now," she said.

"Bring it here to me," said the old woman.

She did.

"Take off the paper now," said the old woman.

She did. The old woman caught the saucepan by the handle and hit it against the wall. It came out yellow. The butter had turned yellow when it began to freeze.

"Oh, isn't it very yellow!" said the girl.

"Never you mind," said the old woman.

The girl then hid the money in a safe place.

When the son came home from Mass the old woman told him to go for the priest, that she was unwell. The priest came and heard her confession; he then annointed her, and she was dead the following day. The son gave her as decent a burial as any old woman got.

Shortly after her death, the son began to complain, wondering if his mother had left any money.

"If she did," said the girl, "what are you telling me for? Why didn't you ask her when she was alive if she had money?"

The girl stayed in the house for a year for fear she might be suspected. When she left, she brought the money with her.

The old woman had remorse when the girl told her about the yellow on the wall. It was the remorse that killed her. It broke her heart that the money was gone. The girl did better for herself than the old woman who tried to melt the money. There are some old people who don't like to leave anything behind them.

THE OLD MAN WHO HAD THE PILLOW (1)

There was this man, a strong man, well off, with money and everything. He told his wife one day that she should make him a pillow to put under his head, a nice light pillow he could bring with him anywhere he wanted to rest. She made the pillow the way he told her to. When death was approaching, the priest came to him, and when he was ready to meet God, he told his wife to put the pillow under his head in the coffin when he would die. The wife said she would.

When he died and was laid in his coffin, the pillow was placed under his head.

The family thought the mother had the money, and she showed no concern. The family asked her where the money was. The mother said she knew nothing about it, "but he told me," she said, "to make a pillow for him and to place it under his head when he died, and maybe that's where the money is," she said. "I think that's where the money is," she said, "because he was very attached to it."

"If you think that's where the money is," said the family, "shouldn't we speak to the priest about it?"

They went to the priest and told him they suspected the money was in the pillow. The priest said that if they did, it was easy to get it out of there and that it was a bigger sin to leave it there than to take it out. The priest went along with them, and they took the lid off the coffin. When the priest looked down at the corpse, it was turned upside down and the pillow in his mouth.

"It's a devil," said the priest, "close the coffin. Let him keep it." They did that.

A TREASURY LIAM DE BARRA FOUND (1)

Liam de Barra was living in Cill Chiaráin. A sister of his was married to Tomás, the blacksmith, where the convent is now, or a sister of Tomás the blacksmith was married to Liam; I don't know which, but they were in-laws anyhow. My father knew Liam, and they both knew one another. My father was coming east along the road one day, and he saw Liam de Barra inside on Tomás's land. He had a spade and was digging a hole. My father went in to welcome him and asked him what he was doing. Liam said he was going to build a house, that Tomás had given him a site for a house. My father knew that Liam had a fine place over where he was. When Liam said he was building a house, he left it at that and my father didn't pursue the matter any further. Liam didn't continue with the work.

My father was coming over to Carna again some days later, and he looked into the hole Liam had made. There were three stones there coming together at the top, and where the pot had been hidden was dug out underneath. Rumor had it that Liam de Barra found a treasure under the stones. Liam had plenty of money, and he hadn't reached the pot when my father was talking to him. If he had, he might have given him some of the money.

THE TREASURE IN LIMERICK (1)

There was a man in Limerick, and a spirit used to visit him and encouraged him to go to a bridge near Boston in America and that he'd get great wealth there on top of the bridge. The spirit visited him three times. The man went over to America and was a long time standing on the bridge. A man came up to him and asked him what he was doing there. "I'm watching you there since morning," he said, "it seems you have nothing else to do," he said.

"Musha," said the Limerick man, "since you asked me, I'll tell you what I'm doing. I'm not getting any peace for a long time now from a spirit that's appearing to me and telling me that I'd get great wealth if I'd come as far as this bridge." He didn't tell him at all where he was from.

"Oh, have sense, whoever you are," said the American to him, "a man like that is coming to me for the past seven years, telling me if I went to Limerick, somewhere in Ireland, that I'd get three pots of gold there. There's a field near Limerick, and there's a little house in the middle of the field, and such and such a man is living there"—and he gave him the name and surname of the man, the name and surname of the Limerick man himself—"and this man has a big tree growing near the house, and he told me if I went to Limerick that I'd get three pots of gold under the tree, and that's a place I'll never go," he said.

The Limerick man didn't let anything on when he got the exact description from the American, and he sailed back home again and found three pots of gold under the tree in his own field in Limerick. Limerick is an ancient place, and there were many treasures buried there.

A BLIND MAN WHO HAD A STOCKING FULL OF GOLD (1)

There was this blind man, and he had three or four sons. He had great wealth, and he had a stocking full of gold he kept hidden in his armpit.

"I was just thinking, my children," he said one day, "that it would do me good if you'd take me out on the bay so that I'd get the smell of the sea."

"Do you know what my father said to us today?" said one of the sons to an elderly man who lived nearby. "That we should take him out in the boat, so that he'd take in the smell of the sea, whatever he meant by that."

"There's a good reason for it," said the old man. "He has a treasure. He wants to throw the treasure in the sea rather than leave it to you. Take him out, but don't go far from the shore. Keep rowing back and forth near the shore, and it will tire you out. But keep going to and fro, and he'll think you're going out to sea, till a good part of the day is gone. Even if he throws the money in the sea then, you'll find it again when the tide goes out; but don't go out on the deep with him."

The following day, the blind man sat into the boat. The family began rowing and making noises with the oars, and when they had been rowing for a good while along by the shore, they turned round and came back again the same way. When they had spent a long time rowing like that, he asked them if they were far from land.

"We have lost sight of land altogether," they said.

"Keep rowing out to sea for another while," he said.

They began rowing again, and they kept near the shore. They were inside a little creek and going around by the sandy shore, but he didn't notice them turning as they were going around. He soon put his hand into his armpit. He pulled out the stocking full of gold and cast it away from him, only to fall on dry land.

"Oh, aren't you an awful man, father, to throw the gold into the sea like that," said the family.

"It wasn't gold at all," he said.

They were trying to make him feel bad by saying he threw it in the sea.

A TREASURE THAT WAS NOT REDEEMED (1)

There was a man in Maíros. He was a young man. Val Mac Donnchadha was his name. He had dreamt three times that there was a pot of gold somewhere. The spirit was telling him where it was. Workmen were building a road near where the pot was hidden, and Val Mac Donnchadha hadn't redeemed the pot.

The spirit appeared to him again: "Micheál Seoighe went very near finding your pot today, or are you going to redeem it?" it said, "or are you going to redeem it?" it said a second time.

"Ah, I don't know," he said.

The spirit departed in a flash of anger.

"You won't see me again," said the spirit.

He never saw him again, and he never redeemed the treasure.

NOTES

1. *Caladh an Chnoic:* landing place of the hill.
2. *Doire Iorrais:* wood of the peninsula.
3. *Cnoc na hÁbhaí:* Hill of the hole.
4. *Crompán Choill Sáile:* Kylesalia (wood of the sea inlet) Creek.
5. *Barr na nÓrán:* hilltop of the fountains.
6. *Roisín na Long:* small peninsula of the ships.

SEVEN

—ᗰᗰ—

SMUGGLERS

TRADING WITH GUERNSEY (4)

Sloops were the boats used by smugglers who traded with Guernsey. They brought tobacco, drink, and clothing from Guernsey, and they didn't have to pay any customs levy there. The boatmen would be gone for two weeks, depending on the weather. The King's boats were watching out for them, and any boat caught by the King's cutter would not be redeemed, nor would its cargo. A boatman who would make the trip to Guernsey was worthy of great respect. There's a place called Cutter's Bog in Aird Thiar (Ard west) where the cutter lay in waiting, watching out for the smugglers. Séamas and Liam Ó Loideáin (Lydon) from Maíros used to go to Guernsey, and men from Iorras Beag (Errisbeg)— three sons of Eoin (son of Micheál) Mac Con Rí. Big Marcas Mac Cualáin from Leitir Mealláin (Lettermullen) went and Tomás Rua Mac Donnchadha (Tomás Rua of the Guinea) from Loch Conaortha (Loughaconeera).

The Martins would buy from the smugglers, as would everybody else who could afford to.

THE SIGNAL FIRE (7)

When a boat was coming from Guernsey with a cargo, a signal fire was lit on a hillock near the bay it was headed for. The fire was a sign that the King's vessel was not in the bay. If the boat's captain wouldn't see the signal fire the night he was coming, he would not come in.

Big Marcas Mac Cualáin used to be coming in from Guernsey to Caladh Ghólaim (Callowgolam) in Leitir Mealláin (Lettermullen). On one occasion he was expected for two weeks, and though the signal fire was lit for him every night, he didn't come. They then gave up lighting the fire and didn't know what had happened to him. He then came in one night, and he thought the folks at home had been neglectful for not having been expecting him because he had been neglectful himself. He came in to Caladh Ghólaim, and the King's vessel was there waiting for him. He was arrested, and the boat was confiscated and all its cargo.

BIG MARCAS Ó CUALÁIN (13)

Big Marcas Ó Cualáin (Folan) was born and reared in Maínis, where Muintir Laidhe (the O'Lees) are living now. It was he who built the house there. He was a boatwright and the captain of a sloop. He had two brothers, and one of them was married to Máire Rua Ní Dhomhnaill (O'Donnell). Big Marcas and Tadhg na Buile (mad Tadhg) were at loggerheads. Tadhg used to burden them with too much flax to be spun, and they had to do that work for Tadhg. They were tired and exhausted at this stage, and Big Marcas and his family left altogether. They brought their furniture and all their possessions with them, put them in the boat, and moved to Leitir Mealláin. The house (in Maínis) was full of Tadhg's flax, and when they were leaving, they set fire to it, and the house and the flax were burnt down.

Marcas's two brothers were boatwrights, and they moved to Leitir Mealláin along with him. The three brothers went to Guernsey for a load. They bought the tobacco, brought it home, and sold it. They were getting on like that till they had put a cargo ashore five times in Caladh Ghólaim bay when the King's vessel came and arrested the captain and his sloop. Big Marcas was the captain of the vessel. The sloop was confiscated together with the cargo of tobacco and a hundred pounds. The two brothers ran away, and they never returned to Leitir Mealláin. One of them settled down in Lochán Beag. Big Marcas Ó Cualáin was my mother's grandfather. May God rest his soul.

EOIN MAC MHICHÍL'S FAMILY (12)

My grandfather had a first cousin called Seán Mac Con Rí. The first cousin's name was Eoin Mac Con Rí, Eoin Mac Mhichíl. He had six sons, and they were known as Eoin Mac Mhichíl's sons. They were living in Muirbhigh (Murvey) to the west of Iorras Beag[1] (Errisbeg). Five of them were ship's captains, and they used to go to Guernsey to buy stuff. There was a man in Dumhaigh Ithir (Dooyeher) at the time to watch out for the men who went to Guernsey. He had a boat and crew and was working for England watching the bay. He was an Ó Ceallaigh (Kelly). One of Eoin Mac Mhichíl's sons was returning from Guernsey with a cargo. When his boat came in between Cruach na Caoile (Deer island) and Leathmhás (Halfmace), the Ó Ceallaigh man challenged him and boarded his vessel. There was very little wind, and Eoin Mac Mhichíl's son wasn't sailing well. He offered Ó Ceallaigh a third of the cargo. That wouldn't do. He offered him half of the cargo. That wouldn't do. He then struck Ó Ceallaigh with his fist and knocked him overboard and hoisted sail again. His own people rescued Ó Ceallaigh and brought him home. Mac Con Rí kept going till he went up by Ceann Reamhar as far as Ros Rua, and he landed his cargo that night. He had customers, and they came to him. The vessel had sailed again by morning, and there was no trace of it.

TWO BROTHERS (4)

The two men from Iorras Beag, Eoin Mac Mhichíl's two sons, had lived apart for so long that they didn't recognize one another when they met. A fight broke out between them, and one of them was getting the better of the other. "If I were at home in Iorras Beag," said the vanquished man, "this wouldn't happen."

"What have you got to do with Iorras Beag?" said the other man.

"That's where I was born and reared," he said.

"Who are your people?"

"I'm Eoin Mac Mhichíl's son."

"If you are, I am a son of his too," said the other man. That was the end of the fighting.

PEADAR BÁN (2)

Peadar Bán Mac Con Rí, a son of Eoin Mac Mhichíl, was smuggling with his brothers. He was drowned while they were on a voyage to Spain. They met a small sailing boat like the one they had themselves. There was a young woman on board. When the two vessels were close to each other, the woman made a small gesture to Peadar Bán. He took such a liking to her that he jumped into the sea thinking he'd be taken aboard the woman's vessel, but he wasn't, and he drowned.

Three weeks from that day his body came ashore in Iorras Mór[2] (Errismore), and the villagers recognized him. They recognized him on account of his long hair; he had long hair, and it was by his hair he was known. But they didn't know at the time how he was drowned, not till they heard about it when the vessel returned from Spain.

SHIPWRECK ON FOREIGNERS' ROCK (3)

Tóna Ó Conaola (Conneely) lived in Leitir Mealláin. That's where he was born and reared. He was a shipwright. He was able to build a boat, to make the sails, and to rig it, and when he had rigged it, he was able to captain it. He traded with Guernsey. He was one day coming back with a load, and as he was coming west over Sceirde (bleak island), he saw the watch boat coming in from the east over Oileán Iarthach Árann. The wind was favorable coming from the land to the north. He headed east toward Great Man's Bay. It was late evening. There's a rock within a half mile of land in the mouth of Great Man's Bay. When it was late and it was dark, the watch boat struck the rock and it was wrecked and the crew were drowned. That rock is called Foreigners' Rock ever since.

Ó Conaola escaped and saved his cargo on that occasion.

OILEÁN AN ANAMA (SOUL ISLAND) (7)

Oileán an Anama is at the mouth of Cuigéal Bay to the east, off Poll Uí Mhuirinn. A vessel was wrecked on the tip of the island, and only one man was drowned. There was a cargo of cotton on board. The naval guards took the cargo off it. The floor timbers and the tiller are still to be seen there.

Oileán an Anama is to the east of Carraig na nGall (rock of the Englishmen) between it and Trá Bháin (white strand).

LIAM Ó LOIDEÁIN (LYDON)

Liam Ó Loideáin was living in Maíros (Moyrus). He was a seafarer. He had a two-mast vessel, a schooner. He traded with Guernsey and Spain from Conamara. He bought rum, indigo, tobacco, brandy, and silk. They got those wares cheap there. When they managed to bring their cargo ashore without

the King's guards confiscating them, they had great profit when
they sold their ware.

Liam had just come ashore in Guernsey one day. He walked
out as if he was looking for a storage man. None of his crew was
with him. He hadn't walked for long when a bulldog was set on
him. He saw the dog coming behind him, and when the dog tried
to jump and bite Liam, he hit him with the heel of his boot in the
throat, and he broke its neck. He had killed the dog with the heel
of his boot without looking behind him. He brought a cargo of
merchandise safely home with him on that same voyage.

He was once coming home from Guernsey, and it was difficult to do it unknown to the King's guards. The cutter spotted
Liam's boat, and it was sailing behind. Ó Loideáin headed for
the Slyne Head Sandbanks in an attempt to lead the cutter astray.
He was a pilot himself, and he knew the area well. He came west
by Bealach na hUilleann.[3] There's a high cliff on both sides of
Bealach na hUilleann, and it's very deep there. He cut the masts
off the boat so that they couldn't be seen, and the crew of the
cutter didn't know where he was. The cutter continued on east
over Slyne Head. There was another boat sailing ahead of them,
and they thought it was Liam Ó Loideáin, but he had been left
behind by them in Bealach na hUilleann. He made great money
on that voyage.

THE BIOR MAN'S JOURNEY (12)

There was a man of the Mac Donnchadha clan (Mac Donagh) in
the British Army. He deserted and came to live on Bior or Oileán
Biorach (pointed island) at the mouth of Cuan Chill Chiaráin
(Kilkerrin bay). A grandson of this man was a boatman. He sold
all he had and bought a sloop. He went to Guernsey and bought
a load there. On his way home, the King's vessel caught up with
him and the load was taken off him. The cutter's crew confiscated
the cargo, and the boat was given to the Bior man's captain. "The

Bior man's Journey to Guernsey was the worst journey a Carna man ever made." It has become a proverb.

CAPTAIN O'MALLEY (5)

Captain O'Malley had a sloop for trading with Guernsey. He often wrecked a boat while fleeing from the King's boat. He wrecked a boat at the Old Head in County Mayo. He had sold his cargo and unloaded it all except for a big puncheon of rum, and he was putting to sea again. What would he see coming in against him but the cutter. He turned his boat around. He had no way out. He knew the area well, and all he could do was steer the boat into this cove at the Old Head. Help gathered then, and he got the puncheon of rum off the boat. They brought the puncheon to the nearest house. It was too big to fit through the door of the house. They knocked down the sidewall and got the puncheon inside. The boat was wrecked in the cove. O'Malley would rather wreck his boat any day than give it up to the King's crowd.

They used to be trading over and back to Guernsey from all parts. They had no other means of livelihood.

FINE GUERNSEY CLOTH (4)

The people trading between Conamara and Guernsey used to bring home material for men and women they called "fine cloth." It was tailored in this country. Long-tailed coats and knee breeches were worn by the men, and tall hats (*carolines*).[4] I know the tall hats and the silk cravats the men used to wear came from Guernsey. The women used to wear a cape and cloak of the fine cloth and a linen cap trimmed with lace.

There wasn't a man going to Guernsey who wasn't buying clothes there and bringing them home and selling them for profit. There was a certain man in this locality whose name was Old Séamas Mac Donnchadha. He made a great amount of money, and he said he'd go to Guernsey and make even more. He made an arrangement with an Ó Laidhe man who was captain of one of the boats. Captain Ó Laidhe was willing to bring him there and bring back whatever cargo he'd buy. There were many people ordering goods from the captain, and there was one man in particular who ordered a hat with him. The men used to wear three types of hat in Conamara at the time: a low hat with a broad brim, another slightly taller hat with a narrower brim, and a tall hat they used to call a "caroline." This man told the captain to bring him a hat that wasn't as tall as the tall hat or as low as the other hats. I suppose the captain was intent on roguery because he said to this man, "You have my word that it won't be too low or too tall."

They sailed off and didn't stop till they reached Guernsey. They loaded the boat with goods, and Old Séamas bought his own goods, five hundred pounds' worth; he had that much money. When they had everything on board, they sailed out heading for home till they came within sight of the land of Ireland. It then began to blow a gale, and a storm arose from the west. They were thrown off course, and they had to run before the wind up the east coast of Ireland till they came ashore in the north of Ulster. Some of the crew became ill. Old Séamas Mac Donnchadha was very ill. He had to be taken off the vessel. They found someone to take him in and tend to him. He didn't get up off his bed for six or seven weeks, and the people of the house were very good to him. When he got up, the vessel and all the goods were gone, and from that day on, there was no trace of Captain Ó Laidhe or the merchandise. Old Séamas was left high and dry, without a penny in his pocket or a smoke in his pipe. He had to make his way, working a week here and a week there, walking all the way till he came to Conamara. He used to work with a sickle, and he brought the sickle home with him. A year and a day had just passed since the morning he left home till he walked in through Carna Moor again. He was so long gone that everybody thought he was dead. People were going to Mass on Sunday morning when they saw him approaching, and they got an awful fright. We have the old saying ever since then, "Séamas's journey to Guernsey."

NUALA NÍ THIOBÓID AND HER FAMILY (4)

Nuala Ní Thiobóid was married to an O'Malley man in Fínis[5] Island. They had many sons, all fine men. One of the sons was killed while smuggling, in a battle with one of the King's vessels, and it was said that Nuala, his mother, couldn't finish Our Lord's Prayer from then on till her life was nearly over: "Forgive us our trespasses as we forgive those who trespass against us"—she wasn't going to forgive those who killed her son.

The sons were very good-looking. It's still an old saying in the locality, "He's as fine a man as Nuala Ní Thiobóid's sons."

I don't know who Nuala's people were, but there's an old saying, "Many a Theobold is a Joyce."

A daughter of Burke of Cloch an Uabhair[6] eloped with Liam Ó Máille (O'Malley), one of Nuala's family. Burke and some of his people were somewhere one day, and they began to be set upon. Liam Ó Máille was present, but the Burkes didn't recognize him. He saved the Burkes, and that's when Burke accepted O'Malley and gave a dowry to his daughter. There was a song about "Burke of Cloch an Uabhair." He often visited Fínis.

BIG NED JOYCE (7)

Big Ned Joyce lived in Baile na Cille (Ballynakill). He was related to Seán Bán Ó Flaithearta. His mother was a sister of Seán Bán's. They weren't very close to each other despite the near relationship. Big Ned had a sloop, and he used to go to Guernsey to buy stuff. He used to come in to Cuigéal with his cargo. He used to keep a good deal of the cargo at his own house. The bottles and jars were hidden in the sod walls. A great many years later, the children began burning the walls and found a lot of bottles in them, bottles that were smooth all the way up, without any shoulders. There wasn't a drop in them as they had been shattered by the fire.

Big Ned had a tract of land near Clifden and another tract near Leenaun. He moved from Baile na Cille to Clifden or somewhere near it. That's where he's buried. A daughter of this Ned Joyce was the grandmother of Martin Grealish in Iorras Fhlannáin (Errislannan, St. Flannan's peninsula). This Grealish man died in the storyteller's house.

GUERNSEY TOBACCO (5)

> I'm begging the pardon of you who have gathered,
> I've a horrible curse to recite now;
> May he not see tomorrow the person who has it
> And who puts not a grain in my pipe now.
> I remember the time when 'twas easy to find
> Hidden as scraws 'neath the dunghill.

When a load of tobacco came ashore it was hidden till it could be sold. It used to be hidden beneath the dung.

BURKE OF IORRAS BEAG (2)

A Burke from Iorras Beag used to go to Guernsey to buy cargoes, and he used to come in to Roundstone Bay with a load on the sly. The King's vessel was chasing him one night, and Burke got away from the vessel and put the cargo ashore. He had a great boat. He happened to be in Galway some time later, and some of the crew of the King's vessel recognized him. They told their captain to arrest him. "I will not arrest him," said the captain. "He's the best seaman I ever saw."

BRANDY HARBOR (5)

One of the Loideáin (Lydons) from Maíros, together with his brothers, had two hookers (large sailing boats). He was coming home from Guernsey one night with a load of brandy. Between Árainn and Sceirde, he saw the King's vessel and the crew of the vessel saw him and followed him. He headed up the bay, Cill Chiaráin Bay. He turned his boat east by the outer end of Leitir Calaidh (Lettercallow, harbor hillside). He came in beside a cliff in Leitir Calaidh. He put his load on the side of the boat. He put his tackles on the mast and on the cliff till he brought the mast right down against the rock. There was no mast to be seen now by the King's vessel. They came up Cill Chiaráin Bay in the morning looking for him, but they could see nothing, and they went away again. Loideán put out his load of brandy on the cliff, and the place is called Brandy Harbor ever since.

ANTAINE RÉAMOINN MAC DONNCHADHA (11)

Antaine was the son of Réamonn Mór Mac Donnchadha who lived on Oileán Chrapaigh (Crapach, lumpy place) near Ceann Gólaim. He was captain of a vessel, and at that time the Comerfords owned the vessel he had. The Comerfords were from Leitir Mealláin. He went to Spain with a load, and on his return he brought back a load—tobacco, wine, brandy, and all sorts. The King's cutter knew he was coming, and Antaine Réamoinn waited till it was night. When darkness fell, he sailed in and up Bealach an Dorú (way of the fishing line), a narrow channel just wide enough for a boat between Inis Eirc (Inisherk) and Crapach. In the middle of the night, he unloaded his cargo below his father's house, and the vessel had gone out again and was on the deep before daybreak. That's the cargo that put Réamonn Mac Donnchadha on his feet.

This Captain Antaine was drowned near the coast of America while saving other people. At the time Antaine Mac Donnchadha died, the poet Colm de Bhailís was working for Antaine's father, for Réamonn. Colm de Bhailís was sawing that day, and around midday he stopped working and walked into the house. He told Réamonn's wife that he couldn't continue with his work just then.

"What's wrong with you? Are you ill?" she said.

"I'm not," he said, "but there's something up that's not right. Take the ear off me if Antaine is not dead."

Réamonn had gone to Achill. He was gone for two weeks when he came back. The day he came home, he was gloomy and sad. His wife noticed how sad he was.

"Is there something wrong with you?" she said.

"There's nothing," he said.

"There's something," she said. "What is it?"

"Antaine is dead," he said. "This is the paper I got in Achill. The report of his death is there."

When the first Antaine died, his mother had another son and they called him Antaine. He died when he was seven or eight years old. Another son was born after him, and he was called Antaine. The third Antaine lived till he was a man, and he died in America. His mother was an Ó Flaithearta from Árainn. She had twenty-one children.

LONG MHÓR NA MBÚRCACH (THE BURKES' GREAT SHIP) (3)

The Burkes' great ship sails, with fine indigo laden,
I'd give you first share of it, friend of my heart.

— An old song

The great ship belonged to a Burke man who lived in Galway. He captained her himself, and he used to go to Guernsey. She was coming back with a load once, and the King's boat was waiting for her in Sunda Salach.[7] The Burkes' vessel didn't heed it, and the cutter came up alongside her, and the men jumped on board Burke's vessel. There was a battle between the ship's crew and the King's men. Captain Burke was stabbed with a sword and was killed. The ship's crew refused to steer the ship to Galway, and the King's men had to bring her in themselves.

Indigo was in great demand at the time for dying homespun cloth blue. No respectable man was content without a blue short suit: a short jacket, short breeches, and long stockings.

TOBACCO FROM AMERICA (18)

The vessels bringing timber beams from America to Galway eighty years ago used to bring in tobacco secretly. Holes were bored in some of the beams to make them hollow in the middle. They were then filled with tobacco and sealed again so that the tobacco would not bulge and be ruined by the salt water. When Captain Comerford's vessel came into the bay, there would be boats from Bell Harbor and Kinvara waiting for it. The beams with the tobacco would be thrown overboard, and the boats would bring them secretly ashore.

SHIPWRECK (2)

It might have been the third year of the famine when a grain vessel was shipwrecked on Clochar an Fhrancaigh (Frenchman's stony ridge). A French vessel with a cargo of grain was on its way to Galway. This stony ridge (clochar) is to the southwest of Na Foiriúin, and it's called Clochar an Fhrancaigh on account of the shipwreck. Poll Watt (Watt's pool) is in Bealach na Bréige (the way of the lie) on the north side of Na Foiriúin, and there was grain piled six feet high in the pool after the ship was wrecked.[8] All the people had to do was to come with shovels in their boats and fill them up with grain. The grain gathered in the calm spot, and the greater part of it was gathered in Poll Watt.

The people saw rats as big as cats deserting the vessel. That's why the *luch mhór* (big mouse) is called *francach* (Frenchman) since.

The time the grain came, the people were in dire need of it. There were lots of people who didn't sow any potatoes that year, and many would have died only for the grain from the ship that was wrecked.

Another vessel came ashore in Inis Bigir (Bigger's island) after the famine. Life had improved by the time it came. There's a treacherous breaker outside Carraig Áine (Áine's rock) on the west side. It hit that breaker first, and it was thrown into the channel between Carraig Áine and Inis Bigir. It was thrown against the rock, and all a man had to do was to walk into it off the rock. It was on Oíche Chinn an Dá Lá Dhéag (the night of the twelfth day of Christmas) it came. Only one of the crew was lost.

There were all sorts of things on board, and everything was for free. There was coarse linen or canvas for sails (baffity). There was furniture and tackle for horses. There were ropes there in coils. There was no knowing how many coils of rope there were. There were boxes of tea and sugar and butter. There wasn't a thing you could think of that wasn't there. The boiler is still to be seen in Bealach Charraig Áine (Carraig Áine's way). The wood was broken up, and the people carried off the cargo. There were no marine guards at the time.

I heard a man say that he took a big roll of baffity that weighed two hundredweight off the vessel. He didn't want to go too far with it before going back to the vessel for something else. He threw the roll of baffity at the foot of a rock and went back to the vessel, and when he returned, another man had gone off with the roll of baffity. I've often heard him say that. Cóilín Aindriú was his name.

Seán an Chóta brought a coil of rope off the vessel and sold it in Galway for two pounds ten shillings. That was great money because money wasn't plentiful. Even the person who took very little off the vessel took a lot off it. It made people rich in Leitreach Ard, Maíros, the two Ards, Más and Leathmhás, and Dumhaigh Ithir. The Maíros people got most of what was in the vessel. The Loideáin (Lydons) were strong in Maíros and had a great number of men to help them. They got the fattest part of the cargo.

A SHIPWRECKED VESSEL (2)

A vessel was thrown ashore in Leitir Mealláin around the Feast of Saint Brigid about sixty-five or sixty-six years ago. There was a load of timber on board, timber beams. There were very few seafaring men between Roundstone and Leitir Mealláin who didn't come there hoping to get some of the timber. Three men from An Aird said they should go there themselves—Stiofán Thomáis Shéamais, Séamas Sheáin Pheadair, and Tom Rua. On their way over Bealach na Srathrach, a man of the Cualáin (Folan) was on Carraig an tSnáimh (swimming rock), and he said if that's where they were going that he'd join them. They were very pleased because the boat they had was a rowing boat and a fourth man was needed. They were in no hurry, as they wanted it to be nightfall by the time they were in Leitir Mealláin, and so it was. They put two of the men ashore to push out a beam or two. Beams that had fallen off the vessel were in by the coast. The two who went ashore pushed out two beams. They had a punt pole each for pushing them out.

Just when they had tied the two beams to the boat, a shot was fired and the man who was rowing to the fore said he was dead and didn't speak any more. With the next shot that was fired, the man who was rowing to the rear said he was dead, and he fell down. The firing stopped then, and they let go of the beams and headed for home. The Cualán man was talking to them till they came to Bealach na Srathrach. That's when he died. Tom Rua Mac Con Rí died immediately. They put the Cualán man ashore on Oileán Máisean (Mason Island) on their way home. His family came and took him away with them, and they were to be pitied mourning for him.

They brought Tom Rua to An Aird. He was married but had no offspring. He was a weaver. His wife and neighbors grieved sorely for him. He was a great tradesman weaving tweeds, and weavers were very scarce at the time. There was a coroner's inquest on each of the men the following day. The bullet went very near the heart in Mac Con Rí. It went right through him, out through his back. The bullet that killed the other man was found in his thigh. The marine guards were brought before the law, but nothing happened to them.

That same night that Ó Cualáin and Tom Rua were killed, Pádraic Mac Eoinín from Leitreach Ard, himself and his near relations, went to Leitir Mealláin looking for timber beams. His relations put him ashore to push out a beam. He was riding astride the beam when the marine guards started shooting. The people in the boat had their sails hoisted when they heard the shooting—they hadn't lowered them at any stage—and they headed for home. They left Pádraic behind. They thought he was ashore.

When Pádraic heard the shots, he lay down on the beam. The beam was drifting with the wind. The wind was from the southeast, and he was found in the morning near Carraig-a-Meacain, nine miles from where the shipwreck was. It was a winter's night. The wind remained steady. He held on to the beam. Only for he did he was lost. A boat picked him up in the morning, and he wasn't any the worse after the night. I don't think he even caught a cold.

He was a pilot. There wasn't a vessel that came for a load of kelp or marble but Pádraic was waiting for her in Cruach na Caoile (Deer island) to take her up to Aill na gCuil (rock of the flies) just west of Cashel.

At the time the two men were killed in Leitir Mealláin, Seán Ó Briain was putting timber beams overboard off the vessel. A beam fell on him and broke his two legs. Only for that he might have been shot himself for all he knew. There were very few men as fine looking as him in his time or as mild-mannered. Seán Bacach Ó Guairim, the local poet, made a song praising him and his Báibín, Seán Ó Briain's wife:

If a boat was in a storm
And the west wind blowing a gale
We would soon find food and sauces
In the house of Seán Ó Briain.
If I sank down to the bottom
And started blaming the Ó Briains
And then met the woman of the glen
And a huntsman with his gun;
She'd have cream and milk and butter
And so much more besides;
I hereby say that I give the sway
To Báibín Sheáin Uí Bhriain.

NOTES

1. *Iorras Beag*: small peninsula.
2. *Iorras Mór*: big peninsula.
3. *Bealach na hUilleann*: way of the elbow.
4. *Caroline hats*: belonging to the time of Charles I or II. From *Carolus*, Charles.
5. *Fiodh*: wood; *Inis*: island. (Feenish island).
6. *Cloch*: stone; *Uabhar*: pride. (stone of pride).
7. *Sunda Salach*: Foul Sound, between Inis Oírr and Inis Meáin, in the Aran Islands.
8. *Na Foiriúin*: rocks to the west of Maíros. Similar names occur at Slyne Head and off Leitir Mealláin.

EIGHT

—ᗡᗠ—

POOR SCHOLARS

MÁIRTÍN Ó CONAIRE (CONROY) (4)

There was a man in this community called Máirtín Ó Conaire (Conroy). He was known as Máirtín Aodh' Ruairí, and I suppose he was from this locality. He was a schoolmaster, going from village to village. There wasn't a wake in the neighborhood that he wasn't present at, and he'd spend the night telling stories about the Fianna and reciting poems such as "Seanchas na Muice" (The Ancient Lore of the Pig).[1] It was said about a good versifier or storyteller that he surpassed Máirtín Aodh' Ruairí, which goes to show that Máirtín Ó Conaire was very good.

SCHOOLMASTER Ó LAIDHE (2)

A schoolmaster called Brian Ó Laidhe (O'Lee) came to An Aird (Ard) long ago to teach school. It's a hundred years since he was there. He used to teach Irish and, thanks to him, many of the old people were able to read any Irish language book. Anybody in either of the two Ards who wanted to, was able to read Irish, and people in Coillín were learning from him. He held the school in the houses. He might stay in one house for a year if he was kept. The house he stayed in didn't have to pay him a penny except to keep him going, unless they gave him a tip. The neighbors who came to school to him used to give him a little, according to what they could afford. This was before the famine. When the famine came, the schoolmaster had to leave. He didn't leave house or family after him.

SEÁN DE BARRA (2)

Seán de Barra (Barry) came after Brian Ó Laidhe. He was a schoolteacher and was very learned. He had Latin and English, and he was a freemason. He was teaching in An Aird, and his scholars were young men. He asked them one day if they would like to see the devil. They thought he was joking and they said they would. Within five minutes he had brought the devil up through the floor, and all the scholars in the house ran away when they saw him. Seán de Barra went out and called them back and told them not to be afraid, as he had sent him back down again. Some of them came back and more of them did not. In the evening, when they went home to their parents everyone was telling about the wonder he had seen.

"We had better go and tell the priest," said some of the parents.

The priest was nine or ten miles away. He came, and when he was told the story, he went to Seán de Barra.

"I am told," said the priest, "that you are able to bring the devil up through the floor. You may as well do it now till I see if you are able."

Seán began to speak, and within five minutes your man (the devil) put up his two horns.

"Ó, Seán," said the priest, "don't let him come up any further."

"He is there now," said Seán, "and I'll let you put him down yourself."

Seán sent him down the same way again, on the priest's advice.

The priest spoke to the people of the village and told them to run Seán out of the place completely. They didn't give him lodgings any more, and he had to leave.

SEÁN OF THE SCHOOL (2)

Seán na Scoile (Seán of the School) was living in Aird Thiar (Ard West). His little house had a chimney in one gable end. The only means of living he had was the shilling he'd get from those who had it, and those who hadn't would bring him a bag of potatoes as payment for teaching the scholars. He held his school in the little house. After half a year when he'd have collected a pound of money he liked to pay a visit to his own people. They'd be expecting him, and they used to say he might be there in a week's time. When they didn't see him coming, they would think he must have died. In six weeks' time Seán would turn up, having done his month in prison for drunkenness and beating up *peelers*.[2] He used to say that no other man had suffered as much as he had, since they last saw him.

His school was all in English, but he was the best of Irish speakers. He came here from the east. He died fifty-five years ago.

SEÁN OF THE SCHOOL'S FATHER (4)

The teaching of Irish didn't stop altogether until the National Schools began.[3] Seán na Scoile was in An Aird until that time. He had to leave then.

Seán na Scoile's father was an old soldier or a seaman. His name was Uáitéar Mac Donnchadha. He lived in Flood Street in Galway. He was a learned man, and he had only one arm. He used to write letters for people in the town, people who couldn't write themselves.

Seán, the son, was a schoolmaster in Ard. A sod hut is what he had for a school, where the master's house is now. He used to teach Irish and English; catechism was taught in Irish for certain. A penny a week is what a small child had to pay, and from there on up.

There were very learned men in Leitir Mealláin (Lettermullen). Poor scholars were teaching geometry and navigation there. The poor scholar Ó Briain in Clifden was very good.

POOR SCHOLARS IN THE ISLANDS (7)

There was a poor scholar in Leitir Mealláin before my time, in my father's time. I heard tell of him. He used to teach children in the houses, and they paid him a penny a week. Séamas Ó Maoláin (Moylan) was his name.

There was a small house in Baile na Cille (Ballinakill) between my own house and the sea. That's where Seán Ó Briain lived, himself and his old lady. They had no family, just the two of themselves. Seán Ó Briain was teaching school before my time. He had no schoolhouse but the little dwelling house. There was no government school in Gorumna Island at first. Archbishop Mac Hale wouldn't allow it. He was against English and against England.

I, myself, saw a school a poor scholar had in Inis Ní (Inishnee). Ó Cearbhaill (O'Carroll) was his name. Himself and his wife had a little house on the island across from Roundstone pier. The Inis Ní children used to go to him. That's nearly sixty-five years ago.

They didn't teach writing in these schools till a child was a good while at school, and there were many people in the locality who could read but who couldn't write at all. At the time my father was going to school, Irish was being taught. He was able to read Irish, and so was his father before him. My father had an Irish language book by Tadhg Gaelach Ó Súilleabháin.[4] I had that book and that's where I learned *Aighneas an Pheacaigh leis an mBás* (*The Sinner's Contention with Death*).

There were schools in Leitir Mealláin (Lettermullen) long before they were set up in Gorumna. Leitir Mealláin belonged to the Galway diocese, and government schools were allowed in there before Archbishop Mac Hale allowed them into his own diocese of Tuam. When the government schools came, English-speaking masters were put into them. English is the language they all spoke when they came. They weren't able to teach the catechism. It was Pádraic Antoine Mac Donnchadha who used to teach catechism when I was young. When there was early Mass, he used to teach it for half an hour after Mass. When I grew up myself, I used to teach catechism in the church on Sundays. My father taught me how to read it. Mac Hale's Catechism is what I used to have.[5] There was another book before Mac Hale's book, Doctor Kirwan's Catechism. It gave better explanations than Mac Hale's book.

INSTRUCTORS AND READERS

Aibhistín Ó Conaola (Conneely), the father of Seán Mac Con Rí's mother, was living in Dúmhaigh Ithir. He had a son, Seán Aibhistín, and he was a scholar.

Pádraic Eoin Mac Con Rí in Dumhaigh Ithir was able to read Irish, and Máirtín Sheáin Risteáird Mac Donnchadha in An Aird was able to read it.

Beairtle Bán Mac Con Rí in An Aird, the father of Séamas Ó Conaola's wife, used to read Ó Gallchóir's catechism in the chapel on Sundays, and Seán Breathnach from Roisín na Mainiach, known as Seán Phádraic, used to do the same. He had Latin. He was in a confession house one day when the parish priest and the chaplain were there. The parish priest spoke for a very long time. "You'll make a song of it," said the chaplain to him in Latin. Seán understood the Latin.

Micheál Ó hUaithnín in Leathmhás (Halfmace) was able to speak Irish and teach the catechism.

Seán Bheairtle Caona (Keany) in Caladh an Chnoic used to teach catechism in the chapel.[6]

Maitias Mac Craith, known as Maitias na dTamhnacha (of the grassy uplands) used to teach Mac Hale's catechism. Micheál Ó Domhnaill from Leitreach Ard (Letterard) and Máirtín Mac Craith (Máirtín Beag Mháirtín Aodha) from Glinsce (Glinsk) used to teach the same book.

A woman in Cill Chiaráin used to teach catechism. She was a sister of Seán Ó Briain, the storyteller who lived in Loch Conaortha. It was the priest who taught her the catechism, and he put her teaching it in the chapel. He had no other assistant.

The instructors used to read the catechism before Mass or after Mass, and the people memorized it. It was a good practice.

The books they used were a book written by Dr. de Buitléir, a book written by Dr. Ó Gallchóir, Archbishop Mac Hale's book, and Dr. Kirwan's book.[7]

NOTES

1. *Stories about the Fianna:* A large corpus of stories relating to the band of warriors led by the mythical Fionn Mac Cumhaill. The stories, the first of which appear in eighth-century texts, have been very popular in both literature and folklore for over 1,000 years.

2. *Peelers*: Provincial constabularies came into being in Ireland following the Irish Constabulary Act of 1822. The police were commonly referred to as peelers after Sir Robert Peel (1788–1850).

3. National Schools in Ireland were first established under British rule in 1831.

4. Tadhg Gaelach Ó Súilleabháin (1715–1795), poet of pious verse.

5. Dr. John MacHale (1791–1881), Roman Catholic Archbishop of Tuam, prolific translator and political agitator. See Andrews 2001.

6. *Caladh an Chnoic*: Landing Place of the Hill.

7. Dr. James Butler, Archbishop of Cashel, published a catechism in 1775. Augustine Kirwan (1725–1791) published a catechism in 1842, see Mahon 1991. James Gallagher (1681–1751) was Bishop of Raphoe, see Mac Murchaidh 2012.

NINE

—ᗩᗯ—

PRIESTS

There was no parish priest living in Carna long ago, and there was no priest's house in the whole community. The priest lived in the people's houses. The first priest who had a house for himself was a man called Fr. Dónall Ó Máille (O'Malley). He was living in a house where the chapel is built in Carna now. I believe he used to say Mass in the same house. Fr. Éamonn Ó Máille was there before him. He had no house of his own but stayed in people's houses. He was in Aird Thiar for a while, in the house of Máirtín Sheáin Risteáird of the Mac Donnchadha clan. He would put him up for a month when he came around. Signs on him, there was no better-mannered man than him. This priest was in An Aird Mhór (Ardmore) for a while, and he was in Loch Conaortha and in Glinsk. He used to come around once a month to do baptisms. The people who lived far away didn't have Mass every Sunday. It was twelve miles from one end of the parish to the other, from Doire Iorrais to Maíros. Maíros is the old name of the parish. What they count as Iorras Aithneach is everywhere from the hills down to the sea.[1] If a man from the hills sees one of us going the road, he says that's a man from Iorras Aithneach. And if we see a man from the hills going around, we'll say there's a man from the hills.

Fr. Éamonn Ó Máille was a poet. Fr. Peadar Mac Con Bhuí (Conway) came after Fr. Dónall, and it was he who built the church in Carna.

FATHER ÉAMONN Ó MÁILLE (4)

Fr. Éamonn Ó Máille was parish priest in Carna after the famine. He was a decent old-fashioned man. He was going to kill every man, but every man was alive after him. The Archbishop was in Roundstone one day confirming people, and there was a great gathering of priests with him. The parish priest of An Cheathrú Rua (Carraroe) was there, and a keg of poteen had been confiscated from a stable of his. The priest was brought to court, and he was fined heavily. The priests in Conamara were very poor at that time, and the priest in An Cheathrú Rua didn't have much means of paying the fine. The priests who were gathered in Roundstone decided to help him out according to their means. The Archbishop got the collection going. He put a sum of money on the plate, and all the other priests followed suit till it came to Fr. Éamonn Ó Máille. When the plate was passed to him, he said he wouldn't give a halfpenny: "I have the finest parishioners in the diocese of Tuam, but some of that cursed poteen has come in from the parish of Carraroe, and when they drink it, I lose control of them."

When the money was collected, the Carraroe priest thanked the Archbishop and the other priests. He thought he hadn't deserved what Fr. Ó Máille had said, and though the refusal was bad enough the oration was even worse.

"How do you know," said Fr. Ó Máille, "that I wouldn't be better than the whole lot of you priests, the Archbishop included?"

"That's what I would have expected," said the Carraroe priest.

"Get a pen and ink and paper," said Fr. Ó Máille, and it was done.

Then Fr. Éamonn dictated a petition to be sent to the Viceroy. The Carraroe priest wrote it down, and it was sent off. His fine was forgiven, and he had "the fleece and its price" as a result of the petition. (The money that was collected that day was put in a savings deposit, and the big bells in Tuam Cathedral were bought with the proceeds.)

FATHER ÉAMONN AND THE CHAPLAIN (4)

When Fr. Éamonn was getting old. the Archbishop decided to move him, for his own sake, to a better parish than this one where he wouldn't have as much work to do, but Fr. Éamonn didn't like this at all. When he wasn't willing to move, the Archbishop sent him an assistant, a young chaplain. That was fine, and when he came to Carna, the chaplain went to visit Fr. Éamonn and told him he had been sent by the Archbishop as his assistant.

"How," said Fr. Éamonn, "does the Archbishop expect a poor parish like this to feed two of us? Or where do you come from, please?"

"I'm from Caladh na Muc," said the chaplain.

"From Caladh na Muc!" (landing place of the pigs), said Fr. Éamonn. "I wouldn't mind a landing place of a ship or a boat or some decent place! The best thing you could do now is to sail back to Caladh na Muc again and leave me and my parishioners here till I die in their midst."

"GOD BLESS THEM"

There was a mission in Carna in Fr. Éamonn's time. At the end of the mission, the congregation was so big that there wasn't room in the church for them, and the sermon had to be given outside. The missionary was speaking and was praising the parishioners highly. Fr. Éamonn was walking outside and had his ears pricked. When the missionary praised the parishioners very highly, Fr.

Éamonn looked up at him and said, in everybody's hearing, "Say 'God bless them!'"[2]

FATHER TOMÁS Ó MÁILLE (1)

Fr. Tomás Ó Máille was chaplain in Carna. He was a poet, and it was he who translated "The Bells of Shandon" into Irish. He died in the house where Josie Mongan's widow is living at the moment, in Bánrach Ard (high paddock) near Cill Chiaráin. When he died, his people wanted to bury him at home. When the funeral came to the crossroads in Carna, the parishioners wouldn't let it go north. They made the priest's people bury him in the church in Carna. It is said it's not lucky to take a priest out of the parish he dies in.

THE PRIEST OF THE ISLANDS (7)

It was Fr. Aibhistín Ó Duibhir (Fr. Austin Dwyer) who married my father and mother and who baptized me. He was eighteen years in the parish, and he went from this parish to Dunmore (in East Galway). He was a great man for the Irish language and always gave his sermons in Irish. I often heard him giving a sermon. Fr. Peadar Mac Con Bhuí (Conway) was here before him. It was he who built the church in Carna, and he also built a church in Tír an Fhia (Tiernee) on the shore of Cuan an Fhir Mhóir (Greatman's Bay). He went from here to Headford. Fr. Máirtín Ó MáILóid came after Fr. Aibhistín and was also a great man for the Irish language. Fr. Uáitéar Mac Con Bhuí came after that. When Fr. Uáitéar left, Fr. Seán Ó hÉilí came. He, also, had fluent Irish. All the parish priests were very attached to Irish culture in my time.

Fr. Aibhistín was a very lively man. He was here when Nolan and Trench were running for Parliament.[3] Archbishop Mac Hale was on Nolan's side. Fr. Aibhistín said he wouldn't help him unless

Nolan's father reinstated the tenants he had evicted from Port an Chairn.[4] He told the Archbishop that, and the Archbishop spoke to Nolan about it. "I cannot take the land off the man who has it now," said Nolan. A man from Oughterard had the land.

"You can give them holdings in Ballindereen," the Archbishop told him. He did that. He brought the tenants his father had thrown out on the side of the road, he brought them to Ballindereen, and he gave each household a holding. Fr. Aibhistín backed Nolan in the election.

THE PRIEST'S BOY (14)

Fr. Ó Málóid was going home on his sidecar one day after a marriage. He had a driver called Jack. "How much did you get, Jack?" the priest asked the driver. "It's none of your damned business," Jack replied. "How much did you get yourself?"

NOTES

1. *Iorras Aithneach*: "everywhere from the hills down to the sea."
2. *"Say 'God bless them!'"*: to praise someone without invoking God's blessings brings bad luck.
3. John Philip Nolan (1838–1912) of the Irish Parliamentary Party and William Le Poer Trench (1837–1920) of the Conservatives contested the 1872 Westminister by-election for Galway County. Archbishop MacHale and other bishops supported Nolan who was elected, but Trench went to law and unseated Nolan who subsequently regained the seat at the 1874 election.
4. *Port an Chairn:* Port of the Cairn.

TEN

—ɷ—

PEOPLE AND PLACES

God has many people.

—Peadar Ó Cualáin[1]

RAGHNALL (REGINALD) AND HIS HOUND (12)

There's a *leathrach* (broad seaweed) outside Carraig Raghnaill (Raghnall's rock) near Inis Bigir.[2] It's where Raghnall used to fish. The rock is named after him since then, Carraig Raghnaill and Leathrach Raghnaill. It's a great place for wrasse.

This Raghnall was a monk in olden times, and a monk whose name was well known. He had a hound that was as big as a horse foal. A magician came by and cast a spell on the hound. The hound was so big and so fast that he could catch up with any beast in Ireland. The magician envied Raghnall for owning it. It is said by many people that it is still alive on the strand. It runs from the eastern end to the western end, running a race. The strand is half a mile long.

"I was at a funeral one day," said Seosamh Mac Donnchadha, "a young woman in the village who died a few years ago. The funeral went around by the road to Maíros, and two young men took the shortcut out to dig the grave. They dug the grave till they were a few feet down, and then they met with a hard stone wall made of lime and mortar. They had to get tools to dig through it, and it was a difficult job. When they got down three or four feet deeper, what did they come upon but a dog's skull. Everybody was surprised at the likes of it to be there. After going home, we were talking about it. When an old woman in the village who was over eighty years of age heard about it. 'Ha ha,' she said, 'Raghnall's yellow hound is what you met.'

'What about Raghnall's yellow hound?' says I to her.

'There was a kern they used to call Raghnall Mac Donnchadha living in Dumhaigh Ithir' she said, 'and he had a hound that was famous near and far for its intelligence. It was thought to be as clever as a human being. Raghnall was coming home late one night after a long journey, and on his way across Maíros strand, he met with a white-faced dog and it attacked him. The white-faced dog had Raghnall up to his waist in the tide when he heard a hissing sound coming over the strand towards him. What was it but the hound! It attacked the white-faced dog. It kept at it until he had Raghnall between it and his home. They were cutting and tearing each other, and the hound was looking behind it and giving an odd glance at Raghnall. Raghnall realized that the hound wanted him to make for home. He made it home. Between then and morning the hound came in torn to strips, and it died on the hearthstone very soon after. Raghnall was so grief-stricken that he invited neighbors and relations from near and far; he had a wake for the hound and buried it in the Maíros dunes, and Raghnall put a wall and stones on the grave. The place is within the graveyard now, but it wasn't at that time. It seems that the blown sand covered the wall that was built over the dog's grave.'"

THE O'FLAHERTYS OF THE ISLANDS (7)

There is a bay on the west side of Cnoc Chathail Óig (young Cathal's hill), between the hill and Daighinis (or Daimhinis, ox island), where vessels used to come long ago. It's called Cuan Chaisín (little current bay). A vessel came in there long ago. They say it was a Spanish vessel. It was a long time there, and the ship's crew used to go out fowling. Cathal Ó Flaithearta was the captain's name, and he used to go around in this village where the hill is, and he befriended a young woman of the Ó Fíne clan. He then left after being there a good while and didn't return for a year or so. Himself and the young woman got married and had a son, and the name he was given was Cathal Óg. When they were a good while married and the child fairly hardy, he left Cathal Óg with the grandfather and left them enough money for the grandfather to be able to pay someone to rear the child for him. The captain and his wife went away then and neither of them ever returned.

When Cathal Óg grew up to be a man, he got married and had a son. The name they used to call this son was Brian Dubh (black Brian), and he went to live in Leitir Móir (Lettermore). Seán Bán Ó Flaithearta (the father of Sinéad Ní Sheachnasaigh's husband, Éamonn Ó Flaithearta) was a son of Brian Dubh. Seán Bán went to live in Poll Uí Mhuirinn (Ó Muireann's deep pool) in Oileán Gharmna (Gorumna Island). Seán Bán had two other sons and a daughter. Proinnsias, the lawyer, was one of them. He lived in Inis Mhic Cionnaith (Mac Cionnaith's island), and some of his people are still there. The third son was called Liam, and he lived in Baile na Cille (Ballynakill, church village) in Cuigéal (narrow channel).

Seán Bán had a daughter, and she did a trick, hoping to see the picture of the man she would marry. She went out one day to a hillock near Galway Bay. A vessel was coming up the bay on its way to Galway. Miss O'Flaherty had an eyeglass, and she saw the man on board the vessel whose picture she had seen in the trick. She never stopped until she reached Galway, and she told the ship's captain the story. She told him she recognized him from seeing him in the trick. They got married immediately, and she went off to sea with him.

The O'Flahertys were in the islands for a long time until the famine came, and their tenants had nothing to give them. But the hill called Cnoc Chathail Óig was named after Cathal Óg, the son the captain had left behind. The O'Flahertys departed, but the hill is still there and will be for ever.

SINÉAD NÍ SHEACHNASAIGH (7)

Sinéad Ní Sheachnasaigh (O'Shaughnessy) was from Dublin. She was married to Éamonn Ó Flaithearta from Gorumna Island, a son of Seán Bán Ó Flaithearta. Éamonn and his wife settled down in Leitir Móir (Lettermore) where the Garda barrack is now. They were landlords of the following villages: Eanach Mheáin (Annaghvaan, middle moorland), Leitir Móir, Máimín (little pass), Gleann Trasna (crosswise glen), Baile na Cille, Poll Uí Mhuirinn, Seanadh 'ac a' Mheas (slope of Mac a' Mheas), Lios a' Druim (fairy mound of the ridge). The tenants paid their rent to them, and they themselves paid rent to the Ffrenches of Tyrone.

When the tenants had finished the spring sowing, they had to be ready by May Day to go burning kelp. One half of the kelp would go to Éamonn Ó Flaithearta who had big boats for bringing the kelp to Galway, and the other half to the tenant who burnt the kelp. He used to feed the workers while they were working for him. They used to have a camp on Inis Léith[3] and other places where the black seaweed was plentiful, and the workers spent day and night in the camp. Many locals were working in the big boats. The kelp was brought out in the boats, and meal and potatoes brought home in them to feed the men.

Éamonn and Sinéad gave tools of the trade to the weaver who used to come in to them; they gave him a loom. They had boatwrights working for them, and they gave the blacksmith employment in building the boats and the man who made the sails and the ropes. Many is the tradesman the O'Flahertys gave employment to. Éamonn Ó Flaithearta was rich, and he had a good stock of cattle of his own on the land.

Éamonn and Sinéad had two sons, Máirtín Óg and Proinnsias Óg. The father died when they were still very young. The two sons died when they were young men. Proinnsias Óg was so good-looking that he was mentioned in a song, and his mother didn't like to hear the song. Sinéad outlived the husband and the sons. When the sons died, she didn't stay around much longer and she went back to Dublin. She had a brother who was a lawyer who used to often come to Lettermore.

Whiteboys were very prominent on Gorumna Island that time. They sought to set out their own laws, and people were frightened of them. They attempted to fix prices on everything and did not allow anyone to offer better prices than their own on potatoes or oats. Quite a number of them were arrested and sent to prison. Seán Ó Seachnasaigh, Sinéad's brother, defended them in court, and they were acquitted.

Sinéad continued with kelp harvesting after her husband. She owned both the shoreline and the seaweed and half of the kelp accrued to her as a result. When potatoes were scarce, she used to purchase a cargo of potatoes in Inis Gé (Inishkea, off the Mayo coast) for the men who were burning the kelp for her.

The potatoes of Inis Gé
Coming in to Inis Léith
And the man who depends on them
Has grief and woe each day.

The man who depended on them had very little reward in life. When he depended on them, he had to work whether he liked it or not.

Sinéad Ní Sheachnasaigh had a big boat with two masts. It carrried a few score tons. It was a cargo ship, built in Leitir Móir by island boatwrights. It sank on its very first voyage with a load of kelp. It was a great blow and a great loss; there was two score tons of kelp aboard, and the kelp was worth ten pounds a ton. There was a lot of talk about that boat; even if it were an old boat, there would be a lot of talk about it. When a boat is lost at sea, it is said, "Sinéad Ní Sheachnasaigh's boat was a greater loss than it."

—⁂—

A sister of Máilleach na gCaorán[4] was married to Seán Bán Ó Flaithearta. She was Éamonn's mother. The Ó Máille man was living in Na Caoráin in An Cheathrú Rua (Carraroe) before he went to Aran. He was in Aran when Raftery (the poet) composed "Fiach Sheáin Bhradaigh" (the hunting of scoundrel Seán) because he is mentioned in the poem. There was hardly another house in Ireland better than his house. He was a tenant of Colonel Martin, and it was a great honor to the Colonel to have him as a tenant.

This Ó Máille man was trading from Guernsey, and there was always a barrel of wine in the house with the lid off and everybody allowed to drink the fill of his cup from it. When he killed an ox or a sheep, none of it was salted because he used to share the meat, and it was eaten before it needed salt. The Ó Máille man was famous for his generosity, and it is said that fame is not found without loss. He moved to Aran and built a fine house in Cill Éinde. The house is still there. It is near Teampall Bheannáin (St. Bennan's temple).

The Ó Máilles of Slyne Head were related to Máirtín Mór Ó Máille; both belonged to the old Ó Máilles. This Máirtín Mór Ó Máille said a rude word in the company of the Bishop of Galway. The Bishop hit him in the mouth with the back of his hand. He treated the Bishop in some ill-mannered way. The Bishop's first cousin, Sir Thomas Ffrench, challenged Ó Máille to a duel. Ó Máille was killed by the first bullet. When Colonel Martin heard the news, he said that the Ó Máille man would have preferred a hole in his gut than a hole in his honor, "but," he said, "there wouldn't be a hole in either if he had told me."

LYNCH OF BARNA (1)

For many generations back, Leitir Mealláin (Lettermullen) belonged to Línseach Bhearna (Lynch of Barna). In olden days, a long time ago, there was a Lynch in Barna who had two sons, Marcas and Nioclás. He gave all his land to one of them; he gave him Barna, Leitir Mealláin, Cill Chiaráin and Coill Sáile, and all the rest of his land. He gave the other son money. There came a day when he had nothing for himself, and he needed money before he died. He looked for help from the son he gave the money to. That son said, "If you gave your money to me, you shouldn't be looking for it back, but the man you gave your estate to is the one who should give you money." He then sent for the son he had given his estate to. He came. "If you gave your estate to me," he said, "I don't have much money. It's to the man you gave your money to you should go looking for money. There isn't much money that I can make from land."

Neither of them gave him any help. Then the father took off his cap and implored God and the Blessed Virgin Mary that no second son be born into the tribe ever again. A second son wasn't born in the tribe until their time was up. Marcas, the last heir in Barna, had two sons, and people who were versed in traditional lore said their time was up. The youngest boy died as a child, and the eldest son died of yellow fever in Africa.

Línseach Bhearna was always called Nioclás or Marcas. A Marcas came after Nioclás and Nioclás after Marcas.

TADHG Ó HAIRT AND COLONEL MARTIN (4)

Colonel Richard Martin had a servant called Tadhg Ó hAirt. The Colonel used to bring Tadhg with him to England and to France. He couldn't go anywhere without Tadhg.

The Colonel got into debt in London, and he was sent to prison until he'd have paid his debt. When he was in prison, he promised that if he were allowed home he would collect as much money from his tenants in Conamara as would clear all his debt and that his wife would stay in prison in his place until he'd return with the money. He was released, and his wife went to stay in prison until he came back from Conamara.

The Colonel came home to Conamara and Tadhg Ó hAirt along with him to collect as much rent as would release the Colonel's wife from prison. There was a rich Frenchman in London who was in love with the Colonel's wife. When he heard she was locked up, and that the Colonel had gone to Ireland, he came and paid all the debts the Colonel owed to the people who had lent him clothes and money. As soon as the Colonel's wife was released from prison, she eloped with the Frenchman and the two of them went to his country to settle down there. Well and good. He had a fine house in France, a court, and they were nice and quiet there until the Colonel returned to London. When he went back to the prison, he was told that his wife was released some time before that and that the debts had been paid.

It wasn't long before he was told the whole truth, and when he heard that his wife was with the Frenchman, "He'll pay some more," he said to Tadhg Ó hAirt.

Off he went, and the servant along with him, and he didn't delay till he sought out the Frenchman his wife had eloped with. Himself and Tadhg Ó hAirt went up to him, and the Colonel had his sword and his pistol. He challenged the Frenchman, and with the indignation and rage the Colonel was in, he had him shaking in his shirt.

The Frenchman offered him a thousand pounds if he would set him free. The Colonel said he wouldn't accept his money, that he could give it to the servant, that it was his wife and his honor he wanted. The Frenchman gave the servant the money, and the Colonel ordered Tadhg Ó hAirt to go out and distribute the money among the poor in the street. Tadhg went out with the thousand pounds.

When the Colonel and his wife came out to leave, Tadhg Ó hAirt was there before them in the street.

"Where's the money?" said the Colonel.

"It's distributed among the poor in the street," said Tadhg.

"And, you d. . . . , where's the man poorer than myself?" said the Colonel.

PEADAR MÁIRTÍN (4)

Peter Martin who lived in Aird an Chaisleáin (Ard Castle) had for estate the two Ards, left to him by his father, Colonel Richard Martin. He was a judge. There was a man in An Aird, Patsach Sheáin Risteáird Mac Donnchadha. He always had a gun. He killed a seagull one day. Peter Martin heard about it, and he sent for Patsach.

"I heard," he said, "that you killed a poor seagull that was flying by, and what cause did you have to do that?"

"I had cause," said Patsach. "I had one sheep, and I had no other means in the world of getting a pair of stockings except the wool that grew on that sheep. The sheep had a young lamb, and when it was born it wasn't able to stand up. The first time it opened an eye, this seagull came and plucked the eye out, and that's the complaint I had against the seagull."

Peter Martin said, "I was on board a ship once, together with a big crew of men. An awfully bad night came upon us, and we couldn't see land or strand. We saw a seagull, and so we knew we were near land. The seagull saved the ship and the crew. But, because you had that complaint against the seagull," he said, "I'll let you off this time."

Peter Martin was born out of wedlock. He spent part of his life as a sailor. When he came home, the Colonel gave him the two Ards. He was a Protestant. When he died, he was buried in Maíros as a sign of honor because the people had great affection for him.

SÉAMAS BACACH Ó MÁILLE (4)

Séamas Bacach (lame) Ó Máille lived near Ceann Léime (Slyne Head). Clifden wasn't there at the time, nor any other town nearer than Westport or Galway where fishing equipment could be had. The people used to take shortcuts on foot from Slyne Head to Westport, and robbers lurked in lonely places in the hills. Séamas Bacach went to Westport one day and bought everything he wanted. He had a heavy load, and as well as everything else he had a fine roll of leather for making boots. On his way back through a lonely mountain glen, a robber jumped up before him, a big, strong, powerful man, and told Ó Máille to lay down his load. Ó Máille laid it down.

The first thing the robber showed interest in was some of the roll of leather, and he told Ó Máille to cut the makings of a pair of boots for him.

"I've carried it long enough," said Ó Máille, "and the least you can do now is to cut as much as you want for yourself."

The robber drew his knife and bent down to cut the leather. When Ó Máille got him bent down, he set upon him and hit him with his walking stick and went on hitting him till he had well and truly mastered him. He left him stretched on the ground.

Ó Máille lifted his load onto his back, and when he was leaving, the robber lifted his head and said, "Either you are the devil or one of the Ó Máilles of Slyne Head."

"I am one or the other," said Séamas.

RED-HAIRED TOMÁS OF THE GUINEA (4)

Tomás Rua Mac Donnchadha was called Tomás Rua of the Guinea. The reason for the nickname was that his mother sold himself and a brother of his to some people in Galway for a guinea each. The older of the two was put to death in the presence of the other, Tomás Rua. Tomás Rua got up and made off. He escaped with his life, and he came home. "Tomás Rua of the Guinea" stuck to him ever after. Others used to call him "Luach an Ghiní" (the guinea's worth). That could be a hundred and fifty years ago.

It was said that doctors used to buy children in order to study them.

Tomás grew up to be a fine, valiant man, and he spent a long time as a smuggler going to Guernsey.

NINE WOMEN ON SCEIRDE ROCK (2)

Nine women went out to Sceirde Rock picking *creathnach* (tiny-shelled dulse). The boat that landed them on the rock went fishing and was to return for them in the evening, but it couldn't reach them or come near them as the sea was too rough, and they had to go home. For nine nights and nine days no boat came to rescue them—the sea was that wild—and every man whose own relation was out there said they couldn't but be dead. On the morning of the tenth day, the sea had calmed down, and this woman, an Ó Fatharta woman, Seán an Chóta's mother, said she saw them. She was standing on Caorán na hAirde (Ard moorland), and she told the relations not to be worried, that the women were alive, that she had seen them herself going down when the swell receded and picking a handful of dulse and coming back up again to the top of the rock when they'd see the swell return.

The boat went out with four men to take the women off. The nine were alive, as the woman who stood on the moorland had said. Their jaws were swollen from chewing dulse all the time. They weren't as good as they used to be for two weeks after coming home.

It happened in the Autumn. The Ceannaí Fionn (the fair-haired pedlar) put a curse on anybody who would trust an autumn night: "An autumn night got the better of the Ceannaí Fionn."

MAOLRA (MYLES) OF THE BEES (3)

Maolra Bairéad was a strong, energetic stump of a man. He was a top class runner. In his youth he spent most of his time chasing after bees, finding their hives, and taking away their honey. He often collected five gallons of honey from wild bees' nests in the hills all over Conamara. He was able to recognize the bee that had the best hive, and he often followed it for five or six miles.

This is the trick he had for finding the hives: He always had some honey saved. He would cut a rod five or six feet long and tie a flower onto the end of it with a string, the sort of flower he thought the bees liked most for collecting honey from. When he saw the bee, he would reach out to it with the flower on the end of the rod and the flower dipped in honey. The bee used to alight on the flower on the end of the rod, and it would drink the honey off the flower until it had drunk so much that it was barely able to fly. Then Maolra would follow it. It wouldn't stop or alight until it reached the hive with all the honey it had drunk. That's how he used to find the wild bees' hives, and keep up with the bees, and take away the honey.

He was so good a runner that the water kicked up by his feet turned to mist as he ran through a wet swamp of sedge. Not a word of a lie. I often heard that. He used to go to Gleann Chóchan (Glencoaghan) looking for a kiss from a young woman there and come home again the same night. He'd be the first man to have lit a kiln of kelp the following morning after walking all that distance. Gleann Chóchan is twenty miles from Coillín where Maolra lived.

Clever and all as Maolra was, his son Maitias was cleverer. They had a little patch of land on the bank of a lake. When it flooded, the water rose too high on the land. They said to each other that they should let the lake water flow downhill, that it would dry the land, and that it would be of more use to have the lake dry. They went to let the lake water downhill. They brought their spades and began to dig a trench from the lake to the river. When they were about halfway to the river, they found a huge big rock in the path they were taking with the trench. Maolra didn't know from Adam what they should do with the rock, it was so big. He got frustrated and went home to his house and stayed at home until he had had his dinner. Maitias stayed behind on some pretence or other, and he didn't go home at all until Maolra came back. Once Maitias found Maolra gone he began to dig a hole at the other side of the trench, near the rock, and he dug a big deep hole. When he had done that, he gave the rock a shove with the crowbar. Once it was moved, the rock slid down into the hole. When Maolra came back the rock wasn't to be seen, and there was no trace of where it had gone.

He told Maitias he could go and follow a trade, and that he himself would never have thought of the plan Maitias had thought of in getting the rock out of the trench.

They cut the trench as far as the river to let the lake flow freely. There were fish in the lake, and they left a dam uncut at the lake bank. They then fixed a net in the trench, cut the dam, and caught every fish that was in the lake in the net. They had as many fish as made ample payment for them, about three or four barrelfuls when it was salted. And they had dried their land, caught their fish, and had tasty food for the year ahead. They spent the winter contentedly eating potatoes and lake fish.

Loch Mhaolra (Myles's lake) is what the lake used to be called. *Corcach* is what the area that was under the lake is called. It is soft underfoot and it shakes when you walk on it.

MAOLRA (MYLES) AND THE FOX (3)

When a fine day comes, the old fox brings the young cubs out of the den to teach them tricks and skills. Maolra knew this, and he went to watch the foxes one day; he knew well where the den was. When the day got warm, the old fox came out and three young cubs along with him. Maolra stole up on them until he came as near to them as he could, and he caught one of them before the old fox managed to get into the den with them. He brought it home with him and put it in the goose coop; there was a goose in the same coop, but the goose was made safe.

He knew then that the old fox would come looking for the cub. It was the old fox Maolra was after. There was a hinged leaf in the door of the coop and a contraption to keep it shut once the old fox had gone in. The old fox came that same night and went in, and the door leaf closed so that it couldn't come out. Maolra caught it in the morning.

MAOLRA (MYLES) AND THE OTTER (2)

Maolra of the Bees used to wander by the lakes, and anywhere he got the track of an otter, he would dig a hole and have the otter drowned within three days. The hole would be narrow at the top and wide down below. The mouth of the hole would look no different to the rest of the path. He would lay the scraw over the hole and a trapstick underneath the scraw. He would have the loose clay thrown far from the hole. When the otter came along, the minute it stood on the scraw, the trapstick would go down and the otter with it. There would be water in the hole; it would be narrow at the top and wide below, and the otter wouldn't be able to get out of it.

NUALA SHEOIGHE (JOYCE) (2)

There is a very narrow channel between Sceird an Ghairdín and Carraig an Ghairdín (Sceird Garden and Rock Garden). I never heard of anybody leaping across that channel except a woman called Nuala Sheoighe (Joyce). She was picking dulse on the windswept rock called Sceirde, and she cleared the channel in one leap. There is hardly any slope there, and the leap isn't that wide, but when you'd look down it would frighten you, as the channel is so deep. Nuala had nerve. No man ever cleared that channel, but she did.

A MAN OF VIGOUR (2)

Pádraic Bairéad in Aird Thiar (Ard West) had set his fishing nets at Carraig-a-Míle. He went out without his breakfast in a gale one day to lift them. He rowed a boat westward against two men—he rowed a medium sized boat against two other men to Carraig–a–Míle. There were only three in the boat. He rowed with two oars while the other two men rowed with one oar each. They lifted the nets. When he came home, Seán an Chóta was on the pier.

"Tell me Seán," said the Bairéad man, "why didn't you go and lift your nets?"

"My fishing partner didn't turn up," said Seán. "I suppose he thought the gale was too much."

"Would you go west," said Pádraic Bairéad, "if I went with you?"

Seán looked at him, and he didn't speak for a while. He thought he was joking. After a while he said he would. The two went into the boat, and neither one spoke a word to the other, and none of them said "take it easy," or "back," or "keep her going," till they went to Carraig-a-Míle. When Seán caught hold of the net, he asked Pádraic Bairéad, "are you tired?"

"I'm not," he said. "I'd go the same distance again."

"I am as exhausted as I can be," said Seán.

They came home again when they had lifted the nets. It was about two o' clock in the day, and that's the time Pádraic Bairéad ate his meal. That's the man who had the vigor. It has been said that Seán an Chóta was a strong man, but the other man had more vigor.

SEÁN MAC DONNCHADHA (4, 11)

There was a naval guard, one of the Mahers, in Maínis (Mween-ish). He was godfather to Seán Mac Donnchadha in Maínis. This naval guard was very active. Seán became very active himself when he was growing up, and he was nicknamed Maher, after his godfather.

Seán was in Galway selling a horse. He sold the horse and was walking home. Going past Oughterard (Uachtar Ard) he said to himself that it was a bit stupid to be walking and so many horses in stables here. He went into the stable belonging to the officer of the peelers[5] (police) and brought out the officer's horse. He mounted it, and it brought him to Seanachaola (slope of the Keelys, east of Cashel). There was a man in Seanachaola, Maolra Seoighe, who had a public house, and Seán went in there. He stabled the horse and spent a while drinking. When he was leaving, he brought a horse belonging to Maolra Seoighe with him and left the officer's horse in the stable.

When the officer found out that his horse was gone, he sent the peelers everywhere looking for it. Somebody told them that someone went west through Maam crossroads in a shower of sparks. The peelers followed the shower of sparks as far as Maolra's house, and they said they'd have a drink themselves. They went in, and Maolra told them that Maher had been here and that he had barely left. A peeler went into the stable, and what would he see there but the officer's horse. Maolra Seoighe was arrested.

Maolra's wife had three brothers. They got their own horses and went after Maher. It was a Sunday, and Beairtle Chaona's sons were going home from Mass in Carna. They met Maher, and he had a horse. He told them he had taken the horse from Gabhla Hill (near Seanachaola) and that they might as well take the horse with them and let it out on the hill again.

"We'll do that," said one of the Ó Caona sons, and one of them mounted the horse. On their way up by Caladh an Chnoic (landing place of the hill), they met Seán Pheadair Seoighe's sons coming down. They grabbed the rider and asked him where he got the horse.

He asked them were they out of their senses.

"This is Maher's horse," he said.

"Hold on to the horse till we come back," they said.

They had to ride twice as fast to catch Maher before he'd be in Maínis (Mweenish). They didn't stop till they went into Máirtín Ó Loideáin's house in Carna. He was a good friend of theirs and a good friend of Maher's as well. "If you take my advice," he said, "you'll go home and leave Maher alone." They took his advice, and they went home.

They proved that Maolra Seoighe had nothing to do with the horse, that it was Maher did the bad deed, if indeed it was a bad deed. The peelers believed them, and Maolra was set free. A warrant was issued for John Maher. It was sent to the peelers in Roisín an Chalaidh (Rusheenacholla). They wrote back saying that no such man as John Maher was to be found in the Carna community. That was the end of that.

Maher Sheáin Shéamais was that man's name. His grandfather was Séamas Mac Donnchadha who lost the money in Guernsey.

MICHEÁL MAC EOIN'S WAY (2)

Micheál Mac Eoin and a man of the Mac Con Rí clan—Feichín Beag—rigged themselves out to go killing basking sharks. Feichín Beag was in the bows, sitting on the bow thwart looking out at the sea.

"I have seen something," he said, "that I've never seen this early in the year before—a basking shark going up between Cruach na Caoile and Cruach na Cara."

It was on their way down at Liath Brás that they saw it. Feichín Beag stood by the stempiece at the end of the bowsprit.

"There's a stripe running along under this one's back," said Micheál Mac Eoin, "that's where the spear is to go."

It was Feichín had the spear. As soon as they drew up close, Feichín Beag drove the spear into it as far as it could go. He speared it on the first attempt.

He stepped down onto the foresheets and began paying out cable to the basking shark, and as soon as the shark came to the end of the cable, it was dragging the boat so fast that the bow was sunk down to the bowsprit hole, even though all the ballast had been moved back onto the stern thwart. It took it only a half an hour from the time it was speared till it was clearing the back end of Sceirde Mór. It went out between two rocks to the west of Sceirde where only a fishing boat could go, and it brought the boat along with it. The boat didn't hit the rock. It came safely through the channel. Micheál Mac Eoin was at the helm. The basking shark hadn't gone the length of two fishing nets when its dead body arose to the surface of the sea. They hauled up the cable till they came to the basking shark, tied it at the front and at the rear, cut the liver and the oil out of it, and brought them into the boat. Then they let the fish drop to the bottom.

They hoisted their sails and, with an easterly wind and a southerly wind, they headed for Slyne Head and on to Westport to sell the oil there. They were moored there by twelve o'clock on the following day, and each of them had earned thirty pounds. It took them two days to come home on account of the wind turning against them. They were inside in Dumhaigh Ithir and had moored the boat within an hour of sundown on the third day. The channel between the two rocks has been called Bealach Mhichíl Mhic Eoin (Micheál Mac Eoin's Way) ever since, and the eastern rock is called Carraig Mhichíl Mhic Eoin.

Explanation: The ballast is moved to the back of the boat so that the bow of the boat is raised because the basking shark keeps on going deeper until it reaches the bottom. If it is speared in very deep water, it might go twelve miles before dying. If it is speared in shallow water, it will kill itself in one hour or less against the bottom. It will hit the bottom.

There were a hundred and twenty fathoms of rope attached to the spear that Feichín had stuck in the shark, and he didn't cut the rope because it seemed to him that the man steering would be able to turn the boat if the shark hit the rock. The shark went straight out the channel and brought the boat with it. They have a hatchet laid on the breasthook in the bow of the boat to cut the rope if there's any danger that the shark would drown the boat.

A WOMAN WALKER (3)

There was a woman in Aird Thiar. She was married to an Ó Caola man. Her husband needed the makings of a sail and oars, and he had no way of going to Galway in a boat. The wife said she'd go the roundabout way to Galway on foot. She went there on foot. She bought the makings of a sail of the coarse linen they had at the time. She bought enough *adhairí* to go on the edge of the sail—the *adhaire* is a heavy hempen rope. She bought the makings of two oars of larch, and larch is heavy. She spent the night in Galway, and early next morning she hit the road west. The sail and the *adhairí* were tied on her back, and the timber was on her shoulder. She was home in daylight the same day.

This woman was a daughter of the Ó Fatharta man who was burning kelp when Father Maolra gave him his coat while fleeing from the Yeoman out of Carna. Seán an Chóta was a son of hers, the biggest man we remember seeing.

A MAN WHO CUT A CABLE (1)

His name was Seán Shéamais, of the Mac Donnchadha clan. A Revenue vessel came into Aird Bay. There's a deep anchorage in from Bealach na Srathrach (straddle way), between Oileán Máisean and Maínis. This cutter came in with its crew intent on searching for poteen the following day. Seán Shéamais was living in Maínis, himself and three brothers: Giolla, Ciardhubhán, and Séamas Óg. When night fell, Seán Shéamais swam out to the cutter with a good knife. He cut the cable, and the people on board the vessel didn't hear him cutting it. When he had cut the cable, he came back in again safely. There was no holding the vessel when the cable was cut, and it drifted with the wind until it grounded on a rock in Maínis. When the tide came under it again, it floated off.

LOVABLE PEOPLE (2)

Fighting trouble broke out here long ago between the Ó Domhnaill clan—Micheál Mac Taidhg's sons—and Peadar Seoighe's (Peadar Chartair's) sons. They had herring nets out, and the nets got entangled in one another. The Seoighe sons were first to lift their nets, and they had to cut the Ó Domhnaill's nets in order to disentangle their own. When the Ó Domhnaill sons came, the Seoighe sons were about to head for home. The Ó Domhnaill sons knew it was the Seoighe sons had cut their nets. They left the nets there and went after the Seoighe lads to have revenge on them for what they had done.

"Pull faster," said one of the Seoighe lads. "These fellows are following us to kill us."

There wasn't a boat at that time that didn't have stones placed inside it for fear trouble might break out, and a man would have nothing to frighten his enemy with.

One of the Seoighe sons broke an oar, and the Ó Domhnaill sons caught up with them. One of them picked up a stone and hit the Seoighe lad on top of the head with it. He thought he had killed him outright. There was no more to it. They turned back and went to lift their nets. The Seoighe man brought him to court, and it came up in the sessions. The day the whole lot of them were on their way to the sessions, the Ó Domhnaill clan came upon a cow belonging to the Seoighe family drowning in a boghole. It would never have got out of there and would suffocate unless it was rescued.

"Does anyone know who owns the cow?" said the father to the sons.

"I know," said one of the sons, "that it belongs to Peadar Seoighe."

"Strip off and pull the cow out of the hole," said the father. "That cow didn't do anybody any harm. She doesn't mind who drinks her milk."

They pulled the cow out. When they had dried it, up on the hillock, what did they see coming towards them but Peadar Seoighe and his sons.

"Don't go any further," said Peadar Seoighe to the Ó Domhnaill clan when he saw they had saved the cow, "there will be no court case."

The six of them walked home, chatting and talking. They shook hands with one another, and there was no more about it. There isn't a day since, that the people don't quote the parable, saying it's a great wonder that more don't follow the example of the Ó Domhnaill and the Seoighe clans. Both lots were lovable people.

LÚCÁS Ó LAIDHE (O'LEE) (4)

Lúcás Ó Laidhe was very near being a doctor when he had to go on the run. He came to An Aird well over a hundred years ago. He settled down there and married Éilís Nic Dhonncha, the daughter of Maolra Mac Risteáird and Máire Laighléis (Lawless). Lúcás and Éilís had two sons and a daughter, Brian, Pádraic, and Máire. Brian had a sailing boat, "The Ó Conaill." Daniel O'Connell was in his prime when Brian was alive. Máire married and had a daughter who married Joseph Maude's father in Cill Bhriocáin in Ros Muc. When this woman was dying in Cill Bhriocáin, she sent for Josie Mongan's mother. She came. "I hope," said the Maude woman, "that you won't leave my bones here, but that I'll be buried in Maíros. If you don't consider it worth while doing that, lay my coffin on the tide and I'll go ashore there myself."

Ó CAODHÁIN AND GOOD LUCK (1)

I knew a Tomás Ó Mainnín who lived in Galway. He was from Coill an Bhogaigh.[6] He married an Ó Ceallaigh woman, Bríd Ní Cheallaigh from Aird an Chaisleáin (Ard Castle). He had a house in Flood Street. He had four milch cows. He was steward to the man who had the fair of Cnoc an Doláin and the lighthouse on Oileán na gCaorach (Mutton Island) in Galway Bay.[7] The Cnoc an Doláin fair was an old fair, and there was no other fair to speak of in Galway at the time. That's where the fair was when the people from Annaghdown were drowned.[8]

This Tomás had a brother, Liam Ó Mainnín. He was married to a second cousin of my mother, Mairéad Nic Dhonnchadha. I spent three months with him in Galway. The Ó Dochartaigh man who was killed in Carraigín (small rock) near Craughwell (in East Galway) was a first cousin of theirs. He was killed over a holding of land he had taken lease of. His horse was let out of the stable at night, and when he came out after the horse he was shot.

One of these Ó Dochartaigh men was rich. He had a daughter. She married an Ó Caodháin man who had a shop in Galway. This Ó Caodháin had a stone and a half of sovereigns. That was the weight of the gold he had. He went to the bank one day with three sovereigns to get sixty shillings for them. He handed them in to the clerk, and the clerk handed him out three paper bags. When he came home and opened the three bags, there were sixty sovereigns in the bags.

"What will I do with them?" he said to his wife.

"What would you do but bring them back," she said.

He walked up to the bank again, and he told the clerk he had made a mistake, that he gave him sixty sovereigns instead of sixty shillings.

"You're a peculiar man," said the clerk when he had laid the sixty sovereigns in a safe place, "and bad luck to you that didn't keep it when you had it."

From that day on he got poorer and poorer. There wasn't a place he set hand or foot but bad luck followed him, once he had turned his back on his good luck.

Anybody who has good luck and then turns his back on it has no use talking.

PÁDRAIC SHORT ARM Ó SÚILLEABHÁIN (1)

Pádraic Baclámhach Ó Súilleabháin (O'Sullivan) lived in Doire Iorrais or in Loch Conaortha. He was a great fighting man. A pedlar came in to him and got the night's lodging from him—he was a decent man. The pedlar spent the night there, and in the morning when they had finished their breakfast, Pádraic Baclámhach said he would have to go and cut a load of heather.

"I'll go with you," said the pedlar.

The pedlar had a walking stick.

"You can do that," said Pádraic Baclámhach, "but I'll have to bring my stick with me."

He brought his stick. The two set off together and on reaching the first level spot of ground, the pedlar stopped and said, "The reason I've come here is to try you out. I've heard you're a good fighting man."

"I've no objection to trying you out," said Pádraic Baclámhach.

The pedlar took off his overcoat and inside the coat he was wearing a gentleman's suit that you could draw through a ring. He was a gentleman, and had come to try out Pádraic Baclámhach.

They attacked one another, and Pádraic Baclámhach didn't allow as much as one blow of the stick to touch him the way he protected himself, but he left the other man with a red skin, red with his blood. He had him raw-topped and flayed. The pedlar got what he deserved.

"You may as well come home with me again," said Pádraic Baclámhach to him, "and stay until you're healed."

He went home with Pádraic Baclámhach and stayed with him until he was healed in a week or two, and Pádraic feeding him. Pádraic was more of a gentleman than the pedlar was.

There was some defect in Pádraic's arm.

SEÁN Ó DONNCHADHA

Na Foiriúin are to the north of Carraig-a-Meacain, and there's a big stony beach on top of each of them and white stones with nothing growing on them. They are submerged by the spring tides, but the swell still breaks over them. When there's a big ebb, there's nothing but a ford between them, and the oarweed and strapwrack and everything is left dry. There's black seaweed there, bladderwrack. *Creathnach* (tiny-shelled dulse) grows underneath that black seaweed, and mussels grow on the flagstones.

There was a man in Aird Mhóir (Ardmore) called Seán Ó Donnchadha. He was going fishing for gurnet one day, and he brought his wife with him in the boat and another man, Síomón Ó Mongáin. Bairbre Ní Churraoin (Bairbre Labhráis) was his wife's name. Seán put the two of them ashore on the Foiriúin to collect dulse, and he went further out on the bay himself, fishing for gurnet.

When the two on the island had collected the dulse, they saw the tide coming in. They brought the dulse with them to the top of the stony beach, and Síomón Ó Mongáin began building a cairn of stones for the two of them to stand on. The tide kept rising around them. They saw a boat coming from Ceann Gólaim (Golam Head) to the east, and the boatman saw them. Peaits

Ó Mongáin was the man in the boat, and he knew the two were trapped. He came towards them, and threw them a rope as he couldn't land the big boat on the beach. Bairbre came out on the rope first, and he then threw the rope to Síomón so that he came out. He brought them to Cill Chiaráin (Kilkerrin) and put them ashore there.

Seán Ó Donnchadha who was fishing for gurnet forgot all about them. He didn't come back until their story was told, and when he came there was no sight of the beach or anything. All was submerged, and he thought his wife and Síomón were drowned. But when he didn't come, God sent them another man.

(Micilín (1) heard this story from the Burke man's wife in Roisín na Mainiach, Bairbre Labhráis's aunt. When Micilín had finished the little story, Pádraic Ó Flaithearta said, "When I am as old as you, Micilín, people will be coming down from Dublin asking me, 'Did you know Micilín Pháidín? What sort of man was he?'")

CROTTY (2)

There was a man whose nickname was Crotty, Séamas Ó hUaithnín (Greene) from Aird Thiar (Ard West). He was married to Máire Mhuimhneach (*muimhneach*, from Munster, from Clare), a woman who came here during the famine. He saw a big eel on the mud one Sunday morning, on the Coillín (Cuilleen) mud. There was a big ebb, and the eel was left high and dry. The tide had left it there. He went out to bring in the eel. When he got near the eel, he sank to his two armpits in the mud. He wasn't able to reach the eel, and he wasn't able to come back.

Marcas Ó Laidhe was going to first Mass, and Crotty shouted high and low at him to come and bring him some device to get him out.

"You know, you know," said Marcas, "who asked you to go there? I wouldn't miss Mass for you," and he left Crotty in the mud.

There was an Ó hUaithnín man (Seán Phádraig Bháin) going out to Mass, and Crotty shouted at him with all his might. Seán wasn't as interested in the Mass as Marcas Ó Laidhe was. He got a rope and threw it to Crotty. He tied the rope under his two armpits, and Seán Phádraig Bháin pulled him out of the mud. But he didn't bother with the eel; he wasn't able to.

THE SOLDIER (2)

Seán Ó Briain had a brother, the Seán whose two legs were broken on the shipwreck in Leitir Mealláin (Lettermullen). The brother was finer and better looking than Seán. At the time of the famine, he enlisted in the British Army sooner than starve to death, himself and an Ó hUaithnín man from the same village, Meall Rua (red hillock) in Maínis. War was suddenly declared on England, and the two had to go to the front. The night the two were supposed to go to war, an army captain, himself and his daughter, were walking around looking at the soldiers, and the daughter took a liking to this Ó Briain man. She said she had never seen a man she liked better than him.

"I'll buy him out of the army if you fancy him," said the father.

"I do," she said.

"Beckon him over," said the father, "and let yourself and himself go for a walk together until you see how you like him."

She beckoned to him, and he came. The father went home. Herself and the Ó Briain man walked for two miles before they turned back. When they were within ten footsteps of her father's house and about to part, she told him she was foolish to walk that far with him.

That's when he embraced her, to get a kiss from her.

"You're too late now," she said.

The Ó Briain man was too mannerly for her, and he thought that a lady like her must have thought it was cowardly to be like that. He thought all along that she was only making fun, and only for that he would have been very willing.

The following day he went to war. The battle began. Very soon his thigh was broken, and he had fallen. The two sides attacked one another and began stabbing one another. Ó hUaithnín saw a man coming at Ó Briain and pinning him to the ground with his bayonet. It was Ó hUaithnín who gave the account of his death. He had escaped with his own life.

THE PEDLAR Ó FATHARTA (2)

The pedlar Ó Fatharta used to come around here long ago. He was a gentleman, and he had a world of charms. He had a charm for banishing mice, but he used to say that he'd have to banish them to where they would get plenty to eat. He had the charm written down like a summons, and how he served it was to present it to the queen of the mice. The king or queen would then order the mice to leave, and they would leave one by one. If they weren't banished to a good place, they would return and do seven times as much mischief as they had done before. (Seosamh Ó Briain from Ennistymon tells me that there was a charms man near that town, and that a lot of people used to come to him for a charm. He used to have the charm written on a piece of paper, and he'd give the paper to whoever had the illness or the trouble.)

CEOINÍN THE PILOT (1)

Pádraic Ó Ceoinín (Jennings) from Leitreach Ard (Letterard) had the boat loaded in Galway. There was a ship's captain there, and he wanted a pilot. He was talking to Tommy Réamoinn Mac Donnchadha on the street, inquiring as to where he would get a pilot. He was going to Blacksod Bay. Pádraic Ó Ceoinín happened to be walking up the street.

"This man approaching is the best pilot in County Galway, if he'll go with you," said Tommy Réamoinn when he saw Pádraic.

Tommy Réamoinn then spoke to Pádraic.

"How can I go with him," said Pádraic, "when I have a load in my boat to be brought to a man from Roundstone."

"Never mind that," said Tommy Réamoinn, "if he gives you good money for going with him. How much will you give him?" he said to the captain.

"Three pounds," said the captain.

Ceoinín accepted and went with him. He went aboard the vessel. When they were passing Black Head, the captain put Ceoinín steering the vessel. They were sailing westward, as far west as Oileán Iarthach (Rock Island, western island), the outermost island of Árainn, and Ceoinín saw sea spray rising sky-high.

"It looks like the night is going to be bad," he said. "I know where there's a good deep anchorage."

"If you do," said the captain, "go there."

Ceoinín steered for Caisín to spend the night there. When they were at anchor in Caisín bay, Pádraic Ó Ceoinín began to talk about the seething sea he saw at Oileán Iarthach.

"That wasn't a seething sea at all," said the captain, "but two grampuses fighting, and they won't stop till one of them kills the other."

They spent the night on Caisín, and in the morning they sailed again till they were going west of Cruach na Caoile (Deer Island). They could see the two grampuses again, and one of them was fairly weak. But Pádraic didn't see the end of the fight.

There's a hole in the grampus's forehead and a lid on the hole. When it opens the lid, it is able to send ten barrelfuls of water high in the air. I saw it myself.

Pádraic went to Blacksod Bay with the vessel, loaded his cargo there, and brought it back home again. The captain gave Ceoinín five pounds and told him there was no better pilot.

SEÁN OF THE BRUSHES (1)

There were two men in Limerick, and both of them wanted to be Lord Mayor. When the votes were counted, each of them had the same number. There was a judicious man there who said neither of them should be appointed, as neither of them had beaten the other.

"Will you accept my judgement now?" he said to the people of Limerick.

"We will," they all said.

"Forget about these two men from now on," he said, "but keep watching the bridge of Limerick, and the first man who comes across the bridge, stop him, bring him with you, and make him Lord Mayor."

They kept watching the bridge then, and it wasn't long until they saw him coming with a load of brushes, this man called Seán na Scuab (Seán of the Brushes). Out they went to meet him, a good crowd of them. They threw the brushes away and carried him off with them. They brought him into a shop, bought him a watch and everything that suited him until he was turned into a gentleman all of a sudden, and they made Lord Mayor of him.

He had a wife, Máire. When she heard that he was Lord Mayor, she came to see him.

"Upon my soul, Seán, I don't recognize you," she said.

"To tell you the truth, Máire, I'm not surprised that you don't," said he. "I don't recognize myself either."

There wasn't a man, before or after him, who did the job better than Seán na Scuab.

THE GALLOWS IN LIMERICK (4)

The boatmen used to be trading with Limerick, bringing cargoes in and bringing cargoes out. Oats and kelp used to be sent to Limerick from Conamara. A group of boatmen were delayed in harbor in Limerick. The day they were there, a man was to be hanged. The place people were hanged long ago was in the middle of the town, and the world of people used to gather to watch the hanging. The hangman on this particular day was a man with a big white bald head without as much as one hair on it. One of the boatmen said it would be a nice spot to throw a stone at. Another one of them stooped down, picked up a pebble, threw it at the hangman, and hit him on the bald head. Blood flowed down from the bald head, but the hangman wasn't killed. There was great commotion then with the sheriff and the cavalry, soldiers and policemen looking for the man who threw the pebble, but they failed to find him. The Conamara men had lots of laughter when the battle was over.

OH, MY BOAT! (1)

A fishing boat weighing no more than six tons, from Claddagh in Galway, was fishing in Galway Bay. A gale arose, and she was running before the wind. She was going for four or five days. When they didn't know where they were, the crew put stones in a basket and let it out at the bow of the boat with a rope tied to the two strap handles to keep weight on the bow as the big swells were bearing down on her, and they wanted to keep the bow of the boat to the wind.

A large vessel on its way to America saw the fishing boat, and she lowered a long boat and took the crew on board. They left the sailing boat there in the sea with her bow to the wind. When they were on board and the vessel on its way again, the fishing boat sank to the bottom.

The man who owned her, when he saw her sinking, said "Oh, my boat!" and he died instantly.

He was thrown overboard then, and he went down with the boat.

The crew went to America on the ship. Some of them stayed there, and one man came home. Mac Gabhann was his name, and I heard him telling the story.

THE GOOD LOOKS OF THE ARD PEOPLE (4)

The merchant who had walked all Ireland used to say that the best looking young men and women in the country were in Ard. Fr. Éamonn Ó Máille and the priest of An Cheathrú Rua (Carraroe) were going to Clifden on two horses. Going west by Half Way House, Fr. Éamonn drove his horse down to a water hole to give it a drink.

"Don't let your horse drink that," said the other priest. "It's dirty."

"Ha!" said Fr. Éamonn, in sharp dispute, "there's a townland in my parish, and I think the best looking and the healthiest men and women in Ireland are there, and they never had a drink of water as good as there is in this water hole." (Bog water is what they drank.)

MARRIAGE FAR FROM HOME (4)

The basking shark fishery brought men from Conamara far from home, and they got to know the coastal towns from Limerick to Killybegs. Some of them became well to do from the trade, and many of them got rich on it. They were living off the sea, and they had no interest in working the land themselves. Spalpeens (migratory farm laborers) from east Galway used to do the land work in those times. Spalpeens were coming to the west, instead of going to the east as they do nowadays. They often married far from home and settled down far from home too. I've heard of men who married women from Galway and of men who married women from the north—Inishbofin, Cleggan, Bun Dorcha.

Some of the men married in County Clare and stayed there. People were moving here and there at that time. They weren't a bit afraid of migrating.

THE CALL ROCK (4)

The rock is on the edge of Bealach na Srathrach, between Oileán Máisean and Maínis. People used to stand on this rock when calling the island people to put out a boat for them. There's a rock called An tSrathair (the straddle), Mullán na Srathrach (straddle hillock), in the middle of the channel. Carraig an tSnáimh (swimming rock) is in on the tip of the island.

Micil Áine Ní Loideáin was an Ó Clochartaigh. He lived on Oileán Máisean. When he was going to the island, he wouldn't wait for a boat to be pushed out unless there was one handy, but he would swim from Carraig na Blao to Carraig an tSnáimh on the island. He was drowned later however. He used to ship seaweed, and he hit a rock one night in Kinvara Bay or The Weir. Many men were drowned while shipping seaweed. Seaweed will never again be shipped.

—⁓—

Carraig na mBan (women's rock) is at Meall Rua in Maínis to the west. There's a channel between it and the land.

A PRIEST OF THE MAC CON RÍ CLAN (4)

The Mac Con Rí clan are a long time in Conamara. There was a group of them in Ard. They were weavers, linen weavers and wool weavers both. They used to make tablecloths, towels, sheets, and all sorts. One of this tribe settled down in Galway city. He was a well-to-do merchant and had weavers working for him. He had a son a priest. They say he was the first man from the Carna community to become a priest. The priest was drowned on his way to France. May God have mercy on his soul.

THE RAM'S STONE IN INISHBOFIN (4)

Tomás Mac Con Rí, who was reared in Inis Ní (Inishnee), was the best storyteller and *seanchaí* (custodian of traditional lore) I ever heard. He had only one fault—he always put a Mac Con Rí man ahead of all other men in his stories. I heard him telling a tale of valor once about an Ó Clochartaigh man, but Ó Clochartaigh's mother was of the Mac Con Rí clan.

Once when Conamara men used to fish for basking sharks, they were delayed in harbor in Inishbofin. They used to go visiting or play tricks or perform feats of strength whenever they were delayed in harbor. There was a big stone in Inisbofin that people used to lift in days gone by, the Ram's Stone. This Ó Clochartaigh man was in Inishbofin with the others who were delayed in harbor. Nobody had lifted the stone for many years, but Ó Clochartaigh lifted it this day.

When they gathered that night in the house where they were visiting, it was told that Ó Clochartaigh had lifted the big stone. There was an old woman in the chimney-corner who was so old that she had lost her eyesight. When she heard that the Ram's Stone had been lifted by a Conamara man, she said she wouldn't believe it because that stone hadn't been lifted since a brother of her own lifted it about four score years before that.

Everybody said the stone had been lifted and that the man who lifted it was in the house.

"If he is," she said, "let him come here till I shake his hand."

A man who was there came and shook hands with her.

"This man didn't lift the Ram's Stone," she said.

Another man came and gave her his hand, and she told him the same thing. One by one they all came, and she said the same thing to each until the last man came, and when he gave her his hand, she kissed his hand.

"This is the hand of the man who lifted it, if it was lifted today," she said.

The Ó Clochartaigh man was the last man. He was from Iorras Mór.

MICHEÁL Ó CADHAIN'S STICK (1)

Carraig Chearc (hen rock) is this side of Slyne Head. Micil Eoin Ó Cadhain from Galway built his own boat. He was going to Clifden with a cargo of flour, and he went off course in a fog. The boat was wrecked on Carraig Chearc. He swam ashore onto the rock, himself and the boatman. He went back to the boat for something, but he didn't return. He was drowned. The boatman tried to stop him from going back, but he wouldn't stay.

This Micheál Ó Cadhain was lame, and he had brought his walking stick with him out of the boat. While the two of them were on Carraig Chearc, the boatman was whining that they didn't have the price of their dinner.

"Bad cess to you!" said Micheál Ó Cadhain to him. "Your belly is what you're thinking of. Here's my walking stick," he said, "and whatever house you'll go into, it will be recognized and you'll get plenty to eat there."

BULK ROCK IN ROISÍN AN BHOLGÁIN (1)

"Téagar" (Bulk) was a brother or an uncle of Bairbre Ghiolla. He lived in Roisín an Bholgáin. Téagar Rock was named after him. It's in the mouth of the lagoon in Roisín an Bholgáin. Téagar was of the Conaola clan. Téagar had a brother whose nickname was "Duine Uasal" (Gentleman), and "Duine Uasal" had a son called Beairtle Uasail. Beairtle Uasail's daughter was married to Tóna (Antaine) Mac Donnchadha. Tóna was always rubbing shoulders with the guesthouse people. Tóna was a boastful man. He had a brother, Seán Mór Mac Donnchadha, who was never beaten as a dancer. He was declared champion wherever he went. He was a boatman until he went to America, and there wasn't a better boatman to be found.

"I'll love you tomorrow!" as the Aran woman said to Seán Mór when she saw him dancing—that's an old saying ever since Seán Mór's time.

JACK THE MUNSTERMAN (1)

He was a man who came into this locality long ago. He was a Munsterman (Clareman). Jack the Munsterman they used to call him. He was on the run with the peelers (police) after him. Three of them captured him. The three were taking him to the barrack to make a prisoner of him. They were going along by a low stone wall. He told them to release him as he had an urgent need, and they did. He gave a blow with each hand to two of them and knocked them down. The third man didn't interfere. When he didn't, Jack jumped over the wall and ran, and he came to this part of the country. I didn't hear that he was ever caught after that. My father saw him. He said that there wasn't a house in Roisín na Mainiach long ago that Jack the Munsterman wasn't able to come at it with a run and jump over the top of it. They used to say that he had wings on his heart; he was such a fine man. He was a good-looking man.

Ó CLOCHARTAIGH OF CRUACH CHAOLAINN (2)

Micheál Phádraic Dhonncha Ó Clochartaigh lived in Cruach Chaolainn. The house was above the shoreline on the eastern side of the island. He was a bailiff for Berridge looking after the deer, a hundred or so of them.[9] This man didn't have any boat, but when he needed one, he would light a signal fire on the corner of the island. There was a man on the mainland to the north in Leitreach Ard (Letterard) who would go over to him with a boat. It was this same man who brought him turf. There's nobody on Cruach Chaolainn now. Ó Clochartaigh's family went to America. When they left, they had no English.

THE CURRAOIN PEOPLE'S FLAGSTONES (1)

There are three of them. They are in Trá na Muice (pig strand) in Fínis (Feenish), outside Aill an Chipín (stick rock). Three men from Cill Chiaráin came cutting seaweed under the rock. These flagstones are in shallows, and there's a wave over them with the slightest tide. The three men had loaded the boat, and when they left the shore of the island, they went over the flagstones. The wave broke, and the boat was sunk on the flagstones. The three men in the boat were drowned. Two of them were Curraoin (Curran) people, and the stones are called the Curraoin People's Flagstones ever since.

THE ROCKS OF ROISÍN AN BHOLGÁIN (1)

Carraig Théagair, Carraig an tSrutha (stream rock), Carraig Pheadair that's in the middle of the Stream, Carraig na hEirimiste, Carraig Choilm, Carraig an Spiocáin (there's a white spike in its top), Carraig na gClochartach, Leacracha Chlann Philipe— these are the rocks of Roisín an Bholgáin.

There was a man in Fínis, Pilib (Philip) was his name. He had a son and a daughter. The son and the daughter came out in a boat one day to Roisín an Bholgáin to cut black seaweed. They had the boat pulled up on a flagstone and were cutting seaweed on the same flagstone when the boat drifted off. The wind was from the north. The son swam after the boat, and he was drowned. The daughter was drowned on the flagstone when nobody came to her rescue before the tide came in. The place is called Leacracha Chlann Philipe (Flagstones of Pilib's Children).

I saw two young lads from Fínis (Feenish) on the same flagstones, and their boat drifted off. I heard their shouts myself. The father of one of them was nearby, and I told him somebody was shouting. The two of us went down. There was an old wreck of a rowing boat in Crompán Pier (small inlet), and we fixed two oars on it and barely made it in time. When the swell came in, they were being lifted off the flagstone. They were sitting down and holding on to the seaweed. We took them off the flagstone. One of the youngsters was a Mac Con Iomaire, and the other was an Ó Maoilchiaráin. They were thankful to me.

THE HAG OF CLIFDEN (4)

The Aran people were inclined to go to law about land because land was scarce on Aran, and it was good land. A man in Aran was in trouble about a neighbor's field. He wanted to bring the neighbor to court. He went to Galway to see an attorney, and told him his concern. The attorney told him he wasn't able to give him any advice until he had consulted a counsel, and the counsel's advice was not to go ahead with the law, that he had no case.[10]

The Aran man wasn't satisfied or happy with the advice, and he didn't stop until he went to Clifden to the Hag of the Herb. He told her his business, and she told him to go ahead with the case and that he would win. He did, and he won.

Everybody will tell you that the Hag of Clifden had the gift of prophesy, whomsoever she was getting it from. The Aran people had great belief in her and so did the Conamara people, and people were coming to her from near and far.

Long ago if a man was going to build a new house, he would go to the Hag of Clifden looking for advice. He would tell her where he intended to build the house. If she told him not to build the house there, he would leave the place well alone and wouldn't build a house there. She would tell him everything about the place, things he could see for himself, and she was never in the place.

SLYNE HEAD (4)

There wasn't a year before the lighthouses were built that vessels weren't sinking at Slyne Head. Wooden sailboats were in use at that time, and many of them were being lost.

There was a man from Conamara in England, and he came into a house where there was an old woman with a child in a cradle. She was crooning a song to the child, and in the crooning she said, "It's a poor job I'm at, rearing you for Slyne Head."

"How do you know about Slyne Head?" said the Conamara man.

"That's where," she said, "this boy's father was drowned, and his grandfather, and I'm afraid it's where he'll be drowned himself."

There was so much stuff drifting in from the shipwrecked vessels that people used to walk the shore hoping to salvage wreckage. Anything cast ashore was salvage. There was timber and oil and flour, rum, and everything the vessels used to carry.

THE LAGOON (1)

Long ago a weaver was the only person living in Roisín na Mainiach. There's many a house there now. There were five times as many people living there in my memory. The lagoon to the east of the convent was all peat turf. A boatman used to come from Galway to buy turf there. He'd come in on the tide when the water was deep. When he would have moored his boat, the tide would have ebbed, and when he'd see the lagoon all around him full of rocks and big cliffs, he'd begin to cry, thinking he'd never leave the place, that the tide wouldn't come in there again.

ROISÍN NA MAINIACH (1)

There was deep turf in Roisín na Mainiach (Rusheennamanagh). No other townland in the country had more turf than it. There won't be turf there for much longer; it has been cut. You would think I'm not that old, but I saw bogland there and it would quiver underneath you when you'd walk out on it, and the lapwings flying off their nests. The turf has now been cut and a road built out into it. The people had an income and plenty of money as long as they had turf.

They used to send black seaweed to Kinvara. Long ago they wouldn't put it on the potatoes, thinking it would rot them; they cut strapwrack and put it on them instead. The black seaweed was sent in big boats to Kinvara and the Weir, outside Ardtamhnach (high arable patch). Ardfhraoch is inland to the north of the Weir.

EOCHAILL, CREIG MHÓR, CNOCÁN AN AIRGID (2)

"If you go to Aran, go to Eochaill," said the father to the son; "if you go to Maínis, go to Creig Mhór; if you go to Iorras Mór, go to Cnocán an Airgid (Silver Hill)."

NOTES

1. Peadar Ó Cualáin (c1835–1930) was the originator of the collection of traditional lore, *Peadar Chois Fhairrge*, compiled by Mac Giollarnáth and published in 1937.
2. *Inis Bigir*: perhaps from *bigil/vigil*, connecting with the holy well or the old chapel on the island.
3. *Inis Léith*: grey island, an islet off Leitir Móir.
4. Ó Máille of the moorland hills.
5. Synonymous with members of the Irish Constabulary, described as the Royal Irish Constabulary from 1836. The Irish Constabulary Act of 1822 established the first provincial police forces in Ireland and is

associated with Sir Robert Peel (1788–1850), who was appointed Chief Sec-
retary for Ireland in 1812.

6. Near Gorteen, Ballymacward, East Galway.

7. Fair Hill in Galway city.

8. On September 4, 1828, eleven men and eight women were drowned
in Lough Corrib while on their way from Annaghdown to Fair Hill in Galway. It is thought that the boat was holed by a sheep's hoof.

9. Richard Berridge acquired ownership of Ballynahinch estate in 1872
from the Law Life Assurance Society and acquired other holdings in Co.
Galway. Berridge built sporting lodges at Lough Inagh, Screebe, and Fer-
moyle. Cf. http://landedestates.nuigalway.ie/.

10. The distinction between solicitor (attorney) and barrister (counsel)
still remains in the Irish legal system.

ELEVEN

BOATMEN AND TIMBER

BOATWRIGHTS (4)

It was in this region that boats were being built. There were lots of good boatwrights in Conamara. There's no boatwright there now except for a man in Maínis (Mweenish) and a man in Inis Ní (Inishnee). There was no currach long ago. The boats were from four or five tons, up to sixteen tons. Every bay was full of boats at that time. People were going to the woods buying oak, to Roxborough and to Ráisin, to County Clare, to Cill Charnáin, and to Ballyglunin fen in East Galway.[1] There were all sorts of timber coming ashore—red pine, yellow pine, and teak, and an enormous amount of timber beams. The boatwrights had plenty of timber. They used to buy the tackles, the sheaves, and the nails in Galway.

There was a smith in Roisín an Chalaidh once who was able to keep four craftsmen at work making nails. He was a whitesmith, and he was able to make a lock and key. Some of the Guairim clan were smiths, and they used to work for the boatwrights.

No matter how skillful a man is, he's not able to build a boat without learning the trade.

The first man of the Mac Con Uladh clan who came to Conamara was making nails for the boatwrights. It was he who brought the first mule to Conamara. The mule had a great age. There's an old saying: "as old as Mac Con Uladh's mule."

—⁓—

The *gleoiteog* is a boat of between five and seven tons. At first it used to have two sails. It was a long time before a jib was added. That's why the middle sail is called the foresail. Maybe there was an odd jib there a hundred years ago. There was no *púcán* (an open boat with mainsail and jib) at that time. The *bád mór* (big boat or hooker) weighed up to sixteen tons. It used to be called a hooker. The sloops were bigger than the hookers. They used to go to the coast of France and to Guernsey.

BOATMEN (4)

No boatman was worthy of respect in the old days unless he had fished for one or two seasons at the basking shark bank or had made a trip to Guernsey. The shark bank is to the west of Inishbofin. There were usually five or six men in the basking shark fishing boat, a boat of six or seven tons. The basking shark couldn't be caught until *lacht*—sleep—came over it, and it would rise to the surface. The good sailing boat would be first to the basking sharks, and the other boats would follow. Each boat crew had a spearman. The spearman had the skill, and he would get a share and a half of the proceeds for his skill. He would have to own the spear. It was his own.

A basking shark would pay the expenses and leave forty or sixty pounds extra to be shared. They used to sell the oil in Westport. A good basking shark was worth sixty pounds. The oil was extracted from the liver, and there was an apparatus in Westport for melting the liver. Basking shark's oil is what used to be burnt in the lighthouses in the early days.

The boatmen in the old days were strong, well-built, chosen men, and the boatmen before them were stronger still. They were able to go to Sligo and to Limerick from Iorras Aithneach, and very few of their boats had a compass. They used to watch out for the boat with a compass. The boatmen were good pilots, and one of them was often taken off his boat to bring a vessel into Sligo or Galway.

There was a vessel going to Sligo once, and when they were going past the basking shark bank, they asked a man from an Iorras Aithneach boat to come with them to Sligo, that they needed a pilot. The boat moved in close to the vessel, and they were told the boatman was willing to do the piloting for them. There was a man on board the vessel who spoke Irish. None of the boatmen could speak English.

"Ask him," said the ship's captain, "if he's able to box the compass."

He was asked.

"I am," said the boatman.

"Let him read the compass," said the captain, "until I see."

The boatman began reading it (in Irish) at point north. "My father," he said, "my father's father, my father's grandfather, my father's grandfather's father."

Then he turned to his mother, "My mother, my mother's mother, my mother's grandmother."

What he said sounded like the points of the compass, and he was allowed on board and he brought the vessel to Sligo.

There was good payment to be got for piloting.

THE BOATMEN'S WIVES (2, 5)

Caitlín Ní Chualáin was a boatwoman. She was married to Pádraic Ó Conaola on Oileán Máisean (Mason Island). Pádraic was nicknamed "An Bádóir" (the boatman), and his son is called Colm an Bhádóra (Colm of the boatman). Caitlín used to be in the boat with Pádraic. She ran a load of seaweed to the Weir with him. She was as good as any man in a boat.

Méirín Shéamais Mhicil was married to a Mac Con Rí man on Oileán Máisean. She was of the Mac Con Rí clan herself as well. Her husband was west in Iorras Mór once, and she felt lonely. She put to sea in the sailing boat from Oileán Máisean and sailed westward on her own, without another soul, until she landed in Iorras Mór. She spent a while of the day talking to her husband and sailed back home again in the evening without another soul in the boat with her.

Seán Ó Lorcáin in Daighinis had a sister who used to work in the boat with him, running seaweed and running turf.

THE PILOT OF CAISÍN BAY (2, 5)

Seán Ó Lorcáin in Daighinis, Leitir Mealláin, was a pilot who went aboard the vessels. He would see the vessel coming into the bay from the west, with the flag raised to request a pilot. He would go out and be paid for bringing the vessel to Galway or Cill Chiaráin or any other bay where they would be taking cargo. Seán was able to swim like a cormorant. He was on a vessel in Cill Chiaráin one day when a fight broke out between the captain and one of the sailors. Seán went to save this man from the captain, and the captain grabbed the hatchet and went after Seán. All Seán had to do was to jump into the sea. He swam in to Cill Chiaráin pier, and the night was dark. He often went to Scotland on a kelp vessel when they were a man short. He used to be talking to himself while going the road when nobody else was talking to him, but if he had company, you would hear him two miles away; his voice was that loud. He was a sporting and a drinking man, and there was no better dancer than him.

MICHEÁL BAIRÉAD (5)

Micheál Bairéad from Foirnis (outer island) in Leitir Mealláin was a boatman. He was an uncle of Máire Ní Dhomhnaill, Caladh

an Chnoic (hill landing place). His brother's son lives in Roundstone and has a sailing boat. Micheál himself never married. He
used to buy kelp and run it to coastal towns. He used to buy
poteen and sell it in Limerick and County Clare. He went out
one night with a load of poteen, himself and another man, to
Brannock Island to the west of Aran.[2] There's a deep channel
between this island and Oileán Iarthach (Rock Island, western
island) where the lighthouse is. They said they would spend the
night there until daybreak. The boat was moored at a place they
call Ceann an Bhalla (head of the wall) with the poteen on board.
Micheál went down to see the boat some time before day. When
the other man came, he found Micheál Bairéad drowned between
the boat and the rock. He was the finest of gentlemen.

TWO WOMEN ON AN ISLAND (11)

There were two women on Oileán Iarthach, Máire Phatsaigh
Thomáis (Diarmaid Ó Cadhain's wife) and Micil Bheite's daughter. The pair of them were able to bring the sailing boat from
Oileán Iarthach (off Ros Muc) to Cill Chiaráin with nobody
else with them. They said that Micil Bheite's daughter was a better woman in a boat than the other woman. She was reared in
the mountains at Leitir Seana (assembly hillside), and the other
woman was reared in Leitir Deiscirt (south hillside). They used
to come across the bay in their boat to Mass in Cill Chiaráin and
go to Cuigéal and to Aird Mhór (Ardmore).

THE BOATMAN IN THE PROTECTION OF GOD (2)

The boatman will put himself in the protection of God and Colmcille when setting out in the morning. An old boatman said to
another man that anybody who does that will never be drowned.
   "It's easy to keep us from drowning so," said the other man.
   "When the day comes, fate will not be thwarted," said the old
boatman in answer.

—⁓—

It has been said that the spumy sea was the holy water Saint Peter had. The fisherman dips the tail of the net in the sea three times before he sets it, and he throws the water into the boat three times, in the name of the Father, of the Son, and of the Holy Ghost.

—⁓—

Colmcille and Mac Dara are the saints of the sea in Iorras Aithneach, especially Colmcille. The man from Iorras Mór will call on Cáillín.

—⁓—

"Thanks be to God and to holy Colmcille for my season!" is what the fisherman would say when he'd see a great catch of fish in the net.

Holy Colmcille and miraculous Mac Dara, they say.

—⁓—

Pádraic Mac Donnchadha (Liam) was fishing with another man one day. The other man brought in a big fish. This is what he said as soon as he brought in the fish:

> I proclaim cold and famine out of Erin,
> My God's deliverance and may He save me,
> And may I live to see this time next year.

The women had the same saying when digging the first of the early potatoes.

THE Ó CONAILL (4)

Lúcás Ó Laidhe had a son whose name was Brian, and Brian had a boat called the "Ó Conaill" (the O'Connell). At that time, it was the most famous boat in Galway Bay for sailing. She never left Galway without saving a half tide in Aird if she had enough wind. She was tacking in the bay one day, and hundreds of other boats along with her because unlike nowadays there were big sailing boats in every bay at that time, from Galway to Slyne Head. There was a full westerly wind, the rarest wind in Galway Bay. All the boats made for land to the south, and when they were going westwards under Oileán Lua, they saw a pleasure boat heave to and her crew eying them keenly. Out of the lot they had chosen the best boat, and they came alongside to speak to them. They asked them if they would please tell them if a boat called the "Ó Conaill" was in the bay today. The master of the Ó Conaill was an elderly man by the name of Réamonn Ó Flaithearta, and his shipmate was a strong, able, and agile young man by the name of Parthalán Mac Con Rí. Réamonn thought for a moment when the pleasure boat crew spoke to him, but he soon perked up, stretched out his arm, and patted the boat's quarter, the Ó Conaill's quarter, with the palm of his hand. "Here she is," said he, "and let her not be concealed from poor man or rich."

"I thought so," said the pleasure boat man, "and would you be willing to have a little sailing tack with us?"

"I'll find no fault with that," said Réamonn, "but we'll have to get ourselves ready."

"Thank you," said the pleasure boat man, "and we'll have to do the same."

The two boats heaved to, while they peaked, throated and tackled, and they filled out the sails to the west of Black Head. Réamonn was so eager for sailing—he was on the helm—that he wouldn't break his concentration to look behind him at the other boat.

"How is she doing now?" he asked the shipmate.

"She's coming up by our quarter now," said the other man.

After another while he asked, "How is she now?"

"We have her in our wake stream now," said Parthalán.

After another while he asked, "Where is she now?"

"She is now coming up on our windward quarter," said the shipmate.

They were coming eastwards under the face of Black Head at this stage. To the west of the headland, the sea was very high and the wind was hard. When they had sailed for another while, Réamonn asked Parthalán again, "How are they now?"

"They have dipped the jib fairly deep three times in succession," said Parthalán.

"They'll soon have their fill now," said Réamonn.

The Ó Conaill was going away from them from then on, and the pleasure boat soon got tired of it and continued on ahead till they reached Galway. The gentleman who owned her said he had sailed around the coast of Ireland and that he wasn't beaten at clean sailing until that day. The Galway fishermen were listening to him, and every man of them said it must have been the Ó Conaill he had met up with.

The Ó Conaill was in Galway Bay another day and many other boats along with her. There was a very strong wind, and Réamonn told Parthalán that he should lower the sail and tie a reef. "Liam Ó Laidhe's boat forever!" said Parthalán, "Tomás Ó hAllmhuráin's ropes, Dónall Ó Muir's sailcloth, made by Maolán Caoch (blind Moylan) and well able to carry it!"

BUTTER FOR THE SAIL

There wasn't much butter being sold in this locality long ago. The boatmen needed a lot of butter for the sails and for rubbing on the boats to make them slippery in the sea and to keep them clean. A great amount of butter was also consumed as sauce for the potatoes.

THE WOODS OF CONAMARA (12)

A young man was on his way to buy tobacco for his father back in Letterfrack one day. He met an old man on the road, and the man asked him where he was going.

"I'm going to buy tobacco for my father," said the young man.

"Will you give me a bit of the tobacco when you have bought it?" said the man.

"I will."

"Hurry up and buy it," said the man, "and I'll meet you when you have bought it."

The youth went on his way and bought the tobacco and met the old man again. The young man handed him the tobacco, and the old man cut about the full of his pipe.

"I'm thankful to you," said the old man, "and tell your father when you go home that you gave a bit of the tobacco to a man who told you that he hasn't been in this part of the country since the time he could walk on branches of woods from here to Galway."

—⁊⁊—

It has been said that there was no end to the amount of pine trees in these parts until the world was set on fire. There wasn't either. It is thought the world was first drowned, was then set on fire, and that the third destruction will be the end of it in one go when it will be broken up.

Many of the pine trees and black oak trees have been burned down. The burning is to be seen in the bog stumps. Many of the woods burned down to the stumps. The trees growing on solid ground remained standing until they burned all the way down. The stumps are still there. The trees that are left in the bogs have fallen there, and every bog tree is lying in a southwesterly direction.

BOG WOOD (2)

There was plenty of bog deal in Maíros and plenty of oak and also in Inis Ní (Inishnee). (There were four sorts of wood in the bogs of Inis Ní). South of Cashel, to the west of Barr na gCrompán (head of the creeks), there is a world of burnt stumps.

The trees are still being unearthed. It is difficult work because the place is so soft.

In the old days when there was no oil to be had, there were bog deal candles made of strips of bog deal. Before any roads were built, people used to have a bog deal candle when going out at night to a neighbor's house or to the landing place for boats. A strip of bog deal would bring you two miles of the road on a calm night. On a wild night they used to carry a red ember to light it again if it went out.

Bog deal candles were used in the house, by the housewives when they were spinning or making fishing nets (knitting them) and the poor scholars when they were teaching the children. A bog deal fire would cast light all over the house. When they were about to eat their meal, they would throw a stick of bog deal on the fire to give them light. The strip of bog deal was easily lit. There was oil in it, after digging it out of the bog.

Boats were often built from black oak out of the ground and from the bog deal stumps lying in the bogs. The oak and the bog deal stumps were recommended for the knees in a boat. They would never wear out. They had the natural bend, and they were hard.

The great bog deal was used in the roofs of the old (thatched) houses, as it was going to last till the end of the world. And nothing else was considered for thole pins (in rowing boats) but the black oak and the ironwood.

Pails (*pigíní*) were often made from black oak in the old days. The pail was a small gallon or two-gallon vessel with a handle—one of the boards being taller than the rest. The big cooper in Maínis, Micheál Ó Gaora, used to make them, and an Ó hAllmhuráin man from Iorras Mór, and Seán Mac Con Rí from Iorras Mór. Séamas Ó hUaithnín from Más made some of them.

Vessels for butter were made of black oak. This vessel consisted of just one piece. The hollow was carved out of the oak beam.

The churns around here were made of white pine that came in off the sea, and the tankards were made of the same wood. The disc of the churn dash was made of black oak, and the cup to be put down on the handle of the churn dash. The women used to have little wooden basins made of black oak to skim the cream off the milk. They were made in one piece, a thin piece. They used the same wooden basins to lift the butter from the milk when the churning was done, and to harden the butter in. There are some of them still around.

People used needles of oak for knitting fishing nets. Nothing else was recommended.

In this part of the country, a turner from Iorras Mór used to make flax spinning wheels out of black oak, for spinning flax for fishing nets. Even with the wool spinning wheel, the spindle and wheel were made of black oak. Seáinín Mac Con Rí was the turner's name. He was able to make music pipes. He made them—I heard my mother say he did.

It was on wrecked ships the ironwood was to be found. No beam of it ever came ashore. It doesn't float, it is too heavy. The black oak doesn't float either.

FLAX FOR THE SAILS (4)

Nearly everybody used to sow flax, and the women spent most of their time working with it. The fishing nets were being made from flax, as were the various sorts of ropes used by the fishermen and the sails. And as well as the ropes and sails, people made clothes for themselves from the flax. Weavers were very plentiful. Hardly anything was bought by the people, but everything was made by them.

The first man who bought baffity sails was an Ó Nia (Nee) man from Leitheanach.

The boats and the nets depended on the flax, and the women were always working at it.

The women's work has died out. They used to be carding and spinning yarn, sewing, knitting, working with flax, and weaving ropes and nets.

Wool was scarce among the poor. Poor women went out selling dulse to those who lived in the hills. They used to sell the dulse for wool and have a bag of wool coming home.

NOTES

1. *Creig an Róistín* is Roxborough, near Loughrea, Co. Galway; *Cill Charnáin* is possibly Kilcornan, Clarinbridge, Co. Galway; *Ráisin* (possibly Roisín) is unidentified and unlikely to be Ráistín or Clonmellon, Co. Westmeath, and in probability refers to a plentiful source of timber for boatwrights.

2. *Oileán an Dá Bhruithneog*: a *bruithneog* is a potato roasted in ashes. With white foam encircling it, the island appears like two potatoes roasting in ashes. The Placenames Branch renders this placename as *Oileán Dá Bhranóg*.

TWELVE

—ɯ—

FOOD

In the Autumn when the potatoes were plentiful, a meal of potatoes was dug for the breakfast, and if they had fish, they would put down a pot of it for the family. They would eat the potatoes and the fish and drink milk too if they had milk. There was no bread. For dinner (midday meal), the same. They had nothing else. If it was summer and people had run out of potatoes, they would have Indian meal, Indian meal porridge and milk. There were lots of people who didn't have milk. For supper, potatoes or Indian meal.

They used to boil sloke (*sleabhcán*), tiny-shelled dulse (*creathnach*), another light seaweed called *cáithleach*, and periwinkles and limpets. They would drink some of the gravy with the potatoes. No two of these sauces had the same taste. They used to eat the periwinkles and limpets boiled.

They used to boil charlock (field mustard) and nettles, with a grain of Indian meal mixed through it. That's what they ate in the famine time. Dandelions were eaten but charlock was the easiest to eat if you had a pinch of Indian meal to mix with it. Wild carrots that grew on good land like the ordinary carrot were good to eat, root and leaf. People could eat the root raw because it was sweet. People used to go around with small spades digging them.

There was no talk of flour until they threshed their oats before Christmas. They used to have oaten bread and rye bread for themselves. Every housewife had a crock of butter put by for Christmas. On the night of Christmas Day, the night of New Year's Day, and the night of the Twelfth Day, poor people used to have a meal at night of bread, butter, and milk. Those who didn't have meat in the middle of the day would have a fine bit of fish. A man who sold ten or fifteen hundredweight of oats would buy a hundredweight of flour for Christmas. There was no talk of flour bread again until the following Christmas.

Every household had eggs. The eggs were sold to old traveling women for thread and needles. The old women going west to Clifden used to have big creels of eggs. When they sold the eggs in Clifden, they bought another load there.

Many a person would kill a pig or an ox at Christmas, or a sheep. They often had a goose. They always had fish, an abundance of fish.

The land has gotten much worse and oats don't grow as they used to. In the old days, a man would have twice as many oats sown as he has nowadays, and it also gave twice the crop long ago. People had oatmeal and oaten bread. There's no oatmeal around here at the moment, or a mill. I have seen rye bread in this part of the country myself. Rye is being fed to hens and cattle at present. The people of the islands believe that rye straw has a cure for pine (a cattle disease). They wouldn't buy a sheaf of oats straw if rye straw was to be had.

—◊◊◊—

Every man wanted to grind some corn for Christmas. They used to come to the mill with a bag of oats or a bag of rye to be ground. The payment they gave the miller was the fifth quart (measured with a quart jug). The miller was busy the week before Christmas and especially the day before Christmas. Crowds of people were waiting for their ground meal.

There's an old woman in Leitreach Ard (Letterard) who told me she came to the mill herself the day before Christmas Day with her bag of oats to be ground. There were twenty-seven men there at the mill before her, waiting for their turn to come. She had a plug of tobacco for the miller, and she gave it to him discreetly. He let her off before any of the others.

—⁓—

There was rye and rye bread in these parts long ago. When there was too much pure alcohol (*reibhiléis*) in the barley meal, the bread used to make people drunk.

BARLEY BREAD (1)

It was all barley that was sown in these parts (Iorras Aithneach) long ago. The soil didn't yield oats at that time, and people sowed plenty of barley. They mightn't sow many potatoes at all. If the barley wasn't ground and there was no corn in the house, a woman could grind some herself if someone came in unexpectedly, and she wouldn't let him go out without doing him a favor. She would pull four or five fistfuls out of the corn stack. She would bring those fistfuls into the kitchen. She would light a wisp of straw on the floor. She would put the top of the fistfuls into the flame in order to take the beard off the barley. Singeing is what they used to call that, to burn a thing without doing it any harm. A woman would singe a goose, or a weaver would singe the homespun cloth in the loom. When the barley was singed, she would thresh it to get the grain out. She would put the grain in a pot on the fire to harden it. When she had the grain hard, she would take it out of the pot and put it through a sieve to winnow it. Then she would grind the grain with a quern and make meal out of it. She would put the meal through the sieve again, and all she had to do then was to wet it and make bread. When the bread was baked, she would serve it to the visitor with fresh butter and a drink of milk.

A ton of barley grew from a stone of seed. A neighbor of my father had over a half acre of a field to be sown, and he had only a stone of seed. My father scattered the seed. He scattered it very thinly trying to cover all the ground since there was only that much seed. Each grain was a foot from the next. When the corn came up, the blades were a foot from each other at first. Then it began to thicken up until it was in grain. When it was being cut, there wasn't space for it on the ground and it had to be laid crossways. When it was threshed, there was twenty hundredweight from the stone of seed. My father saw that. It was he who scattered the seed.

QUERN AND MILL (2)

Before people turned to the potatoes, they used to sow oats, and many of them ground it to make wholemeal bread. There was a quern in most houses, and anyone who didn't have one would bring the oats to the mill. People had oatmeal all the time, and there was very little talk of flour. I think it was the flour, and it being cheap, that put an end to the grinding of oats. The soil got worse too, the more it was cultivated. The red seaweed weakens the soil gradually. Red seaweed used to be spread under the potatoes, and it made the soil poorer.

Maolra Bairéad had a mill at Sruthán na mBreac (stream of the trout). Máirtín Ó Cualáin used to have a mill on Coillín river, and there was a mill on Carna river, with oats being ground in all three of them. They are all gone now, and you wouldn't see oatmeal in any house.

POTATOES (4)

Oileán Máisean (Mason Island) was the first place around here where potatoes were grown, and they were grown in Dumhaigh

Ithir after that. People thought potatoes wouldn't grow on moorland, and the people of the townlands used to take conacre on Oileán Máisean until they began to grow potatoes on their own land.[1]

—⚟—

The reason potatoes were not sown in the third year of the famine is that the priest told them it was better to eat the seed potatoes, as they wouldn't grow even if they were sown. There were some people who didn't have seed potatoes to sow or to eat. There were others who took the eyes out of the potatoes and sowed them, and there was never such a crop of potatoes as they had.

THE FISHERMAN'S SEASON (4)

Any man who had a hooker was able to keep himself going very well. The people of Iorras Aithneach didn't work their land themselves at all. Their time was taken up with the sea. Seasonal hired laborers were coming in from County Mayo and Glenamaddy to work the land for them. "Spalpeens" (migrant workers) were coming in from the east in the old days.

The fishermen had five or six seasons in the year. (1) Winter herrings starting around Christmas. (2) Running seaweed in Spring to County Clare. (3) Killing basking sharks in May. (4) Fishing for gurnet until the end of Summer. (5) Autumn herrings during the first week of Autumn. (6) Running turf until the herring season again.

A ship used to come from Dublin to buy the herrings.

HUTS AND BOOLIES (1)

When I was a child, there used to be huts on the hills in the first month of Autumn, and maybe some of the huts would be in use for six weeks. There used to be boolies (milking places in summer pasturage) on Leitir Padhbram, Cnocán an Bhodaigh (in Seanadh Bhuire), Seanadh 'ac Dónaill (MacDonnell's slope), Loch an Bhuí (lake of the yellow, from its sandy beach), Cnoc Mordáin (Mordán's hill), Glionnán (gleannán, little glen), Beitheach Chatha (boghole beechwood), and in Creig na gCon (crag of the hounds).

These are the huts that used to be on the summer pastures: two people from Roisín na Mainiach had a hut over on Cnoc Mordáin—Bab Ní Chadhain (Seán Breathnach's wife) and Peig Nic Con Bhuí (Séamas Nóra Pheadair Mhic Dhonnchadha's wife).

There was a hut in the big stone heap in Cnocán an Bhodaigh (lout's hillock) and a hut on Cloch an Chlochair (stone heap rock) in Leitir Padhbram. The Púiríní (hovels) hut was between two lakes on Dochalla mountain.

There was a hut in Troiscín na Neach on Cnoc Buí (yellow hill). (I spent two autumns in this hut myself.)[2]

Joe's hut was at the neck of Loch Padhbram at the head of the river. There was a hut in Beitheach Chatha and a hut in Tamhnach na gCoileach in Glionnán. There were woodcocks in Tamhnach na gCoileach (*coileach feá*: woodcock). And there was the hut in Scailp (cleft) and the Bródach hut.

The "Bródach" (favorite pet) was the name of the woman who owned this hut. She was a sister of Máirtín Ó Gaora who lived in Leitir Deiscirt and of Neda Rua (red-haired Ned). There was another "Bródach" in Caladh Mhaínse (Callowfeenish), a sister of Marcas an Ghabha and Tomás an Ghabha and Seán an Ghabha and Paitseach. The mothers called the two children Bródach, and the name stuck to them. When one of the mothers would be soothing her own child, she used to say:

> Far nicer is Bródach Uí Ghaora,
> Far nicer is Bródach Uí Ghaora,
> Far nicer is Bródach Uí Ghaora,
> Than Bródach an Ghabha in Caladh Mhaínse.

There was a hut at the Aill Dubh (black cliff) in Caladh Mhaínse and a hut on Tamhnach na mBairéadach (the Barretts' grassy upland) on Cnocán an Bhodaigh. There were three or four huts in Dúleitir (black hillside)—one of those was in the loft (a broad ledge of the hillside) above Loch an Áiléir (lake of the loft). There was a hut at Poll an Athar Peadar in Cluais Ghiorria (hare's ear). Father Peadar Mac Con Bhuí (Conway) was the priest who built the church in Carna. He used to fish at this pool on Abhainn na Scainimhe (gravel river). There are sea trout there. The hut at Loch an Bhuí was the last hut I saw. My mother used to be there.

This is how the huts were made: stone walls in some of them and earthen walls in others, and roofs made of sticks and scraws, with two layers of scraws on top of all of them. A bundle of heather was placed in the windward door. No more than four people could sleep in a hut. A bed of heather or white mountain grass on the floor, it would be as good as any other bed, with bags and clothes thrown over the heather under the people.

At the beginning of the first month of autumn, they'd bring the cattle to the hills. They'd go with the cattle themselves, and one of them would always stay in the huts to milk the cows in the morning and in the evening. They used to have a churn in the hut for the milk, and other smaller vessels. Young calves would accompany the cows, and there might be a sty for the little calves at night. Some of the huts were five miles from home. The milk was sent home every day or every second day. Food was sent out to the people on the booley, potatoes, bread, fish, and butter. They used to churn milk on the booley. I saw my mother doing a churning on the booley. She was at it one day, and it failed her to make the butter with the churn dash. She put the churn on her back (there was a rope around the churn and a breast sling), and she brought the churning home. When she was coming down Leitir Caisil (cashel slope), she laid down the churn on the ground and took the lid off. When she looked into the churn, the butter was made.

I was with her. "Come here," she said, "till you see what I have." There was nothing to be seen in the churn but butter.

It was mostly women and full-grown youths who stayed in the huts.

NOTES

1. Conacre refers to the practice of renting land for only eleven months of the year, thus acquiring no rights to it.

2. Affirmation by Micheál Mac Donnchadha.

THIRTEEN

—ᴍ—

WISPS OF STRAW

THE THREE WELLS OF ROME (1)

When Peter and Paul were beheaded in Rome, Paul's head jumped three times, and three wells of spring water sprang up where the head touched the ground.

THE PHOENIX (1)

There was a bird that used to breed itself from ashes. It used to live for seven years. It would then fly into the side of a cliff, go on fire, and fall dead at the bottom of the cliff. Then it would turn into ashes, and a year later, a young bird would arise from the ashes and would live for seven years until it too would go on fire.

The second bird never lived at the same time as the first, and there was always a year without any bird, the year the ashes were at the bottom of the cliff.

"That would be a great cliff for the bird that used to breed itself from its own ashes"—said the man who told me the story. We were standing at the bottom of a cliff.

THE STONE OF GIFTS (1)

There's a cliff in Glionnán, to the north of Dúleitir. The cliff is very high and a deep hollow underneath. In the middle of this cliff, the raven used to have a nest, so nobody could get to it. A man was lowered down the cliff on a rope and took away the eggs. He brought them home and boiled them and put them back in the nest again. When it had failed the raven to hatch the young birds, it went and got "the stone of gifts" on the north side of Hell and put the stone in the nest along with the eggs. When the time came, the young birds were hatched out, even though the eggs were boiled.

This man went down the cliff again. The ravens had left, and the stone of gifts was left behind them in the nest. The man got the stone and brought it with him, and once he had the stone he had every gift.

RIDDLE (1)

Food that went to three
On the bank of Birds' Lake
The food ate the three
And came back safe.

Answer: A kitten brought by a raven to its chicks. The kitten ate the young birds, and then came home himself.

THE FAIRY'S WISH

What the fairy wanted was:
Dulse from the Dásacha,
Limpets from the Foiriúin,
Three good swallows of the water of Glaise Feá,
The meal farthest from the millstone,
And the milk of the cow that calved last year.

The Dásacha, rocks to the west of Leitir Mealláin. Na Foiriúin, rocks to the west of Maíros. Glaise Feá (beech stream) is near

Cashel. The meal farthest from the millstone, the meal that is most difficult to find. The cow that calved last year, a cow that had a calf last year and no calf since. A milk-giving stripper.

THREE PENCE THE CAT GOT (1)

The cat got three pence. It paid a penny for walking silently, a penny for the housewife's mistake, and a penny for having sight by night as well as by day.

A BIRD'S EGGS THAT HANGED A MAN (1)

A man killed another man on the moor. When the man who was killed was nearly dead, he spoke and he said, "May God and the birds of the air be witness to this deed."

Some time later, a boy was searching for nests in a lonely spot on the moor. He found a nest and eggs in it. Written on the eggs was the name of the man who was killed and the name of the man who killed him. The eggs were brought to a person who could read the writing, and the eggs hanged the man who did the killing.

THE COCK THAT TRAILED A BEAM (1)

There was a man coming into Galway with a bundle of rushes to sell at the market. (People used to put tallow on the rushes long ago to make candles.) When he came onto the street, there was a big bulk of men running after a cock and a man in charge of it.

"What has got into you all?" said the man with the rushes to one of the men running after the cock.

"Don't you see the cock trailing the big beam?" they said.

"He's only trailing a wisp of straw," said the man with the rushes.

The man in charge of the cock approached him when he heard him say it wasn't a beam but a wisp of straw it was trailing. He bought the bundle of rushes off him. When he had parted with the bundle of rushes, he himself thought it was a beam the cock was trailing, and he began to run after the cock in wonderment, the same as the townspeople. He felt the temptation now the same as they did. Once he had parted with the rushes, he was making a beam of the wisp of straw, just the same as everyone else. The four-leaved shamrock was in the bundle of rushes, and the cock's owner knew it was.

THE FOUR-LEAVED SHAMROCK IN
A LOAD OF HEATHER (1)

There was a man coming home from the mountain with a load of heather on his back. He heard two dogs talking to each other—barking.

"The clothes your master has put out to bleach will be stolen tonight," said one of them to the other, "if you come with me, we'll watch over it."

"I won't come with you," said the other one, "and I won't watch over it because they beat me a while ago and put me out."

The man who was listening to them went to the house and warned them that the clothes they had put out to bleach would be stolen that night unless they were brought in.

He had the four-leaved shamrock in the load of heather unknown to him. That's why he understood the barking of the dogs.

THE ROBIN (1)

When the Son of God was on the cross and was bleeding, a robin went and picked moss off the stones to stop the blood. When it was putting the moss on the Savior's wounds, the blood was pouring down on its breast. It has a red breast ever since. God likes it and its lack of shyness. It frequents the churches.

THE SHILLING COBBLER (1)

The shilling cobbler is only a tiny little thing, a little man. If he happened to be in heather, he wouldn't be as tall as the heather.

He has a purse tied around his neck, and if you catch him, all you have to do is take the purse off him. He's not going to do you any harm. Many a person took the purse off him, and he didn't do them any harm. Every time you'll look in the purse, there will be a shilling there.

A PAIR OF QUERNSTONES (8)

A pair of quernstones in the possession of Micheál Mac Donnchadha in Más (Mace) were made when the Slyne Head lighthouse was being built. A stonecutter made them at the lighthouse, and a man from Slyne Head who moved from there to Más brought them with him.

ST. BRIGID'S DAY (1)

I heard my mother say that the feast of St. Brigid used to be as big a holiday as Christmas. There were three holidays at Christmas: Christmas Day, St. Stephen's Day, and St. John's Day. They had three holidays at the feast of St. Brigid: St. Brigid's Day, the feast of Our Lady of the Candles, and St. Caolann's Day.

INFANTS' DAY (2)

There's a day in the week after Christmas called the "Forbidden Day of the Year," and "Infants' Day" is the fourth day after Christmas Day. People are forbidden to begin any new work on that day.

BLOODRED THURSDAY (2)

The Jews went out to kill all the infants, hoping the Son of God would be one of them. They killed them. They killed as many of them as they could, from two years down, on the fourth day of Christmas. That's the reason that ever since then, the fourth day is called "Infants' Day." People don't like to begin any work on that day, and it's called the "Forbidden Day of the Year." It is said that there was so much blood on the ground, after so many infants being killed on the fourth day, that there were rivers of blood. People had to go and dig holes to bury the blood in the ground and cover it. They did that on the fifth day of Christmas, and every year since then the fifth day is called "Bloodred Thursday" when it falls on a Thursday. That day comes only every seventh year.

FEAST DAYS

Little Christmas Day, the first day of the new year, New Year's Day.

The Twelfth Day of Christmas, the sixth day of the first month, the Day of the Big Wind in 1839.

The Night of the Twelfth Day (the fifth day), the three kings came from the Eastern World to see our Savior.

St. Brigid's Day, the Feast of our Lady, and St. Caolann's Day come one after the other.

St. Brigid's Day on the first of February, the Feast of our Lady of the Candles (Candlemas Day) on the second day, and St. Caolann's Day on the third day.

—⁂—

In the old days, they decided not to do any work during the twelve days of Christmas.

THE ARK (1)

She is still as good as she ever was. She is on Mount Sion. There's a cliff underneath her, and the only grip she has on the cliff is about three or four feet, leaning out over the glen, and God's miracle holding her there without rotting since.

THE SIZE OF THE ARK (12)

A hundred and fifty yards was the length of her keel,
And twenty-five yards was her width.
Fifteen feet in each storey, she was three storeys high;
That's the length, width, and height of the Ark.

THE FISHERMAN'S SUPERSTITIONS (2)

A fisherman on his way out fishing doesn't like the first person he
meets to be a woman or a priest or a hare or a fox. The fisherman
doesn't like to meet a red-haired woman, but it wouldn't be too
bad if she had shoes on.

Fishermen don't like to turn a boat against the sun in the
morning. They turn the boat with the sun, on their way out in
the morning. They don't like to turn it against the sun.

Should they meet with an accident in the morning, causing
bleeding, they'd say it was lucky.

PURPLE LOOSESTRIFE AND FERN (1)

A potato under the loosestrife
And famine under the fern.
Land where purple loosestrife grows gives good potatoes.
Land where ferns grow is bad land for potatoes.

THE WHITE-FACED DOG (3)

The king of the otters is the white-faced dog. It's a magic dog. If it
should see a person before the person sees it, that person would
die before the end of the year. It is said that it's seen only every
seventh year. It's a thing that never slept a wink, and nothing can
kill it but cross money.[1] Whoever would have its skin needn't fear
an accident on land or on sea.

NETTING ON LOCH NA SCAINIMHE (1)

I heard my father say he saw seven men netting fish on Oileán an Fhiaich (raven island) on Loch na Scainimhe (gravel lake). Early in the morning he saw them, and when they put the net out into the water, three of them would be dragging it; they'd make a circle and come in again. I heard the same account from an old woman. (I saw this netting being done in the Galway river [Corrib] and plenty of salmon being killed.) The old woman told me they were no earthly men. It seemed to my father that the men were walking on the surface of the water.

THE FOX IN CHARGE OF THE LUNCH (7)

The wolf and the fox were in partnership stealing anything they could, but this particular day they stole a lamb, and they knew there wasn't enough in the lamb for the two of them. Then they made up their mind that one of them should stay and the other should go in search of more.

"I'll give you two choices," said the fox to the wolf. "You go into the wood, and I'll stay in charge of the lunch; or I'll stay in charge of the lunch, and you go into the wood. Take your choice now."

Both choices were the same. The wolf was sent into the wood in both cases. The wolf went into the wood and didn't find anything, and when it came back, the fox had eaten the lamb and had taken himself off.

HOUGHING[2] (3)

I am a man who has slaughtered much
I houghed a hundred and a thousand cows
And pity me God, going before the Lord
I made no restitution, and I never will now.

A FISH THAT SPOKE (2)

A man from Iorras Mór (Errismore) who had killed a creelful of fish, a creelful of cod, brought them out to Clifden to sell them. There was a man walking around there, and he came to where the Iorras Mór man was. He took a fish from the creel and inquired how much he was asking for it. The Iorras Mór man told him. The other man smelled the fish and said all the fish were rotten.

"How could it be rotten," said the Iorras Mór man, "the fish that was caught yesterday?"

"You're a liar!" said the fish. "We're dead for three days."

What did the Iorras Mór man do but grab the creel and fling all the fish like a shot onto the road. He put the creel on his shoulder and went home.

It wasn't the fish that spoke at all but the man who wanted to buy the fish. With some trick, he put the words in the fish's mouth.

THE BROTHERS' LYING MAID (1)

The religious Brothers had a maid, and whenever they told her to do anything she always used to say, "Oh, I was just going to do that." Then one day they told her to wash the books.

She said she was just going to wash them. They knew then that she was lying. They never believed her any more.

WHO STOLE THE SHOES? (1)

"Only the Brothers were present, and the shoes disappeared." It was the devil stole their shoes, hoping to put them at loggerheads.

TOBACCO AFTER FOOD (3)

"Tobacco after food, that's on the man of the house."

A beggar man came into a house. He got his meal, and when he was full, he said, "Tobacco after food, that's on the man of the house."

The woman of the house answered him:
"For every vagrant that comes the way
This is little price to pay."
The man of the house spoke:
"The man who invented that toll
May he have neither house nor home."
There were no alms as good as the alms of tobacco.

"The true blessings of God on the souls of all those who departed from you into death, and on your own soul on the last day," is what a person would say after getting a meal or a smoke of tobacco. The people long ago had great belief, and great blessings, and many prayers.

THE TOBACCO PRAYER (1)

Seventeen times the full of St. Patrick's cemetery
St. Brigid's cloak and that of the church,
May the grains of sand in the strand
And the beads of dew on the grass
Be no more numerous than the blessings of God on the souls of
     the dead
Totally and altogether. Amen.

The old women say this prayer when they're smoking tobacco at a wake.

MICHEÁL'S PRAYER (1)

May God give you a long and happy life and the Kingdom of God on the last day.

A PRAYER FOR THE DEAD (1)

"The blessings of God on the souls of the dead."

"And the blessings of God forever," says the second person.

ANOTHER PRAYER (1)

"May you not die in the state of sin!"

PICKING TINY-SHELLED DULSE (5)

There were women picking dulse in Cruach na Caoile (Deer island). They spent the night there. They were afraid because they thought they heard voices. In the morning Cáit Pheadair said,

> If I'd see the time the boat would arrive
> And that my hand would reach its nose
> No sight of Cáit would be seen
> On Caorán na nGall any more.

BIRTH (2)

In a house where a child had just been born, the people of the house wouldn't allow a red ember or a lit pipe out of the house until the child was baptized. I was sent as a young boy to get a red ember in a house where there was a young unbaptized child. I was told I couldn't get it on account of the child being unbaptized; only for that, I could.

GODPARENTS (10)

People who had a child to be baptized would like two people of the one family to be godparents.

LAY BAPTISM (3)

Lay baptism is a baptism a lay person can do. Everybody has an obligation to be able to do a lay baptism in an emergency. In the event of a newborn child, if the mother or father were afraid it mightn't live till the priest would come, the child wouldn't die without baptism.

In the old days, the odd person could be a good age before being baptized.

LAYING OF THUMBS (4)

"It is sad to lay the thumbs on the eyes of a friend."

When a person dies, someone closes his mouth and his eyes. That custom is called "laying of thumbs."

CLUBFOOT (1)

Anybody who is clubfooted or clubhanded, either one, and who falls in the sea, will not sink to the bottom. *Cam reilige* (graveyard crookedness), a crookedness in hand or foot.[3]

THE STRAND THAT DISAPPEARED (1)

There was a fine strand in Iorras Mór where red seaweed used to come ashore. People went collecting the seaweed on the feast of St. Caolann. The following day, there was no strand to be seen. Only rocks were left, and the sea so deep that a boat could sail around them. *Na Searra* is what they're called since. The strand disappeared and revealed the rocks.

LÉIM VILLAGE (3)

Diarmaid and Gráinne were passing through Léim village in Uachtar Ard. Diarmaid cleared the river in one leap. The ground was sloping where he made the leap. He brought a stone with him between his two shins. And Gráinne said his leap was the leap of a lout down a slope. He then turned around and made the leap against the height. That's why the village was called Léim. Diarmaid's Léim (leap) is another name of the village.

DIARMAID'S BED (2)

There's a spot in Meall Rua (reddish hillock), in Maínis, called Diarmaid's Bed.[4]

NOSE RENT (1)

The people by whom the O'Flahertys were dispossessed, the earls of Clanrickard, used to exact rent, and if a man didn't have the rent for them, he was to have his nose cut off.

TUFTY MOUTH (1)

It was Tufty Mouth (Cab an Dosáin) who killed the Fianna in the Battle of the Sheaves.[5]

EAST ON MONDAY AND WEST ON TUESDAY (3)

If a man was going to get married and the wife-to-be was living to the east of him, it would be lucky to go asking for her on a Monday. If she was living to the west of him, he would go asking for her on a Tuesday. If he was going to emigrate, he would do the same thing.

THE ANNIVERSARY OF THE FLOOD (3)

The day before St. Mac Dara's Day, the fifteenth day of July, is the anniversary of the day the Flood began to cover the world. If it rains on that day, it is said that it will be more or less raining for the following forty days. I have noticed that it will rain for most of that time.

YELLOW DROP (1)

Yellow Drop is a fireside trick. A stick is lit, a stick that won't stay lit for long. The person who lights the stick will hand it to another person, and it keeps going round from person to person until the flame goes out. Whoever has the stick in his hand when the flame goes out is laughed at:

The first person says:

Move the drop around.
The second person: What does a drop do?
The first person: Cutting and beating,
Hatchet work
To go nine times
On his wife's turf
To cut turf,
To spread turf,
To put turf out of a boghole,
To poke a boghole,
To close a boghole.
The person in whose two hands the yellow drop dies,
Will be straddled with the creel for the rest of his life.

THE RACE'S HAT (1)

There was a village in Achill, and there was only one hat in the whole village. There was a rocky crossing place on the way out of this village, and there was a bush growing outside the crossing place. The hat used to be hanging on the bush, and each man, when leaving the village, was allowed to wear it for the day. When he'd return home, he'd hang the hat on the bush again until the next man would come and do the same thing. So it was called "the race's hat."

When a utensil or tool is being borrowed from house to house, people say, "You're making the race's hat of it."

SEÁN'S HORSE (11)

"A long standing on weak legs, like Seán Thomáis Mhic Aoidh's horse."

Seán used to be drinking, and he would leave the horse outside the door of the public house for a long time.

TOP OF MY THUMB[6] (1)

The Fianna were going out one morning to save the harvest when they met Top of My Thumb. They started talking to him. He asked them if they were about to save the harvest. They said they were. He asked them which would they prefer, reaping or binding. They said they'd prefer to bind, thinking he was joking.

"I'll go reaping so," he said.

He went reaping, and they went binding the corn after him.

There was so much rivalry between them that as soon as they had bound a sheaf of corn, they'd just throw it over their head, without enough time to even look around. They were killing one another with the sheaves, and they were nearly all killed before they noticed it. That was the biggest battle the Fianna ever fought, the Battle of the Sheaves, where they were killing one another.

Top of My Thumb is also called Tufty Mouth.

THE MOUSE THAT CUT THE CLOTH (10)

There was a sailor on board a vessel, and a mouse had cut his suit of clothes. He had the charm for getting rid of mice, and when he saw the suit was cut, he made the charm. He placed a razor on the deck of the vessel with the sharp edge up. The mice began to come and place their mouth on the razor and go away again. A big mouse came at last and began rubbing its neck on the razor's edge until it cut its throat. That was the one that cut the cloth. The others were swearing they hadn't cut it. The captain was watching. He didn't say a word until he reached land. He then paid this man off and told him to clear off to somewhere else, that he wouldn't have him on the same vessel ever again, not knowing that he wouldn't do to him what he had done to the mouse that cut the cloth.

THE REED WELL IN CRUACH CHAOLAINN (2)

There's a well they call Reed Well at the northernmost point of the island at the top of the shore. You could barely fit a cup into it, but it would keep you going all through the year. You could keep on bailing it until you'd fill a barrel from it, or twenty barrels—it was all the same. It was called Reed Well because people used to bring a reed to sip the water through it when they were thirsty. The fishermen could barely wait to reach the well when they were thirsty after coming west from Carraig-a-Míle.

A WOMAN IN CRUACH CHAOLAINN (1)

A pregnant woman on Cruach Chaolainn went into labor. Herself and her husband were the only two in the house or on the island. When she went into labor, her husband went out in a boat to the mainland to the north to get a midwife. The wife was on her own in the house while she was in labor. When night fell, she was lying down near the fire, with her face to the fire, and a big, black man whom she had never seen before came in, a huge, big, black figure.

"Turn around, wench!" he said.

She didn't turn around. The cock crowed, and the black figure had to leave.

"Oh, you had a narrow escape there," he said, "only for you had the male at your bedside your life would be short."

When the husband and the midwife came in the morning, she had a baby son. The child was well, and she was safe. Even the cock has great power if it has a good voice. A March cock is extremely powerful.

NOTES

1. Cross money: a silver coin with the sign of the cross on it.

2. Houghing: to lame an animal by cutting the hamstrings was a common method of attacking landlords' stock during the Land War, particularly during the initial phase between 1879 and 1882.

3. *Cam reilige*: the result of a mother's fall in a graveyard while pregnant.

4. Many such natural shelters, as well as megalithic tombs, were regarded as having been made by the legendary eloping couple Diarmaid and Gráinne when they were on the run and pursued by Fionn and his followers throughout Ireland.

5. The battle in which nearly all of the Fianna were killed by sheaves of corn they were busily binding and throwing back over their heads, inadvertently killing one another in the process. A little fellow of the underworld Cab an Dosáin (Tufty Mouth) was the sole reaper!

6. A Tom Thumb–like character in Irish myths.

FOURTEEN

—⚏—

CUSTODIANS OF TRADITIONAL LORE AND STORYTELLERS

MICHEÁL MAC DONNCHADHA

It was Micheál Mac Donnchadha who lives in Roisín na Mainiach who told a lot of what's in this book. The neighbors call him
Micheál Phádraic Shéamais Nábla, and that long name brings us
back in history to the Year of the French.[1] The priest who was on
the run in Carna after the Year of the French, Father Myles, was
arrested one day and was locked up for the army to come and take
him away with them. It was Séamas Nábla Mac Donnchadha who
freed the priest from the cellar where he was locked up and allowed him get away. It was Mairéad Ní Iarnáin who told Séamas
that the priest was locked up. Her name and Séamas Nábla's name
are worthy of the respect of the Gael. Micheál Mac Donnchadha,
the storyteller, is the son of a son of Séamas Nábla. I gave a brief
account of his life in *Loinnir Mac Leabhair*, and I'm letting him
tell more about himself and his people in this book.[2]

ON MY GROWING UP (1)

When I was growing up, the people had a hard life, and a harder
life before that again. I spent fourteen years making kelp on Inis

Mhúscraí every summer and autumn.[3] It was like living there for fourteen half years, except that I came in on Saturdays. The island was covered in red seaweed that was being dried. We used to cut seaweed, cutting it dry when there was a great ebb, and when there wasn't a great ebb, cutting it from the boat with a pole called a *croisín*. There was a knife at the end of the pole. You'd push the *croisín* down into the water, turn the knife among the strapwrack, and then give the *croisín* a twist so that it would get a grip on the strapwrack.You could then pull the strapwrack off the flagstone. Two strong men who'd have a good boat would cut three tons of strapwrack in one day. There wasn't a dry stitch of clothes on me from Monday till Saturday.

We used to be burning kelp on the island night and day. When we'd have burnt one kiln, we'd set up another one. I spent six nights and six days without sleeping a wink one year while burning the kelp. It was awful slavery. There was no slavery like it, burning it in the face of the fire all the time and raking it with kelp rakes. The juice used to run out of the kiln, and if you weren't careful, it would ooze over the walls. Myself and another man made nine tons and sixteen hundredweight of kelp one year. Five pounds ten shillings a ton is what we got for that kelp.

There was a house on the island for the bailiff and the kelp workers. Myself and the bailiff stayed on the island on a Saturday night. When it was time to go to bed, we went to bed. The house had a half door. There was a big press in the house, and we put it against the half door, as the high wind used to blow the door in. We were barely in bed when the press was lifted and thrown against the wall on the other side of the house. We put it against the half door again. We fell into a deep sleep, and we didn't wake up until twelve o' clock on Monday morning. We were woken up by six people, two of mine and four of the bailiff's, who came in on Monday. They thought we were dead when they saw the boats and didn't see ourselves around. They saw two loads of seaweed that we were to spread out on Saturday. I believe we'd have slept till Monday night if they hadn't woken us. That sleep was nearly as great as the sleep of the Doire an Fhéich women.

There were three women in Doire an Fhéich (Derrynea, wood of the raven, near Casla). They cut seaweed and burnt it on Monday. They left the kelp to cool on Tuesday till Wednesday. They brought the kelp in three creels to Galway, with the creels on their back, and they sold it in Galway. They placed the odds and ends they bought in Galway in the creels, and they began their walk home, the three of them together. They were in no hurry walking home, and they took it nice and easy. When they had passed the Ros an Mhíl boreen on their way west, they saw a man on the right-hand side—nothing bad ever came from the right-hand side. One of the women was devout and had many holy prayers. When she started saying those prayers, their fear disappeared and they didn't see the man any more. A good part of the night was gone when they came home. They were tired and hungry. They began to put themselves in order, and it was nearly daybreak when they went to bed on Thursday morning. They then slept from Thursday morning till Sunday morning. Myself and the bailiff nearly slept for as long as them in Inis Mhúscraí.

I spent years cutting seaweed on the County Clare shore in April, and in Na Forbacha (Furbo) at Cnocán na gCailleach (hags' hillock), and selling it in Galway. I cut seaweed at Oileán Lua in Béal Achrais, at Carraig an Duilisc (dulse rock), at Carraig Fhada (long rock), and at Oileán Fiadh (deer island), on both sides of Ardtamhnach (grassy upland), and near Pointe na Corann (Weir point), and at Oileán Eide (Island Eddy, at the head of Galway Bay) on the south side of Tawin.[4]

We used to unload the boatful of seaweed every evening in Galway and sell it to the carters from Tuam and from Abbey. When I was one of four in a boat, I would get one fourth, about eight shillings a day some years. There were some days I got five shillings.

MY MOTHER'S FATHER (1)

The men of Aird (Ard) used to go to Sceirde long ago to kill birds such as shags and cormorants. Seven of them went to Sceirde in a rowing boat. There was Máirtín Mac Donnchadha (my mother's father), and her brother Micheál, and five others. They had a rowing boat; no other boat would do. Five of them got out of the boat in the middle of the night. Máirtín Mac Donnchadha and another man stayed in the boat. The two men in the boat soon heard the dogs barking. The roosters soon began to crow. When the roosters began to crow, it wasn't long till the geese and ducks began to speak quite near them. The sea began to seethe, and they had to be off and leave the five inside on Sceirde. They just turned the back of the boat to the wind and went home. They had a following wind, and they came safely home.

The following day it was blowing a gale. Four men went out in a sailing boat to see if the five men on Sceirde were alive. When the five on Sceirde saw the boat, they began to wave their arms, telling them to go home. They went home that day.

The following day, or second day, was kindlier, but the sea was seething still. They went out again and brought bread and water with them for the five men. They went in as near as they could, and they tied a line to the two barrels containing the water and the bread. There was a sinker tied to the other end of the line, and they threw the sinker ashore. The five caught hold of the sinker and pulled in the two barrels.

The following day, the third, they went out again, and the sea had calmed. They had a rowing boat, and they went in and brought the five men safely home. They had killed an enormous amount of birds, fully grown cormorants, young cormorants, and shags.

The nights they were on Sceirde, the men took off their boots and killed the birds when they were asleep. It was the birds kept them alive at night. The birds were heaped on top of them, and their down kept them warm. Seabirds' down is wonderful. They brought the load of birds home, and they ate them. This all happened to Máirtín when he was young. He died about fifty years ago. He was some years over the hundred when he died. He died in Bearna (Barna). He's buried there.

A WOMAN IN SEARCH OF A POEM (1)

Micheál Mac Donnchadha's mother's mother knew Donncha Mór's Poem. His mother didn't know this poem, and she wanted to learn it. Her mother was dead at the time, and a sister of hers who knew the poem was dead too, but a son of that sister was alive and living back west in Más (Mace). She thought he might know Donncha Mór's Poem. She set out one day and walked back to Más, five miles, to her sister's son, to see if he knew the poem. He knew two-thirds of the poem, the beginning and the end, but he didn't know all of it. "All I know of it," said Micheál, "is what I heard from my mother. 'The people of God are a long time poor,' that's the beginning of the poem. Maybe Marcas Ó Maoilchiaráin in Ros Rua would know all of it."

Micheál Mac Donnchadha's grandmother who had known Donncha Mór's Poem was of the Maoilchiaráin clan. Her name was Bríd Ní Mhaoilchiaráin, Bríd Phádraic. She was married to Máirtín Réamoinn Mac Donnchadha, the storyteller's grandfather. He had a world of stories and religious verses and songs, and his wife was as good as himself.

MY GRANDMOTHER (1)

Máire Ni Mhaoilchiaráin Phádraic used to have a voice coming to her at night, whispering a holy song in her ear. When she'd wake up, she'd have songs she had never heard before. Máire Phádraic had lots of holy songs, and she had Donncha Mór's Poem, and her family had it after her. She married Liam Dhiarmaid Ó hUaithnín (Greene), and they had a big family. One of their grandsons is alive and living in Liam Mhaitiais's house. Páidín Shéamais Liam, another one of them, is living in Más.

Máire had a sister, Bríd Ní Mhaoilchiaráin Phádraic. Bríd married Máirtín Réamoinn Mac Donnchadha. They had a daughter, Bríd Nic Dhonnchadha. This Bríd was my mother. I've never heard that the Ó Maoilchiaráin clan were not as long in this part of the country as any of the other clans.

MICHEÁL'S GRANDFATHER (4)

Brídín Mháirtín Réamoinn Nic Dhonnchadha was the name of Micilín Pháidín Shéamais Nábla's mother. Her father, Máirtín Réamoinn, used to go all around the countryside applying charms and cures, including the cure for *cleithín*.[5] There weren't many doctors around at the time. There was a charm for belly-ache, a charm for hunting, a charm for toothache, a charm for a sprain—sprain-thread was available from the weavers—a charm for sore eyes, a charm for "the rose," a charm for blood-stopping, and a charm for the evil eye.[6] They had a charm for a person who was on the run to "blind" those who were in pursuit.

Máirtín Réamoinn had all of those charms, and people were coming to him for them. He was in great demand, and he had to visit people who were bedridden. He had the charms in the form of little poems. He had long old poems as well, and a world of stories. I saw the man myself, and he was a fine, good-looking man. When he came into a house, he wouldn't be told to leave, and if he'd spend the night in a house, he wouldn't be alone there but with a great company gathered listening to him. Réamonn Mac Donnchadha lived in Dumhaigh Ithir. Máirtín lived in Aird Thoir for a while, near the castle. People didn't spend all their life in the same place in the old days.

Micilín's mother had the charms.

Micheál (Micilín) Mac Donnchadha's forefathers were: Pádraic, Seámas (Nábla), Seámas, Seán, Éamonn, Seán.

There's a field beside Loch na Lannach (mullet lake) called Seán Mac Éamoinn's Field. That's where Seán Éamoinn had his house.

A PRAYER MICHEÁL USED TO SAY

May help and friends
And God's grace greet us;
Help each time
And all times we need it.
In the Sacrament of Penance
May God redeem us,
And protect my soul,
Mary Mother of Jesus.

PÁDRAIC MAC DONNCHADHA (LIAM)

Pádraic's father, Liam Mac Donnchadha, had a house and a small holding in Roisín an tSamha (small point of the sorrel, near Carna). Times were bad when Pádraic was a three-year-old. People were being sent to America for free, those who were willing to go. Liam Mac Donnchadha sold all he had in Roisín an tSamha. He sent some of his daughters to an orphanage in Clifden, and he went to America on the free emigration scheme. He brought his wife with him, one daughter, and Pádraic. They went to Pittsburgh and lived there for two and a half years, and then came home again. The reason the father had for coming home was that he got sunstroke. When they came home, they settled down in a house belonging to a brother of theirs in Roisín an tSamha. They had no land and were paying for yearly conacre until Liam, the father, had died and Pádraic was a hardy youth. A part of Coillín was commonage at the time. Pádraic's mother and himself set out one day, got some help together, and built a house on the edge of the commonage in Coillín. Robinson, the agent, was away, and they could not be summoned until he returned. When Robinson came home, he was informed. Máirtín Ó Loideáin spoke to him, and the priest wrote to him asking him to give Pádraic's mother a holding. Even though he was a Protestant, he was very obliging to the priests. He came to Coillín, and he saw the house. He allowed the widow to stay, and he levied a rent of one pound on her.

Pádraic had the same small house until he put a slated roof on it last year (1933), and it is now a solid house. It is built on a flagstone. There's a great flagstone, without any sod on it, stretching twenty yards from the door out to the road. The small holding is below the house in the glen to the northwest. It is bad land except where he has cleared and worked it. He usually has about an acre of potatoes sown. He doesn't have enough for himself, and he has bought fields for the cow inside in Aird.

Pádraic was going to school till he was twelve years old. He never had a master who could speak Irish. There never was an Irish-speaking schoolmaster in Aird school until the Puirséal (Purcell) man who is now in Belclare came, the man who was there before Seán Ó Conchúir. Those two men are famous far and wide for teaching Irish. Many a boy and girl have been sent to college by Ó Conchúir (O'Connor).

Like all Irish people, Pádraic's people are scattered now, some of them in America and some here at home. A sister who was in America is married in Tyrone and is well off in life. Pádraic is in Coillín, a daughter of his is in America, and another daughter in County Monaghan. He has young children of his own going to school yet.

PÁDRAIC TELLING ABOUT HIS MOTHER

I never saw a woman who had a harder life than my mother. When herself and my father were living in Roisín an tSamha, they were making kelp one year in Inis Bigir. They used to walk from Roisín an tSamha every morning to Inis Bigir and walk home again in the evening after spending the day burning kelp. When they had the kelp ready to sell, there wasn't a buyer nearer than Cashel. They loaded the kelp into a rowing boat and brought it to Cashel. Hazel was to be the buyer. There was a spy there before them who told Hazel they had put black seaweed in the kelp—and they didn't, or anything else but strapwrack and red seaweed. Hazel said he wouldn't buy the kelp, and he didn't. They put out the boat, knowing there would be a buyer in Cill Chiaráin the following day, and they would go there. They brought the kelp from Cashel to Cill Chiaráin that day. They spent the night there. Hazel was the buyer in Cill Chiaráin again the following day. When he saw the kelp: "That's the kelp I refused yesterday," he said. "I won't buy it."

They heard in Cill Chiaráin that there would be a buyer in Leitir Mealláin the following day. They put out the boat from Cill Chiaráin pier and headed off over to Leitir Mealláin. My mother, together with my father, rowed the boat from Inis Bigir to Cashel and from Cashel to Cill Chiaráin and from Cill Chiaráin to Leitir Mealláin. There was a different buyer in Leitir Mealláin, and he bought the kelp from them. He said he hadn't seen better kelp that year, and they got a good price from him.

They had to row the boat back to Carna. May the Lord have mercy on my mother's soul. She had a hard life.

My mother spent a night on St. Mac Dara's Island. The reason she spent a night on the island was that Tom Labhráis had promised to put herself and another woman ashore on Cruach na Cara (St. Mac Dara's Island) to pick dulse, as he had business in Roundstone himself. He had planned to put them ashore on his way west past the island, and pick them up again on his way back. My mother's companion wasn't able to go, and my mother said she would go on her own, as she hardly ever saw a day that somebody from the townlands wasn't picking dulse there. Tom

Labhráis put her ashore on the island and went on his way to Roundstone himself. There were other women on the island picking dulse, and when the ebb was spent (i.e., when the tide was turning), everybody was going home. She could get a way home with them, but she would have to carry the dulse for two miles. "I'll wait for the man who left me here," she said in her own mind because he had promised to collect her again. Evening was approaching, and she saw no sign of a boat coming until night had nearly fallen. That was when she saw Tom Labhráis coming down by Ceann Mása (Mace Head), and she said in her own mind that he didn't seem to be coming to collect her. "I suppose," she said, "yourself and the man with you are drunk, and you don't remember I ever existed." The man knew she existed all right, but he thought she had gone home in one of the other boats and wasn't waiting for him.

"We have done a bad deed," said the boatman who was with Tom Labhráis, "if we have left the woman on St. Mac Dara's Island tonight."

"Don't you know," said Tom Labhráis, "a woman whose husband's people were working on the island wouldn't let night fall on her, waiting for us."

When the boat landed, my father was at the landing place, and he saw that my mother was not on board. He asked them if they had any word of her.

"We haven't," said Tom Labhráis, "but don't you know she came out in a boat from Aird Thiar."

My father set off to find out if she had. It was a short summer's night, and he didn't stop till he had walked into Ard West and, as day was dawning, he woke up the houses where he thought she might be. Nobody had heard any word of her. They pushed out a boat. The tide was low, and four of them went to St. Mac Dara's Island, and my father was afraid to come up out of the boat, for fear he might find her dead, until somebody else brought him the news. The other men went to walk the island, and they decided to go to the chapel first. They felt certain that if she was alive at all, it was there they would find her. There she was, sitting at the church gable, where everybody believes Mac Dara is buried. Mac Dara is buried at the east gable of the chapel. The spot is called Mac Dara's Bed. She heard them immediately, and she told them she was neither cold nor hungry nor afraid.

"I was saying my prayers," she said, "but I didn't feel sleepy at all. I knew I was in no danger because I trusted the saint who used to live on the island."

She walked down to the boat with them and showed them a big bag she had packed with dulse. They brought herself and the dulse with them and brought her into Aird Thiar, where she got a meal, and herself and her husband went home to Roisín an tSamha. The sun was not long up when they arrived.

Seán Bacach Ó Guairim, the poet, was married to an aunt of my mother, said Pádraic Mac Donnchadha (Liam). My mother knew Seán's songs.

The poet was in Galway one day. He came into a shop there. The woman of the shop had a suspicion it was him.

"Are you Seán Bacach Ó Guairim?" she said.

"Unmannerly women and senseless children call me that," he replied, "but my name is Seán Ó Guairim from Leitreach Ard. I am not lame, but I have a step when I'm walking."

May the Lord have mercy on his soul. Amen.

A WOMAN SPINNER

Pádraic Mac Donnchadha's mother used to spin for others. She earned seven shillings for spinning a stone of wool.

PÁDRAIC TELLING ABOUT HIS TUTOR

All the stories that I heard, it was from a man living in Aird an Chaisleáin I heard them. Pádraic Ó Maoilchiaráin was his name. He was the strongest man this side of Galway. When he was twenty years old, his father and two brothers were drowned when coming down from Ros Rua (reddish promontory) with a load of seaweed in a small sailing boat. The day was bad, and the boat was too deep in the water. They came too near the land in a place they call Campainn to the north of Ceann Mása. It's a shallow place, and the waves break there. It drowned the boat, the father, and the two sons. The boat was thrown onto the shore, and the following morning Pádraic heard the boat was there and that it was wrecked. He was the second youngest son. He went to get the sail and the mast out of the boat. He tied the sails to the mast with the lanyards and hoisted them onto his shoulder, and he only took one rest until he reached his own house in Aird. They were over two and a half hundredweight, and Pádraic was no more than twenty years at the time.

Himself and an older brother were left on their own, and neither of them ever married. There was no woman in the house as the mother was dead and the sister was married.

The first time I heard him tell a story, he was a few score years old. If there was a wake in any house, he was usually there, and he would be called upon to tell a story to shorten the night. I saw him two nights in a row in the same house, and on account of the two nights he went to bed on Friday evening and didn't wake up until Sunday morning, and only for a next-door neighbor he'd be there still. The neighbor didn't know whether he was in the house or not. He came knocking on the door to see if he was there or if he was alive. That was when he woke up.

He became unwell in the end. He couldn't walk with all the pain in his bones. He was very generous with his stories, and he would last a fortnight telling a story. He didn't need to tell the same story twice. He was able to dress a story in a "suit of heroics" of high-flown speech that would last for ten minutes. He had stories of the Fianna, stories of the fairies, and ancient lore. He saw as many ghosts in his lifetime, if it was true, that half the amount would be a lot! I never heard him reciting poems. It was from him I heard the story of "An Dúradán" (the dim-witted person), "Leadaí an Chraicinn Ghabhair" (the loafer with the goatskin), "Scológ na Féasóige Léithe," (the grey-bearded farmhand), "Triúr Clainne na Bard-scológe," (The Rustic Poet's three children), "An Tarbh Cuthach" (the raging bull), "Táilliúr na hAibhne" (the river tailor), and many more.

He is dead for the past twenty-five years. The sister who was in Leitreach Ard had to take him in, and he spent two years confined to bed before he died. He never did anyone any harm. May the Lord have mercy on him. Amen.

PÁDRAIC TELLING ABOUT MARCAS Ó LAIDHE, STORYTELLER

There was a man in Coillín, Marcas Ó Laidhe, and he had a great many stories. He died thirty years ago. There wasn't a story told in the neighborhood that he wasn't able to tell. It was to him a young man would go when he went visiting. It was in his own house he used to be storytelling. He was the second best man in the locality at saying the family rosary. He had all the old prayers and the catechism. I heard he was the best storyteller in the townlands. The local people used to come visiting every night to listen to him. Pádraic Mac Con Iomaire and Tomás Mac Con Iomaire in Coillín are sons of Marcas Ó Laidhe's daughter. Both of them have stories. Tomás is a fine sensible speaker, but he never left home. Pádraic mostly worked with the sea and is able to tell a story about his own troubles and about what he has seen.

PÁDRAIC TELLING ABOUT HIS GRANDFATHER

My grandfather, Patsach Mór, used to learn from Brian Ó Laidhe and from Seán na Scoile. He was able to read and write Irish. He was granted eighty-eight years of life. He stood six feet, two inches in his bare feet. His mother was a Corbett. She was from Iorras Mór. He never received a blow, and he was never in a court-house. He lived in Aird Thiar, and the means of living they had at that time was, as soon as they had finished the spring sowing, to go out with their fishing line killing gurnet. They might kill two hundred that day. They used to go into Oileán Dá Bhruithneog (Brannock Island) in Aran when night fell. The only facilities they had were the sail of the boat for shelter above them, a pot of Indian meal on the boil, and their fish. The next night they would do the same, and sail to Galway on the third day with their catch. They would sell the fish in Galway. They might get ten shillings a hundred for the fish, and then again they might sell it for five shillings.

The fishermen from Aird were fishing to the west of Aird on a dark night. The weather turned bad, and a storm blew from the north. They had to head out to sea, towards the coast of Kerry, whether they would get that far or not. Four of the boats landed in Malbay (in West Clare), and four boats were lost. Patsach Mór had a hooker, and he landed safely in Aran, himself and the grand-father of Éamonn Mac Con Rí who lives in Más. There was a fisherman from Inis Ní with them, and he had a bad boat. He was sailing beside Patsach Mór's boat when the storm was blowing.

"I had better take you on board," said Patsach Mór. "Your boat won't last much longer."

"No," said the Inis Ní man, "wherever my boat is lost, I'll be lost."

There was a favored man in the boat with the Inis Ní man.[7] That man said he would go on board sooner than be drowned. He bent down to get his fishing line. He hadn't put the fishing line in order when the boat went down, and the two were drowned. He didn't want to go until he had wound up his fishing line. Patsach Mór remembered that much.

Patsach Mór's hooker was a five-ton boat. Unless the day turned very wild entirely, he was able to land it. The small boat of only two or three tons would be lost on a bad day. Fishing with lines was how they killed the gurnet. The gurnet got bigger as they moved further out on the deep. Inside Carraig-a-Míle is where they used to fish for herring. They used to lay out the net at night and come home themselves. They used to lift them the following day.

PÁDRAIC TELLING ABOUT FISHING

I spent three days fishing in Autumn one year. Pádraic Ó Conaire (Conroy) was with me. The boat was his, a *púcán* (open boat with mainsail and jib). I spent two days with Pádraic Ó Conaire until he got tired. He wasn't feeling well. I spent the third day with Seán Ó Gaora (Geary), and we did a lot of sailing. Fishing lines and bait are what we used. I went out the previous night looking for bait. I set a lobsterpot in a stony place in the middle of Coillín Bay where I thought there were plenty of green crabs. There's no better bait for wrasse in the month of September. I put a bit of wrasse in the pot, and the pot was full of green crabs in the morning.

We then sailed out and came to anchor at Dubh-leac (black flagstone) on Sceirde. We had about a stone-weight of periwinkles as well because the green crab is no use unless you put the periwinkle on the hook first as back bait. The periwinkle has the better grip. The shell is taken off the crab, and only a half of it or less is put on the hook. Fishing thread is tied around the crabmeat to keep it on the hook. All the wrasse gather around the crab. The crab is sweet, and it is excellent bait.

We had a fishing line each. We killed thirty-eight each, the first day. They were all fine fish. The second day we had thirty each. The third day we had only eighteen each. They were mostly wrasse and a few pollack. I salted and dried my own lot, and I have them for the winter for as long as it lasts.

Once the Feast of Saint Martin is past, the wrasse loses its sight. Its eyes turn white, and it doesn't see the bait.

It's on a fine day without a breath of wind you would catch a pollack.

April is when the wrasse is fattest. That's when it's full of roe. The wrasse spawns on the edge of the strands, under the edge of the seaweed.

OTTERS THAT ESCAPED FROM PÁDRAIC

I happened to go to the river for a can of water. It was a Sunday morning. There were four otters in one pool in the river. They were swimming around in the pool. When they felt my presence, two of them went upstream and the other two headed downstream. I followed the pair that went downstream till they went into the culvert under the road. I turned back again and saw one of the other pair. I began collecting stones and throwing them at it. I was throwing stones at it till I had a pain in my arm. It would barely have its snout above water when it would drag it down again, and it was difficult to hit it. It was another man, who was asleep in his bed at the time I saw it, who killed it. He skinned it and sold its skin.

The otter is very vicious. If it sinks its teeth it will not let go until it hears the bone cracking. Looking for fish is what brings it to the river. Early in the morning or late at night is when they are usually to be seen. I used to see the path they had made in the snow between two lakes.

PÁDRAIC TELLING ABOUT THE SEAL HE KILLED

I was gathering seaweed one evening. It was the beginning of a spring tide. I saw the seal on the side of a flagstone in the lower shore. It took me a long time to realize it wasn't a bird, until I saw it move. I stepped aside so that it wouldn't see me coming and so that I could go between it and the tide. It saw me, and when it did, it had further to go than I had. There was a great ebb, and the seal had no agility on the strand. I came before it, and it was making straight for me with its mouth open. When it came near enough to me, I stabbed it with the pitchfork. I thought I wasn't making any headway, and I hit it on the snout with the corner of the pitchfork, and it fell as soon as it got the blow. I had left it numbed, and I hit it five or six other blows until I killed it. I got it ready then by tying a rope around it and putting it on my back, and I brought it up onto the grass. I had a donkey for carrying seaweed at neap tide, and I said to myself the donkey would carry it home for me. When I tried to put the seal on the donkey's back, on the first sight of it the donkey upped and ran away. It cast off one of the creels and carried the other creel and the straddle a half mile with him. I followed it and set it up again. I took off my *báinín*[8] and blindfolded the donkey, and it didn't move again until the seal had been fixed and tied on top of the creels. It brought the seal home for me, and I skinned it and took a gallon out of it. The oil is good for the sails of boats. It would make the rough sail as smooth as a silk handkerchief.

PÁDRAIC MAC CON IOMAIRE (3)

Pádraic Mac Con Iomaire was a great traditional storyteller and historian. An Coimisiún Béaloideasa (formerly the Irish Folklore Commission, now Cnuasach Bhéaloideas Éireann/Irish Folklore Collection) has a great collection of the stories he told. He re-members everything he has seen, and he has a keen eye. It's that keen eye that has added such detail to all he has told about the birds. This is himself telling about his forefathers:

It was from Marcas Ó Laidhe, my grandfather, my mother's father, I mostly heard the stories. He lived in Maínis when he was very young and lived in Coillín for some time. He used to fish and work the land. He used to be storytelling to the young men when I was young.

My grandfather, Pádraic Mac Con Iomaire, was about to go to Galway one day. It was the herring season, and they had put the herrings into a cargo boat, a big boat, to bring them to Galway to be sold. The cargo boat was at anchor to the south of Roisín an Chalaidh (little headland of the landing place).

When the herrings had been loaded, my grandfather went home to his house, either to eat his meal or get his clothes. When he came back to go on board the big boat, the boat had sailed east without him. He immediately headed for Galway the roundabout way. The boat had a favorable wind, and she took only a little over six or seven hours to reach Galway. My grandfather was the first man to catch the boat's mooring rope on the quay wall in Galway when she came into the dock.

"The Lord save us!" said the boat's owner. "How did you get here? You must have been with the fairies."

"I was not," said Pádraic. "I walked every step of the way."

"I wouldn't believe," said the boat's owner, "that any racehorse in County Galway could do it."

When death caught up with my grandfather's father, there was no priest in this community. There was only one priest for this community and for Roundstone across the bay to the west. My grandfather walked the roundabout way to Roundstone for the priest, and he heard that he was in Leitir Seanbhaile (rough slope of the old village). He went from Roundstone to Leitir Seanbhaile, and the priest had gone to Leenaun by the time he got there. He followed him to Leenaun and caught up with him there. The priest came twenty-three miles on horseback and anointed the old man and didn't leave the house until he died.

My grandfather walked home. He had walked well over fifty miles that day.

PÁDRAIC MAC CON IOMAIRE TELLING
ABOUT THE KING OF SUNDAY'S WELL

The King of Sunday's Well is what the people around here call the holy well that's at the back of Croagh Patrick. It's within three miles of the Reek to the west, in the parish of Cill an Ghaobhair.[9]

People go on a pilgrimage there on a Sunday morning between the two Feasts of Our Lady in the Autumn.

This is not a long pilgrimage. There are three places for kneeling and praying. Seven Our Fathers, seven Hail Marys, and the Creed are to be said at each kneeling. You'll get up off your knees when you have finished the prayers, and you'll walk seven times around the cairn bareheaded and barefooted, without shoes or socks. You'll go to the next cairn then, and so on. You'll then walk all around the cemetery at the end, and you'll give alms for the poor and offer it up for the souls of the dead that are buried there.

I did the pilgrimage to The King of Sunday's Well myself once. I left Carna about twelve o'clock on a Friday, and I spent that night in a village they call Doire na Cloiche (wood of the stone) to the west of Leenaun on Killary Harbor. The following day I went across the Killary in a small boat. About twelve o' clock on Saturday I was in the village of Cill an Ghaobhair. I spent that night, until it was daybreak at about four o' clock on Sunday morning, in a house in the village. The Penny House they used to call it. They allowed you to spend the night there, without food or bed, if you paid a penny. There might be a few hundred people there through the night. They used to have music and dancing to keep the people from falling asleep. When they got tired dancing, if there was somebody who had a song, he would sing it, and maybe another nine or ten would follow him. Decent company, and the night was merry enough till morning.

In the morning when we went to make the pilgrimage, it was raining. I made the pilgrimage while fasting, without eating anything. When I had finished the pilgrimage, I walked twelve miles to Killary, to Bun Dorcha (Bundorragha, dark end). I came back across in a boat to Doire na Cloiche. There wasn't a bite to eat to be had in the house where I got it on my way over. The chapel was two and a half miles away, and I wanted to go to Mass. I caught the eleven o'clock Mass. I heard Mass. That was the chapel of An Criathrach (the swamp, near Kylemore).

It was still raining. I started walking again after Mass, making my way back home, and I couldn't get a bite to eat till I walked another fifteen miles, till I came to Cúl na Ceártan (smithy's corner, near Recess). I went into a house there. I asked the woman of the house to get me some food, whatever way she could, that I needed it for free or for buying. She had flour in the house—I saw a bag of flour in the corner of the house. She wasn't willing to go baking bread even if she was rewarded for her labor. Her husband came in, and he put a pot of potatoes on the fire and a fish. When the potatoes and fish were boiled, he told me to start eating the potatoes. I ate five or six potatoes and some of the fish. I walked from Cúl na Ceártan till I came to Carna, and it still raining. There was so much rainwater in my clothes and in my boots that I had to take off my boots and walk barefooted, and I wasn't long walking again when the road was hurting the soles of my feet. I had to put on my stockings again to save my feet, and there wasn't a sole left in my stockings that wasn't worn out before I reached home. I had daylight as far as Dúleitir (Dooletter). That's where night fell on me, within a mile of home. I slept easy that night. I was fairly tired. Maybe God rewarded me.

The storyteller explains that, "If someone in your house is unwell and if you promise to make the pilgrimage to The King of Sunday's Well and you make the pilgrimage, the person who is unwell will get well again. I was unwell when I made the pilgrimage, and I got well again."

PÁDRAIC TELLING ABOUT THE
PILGRIMAGE TO CROAGH PATRICK

I made the pilgrimage to Croagh Patrick twice. I went by motorcar to Westport, and I walked the rest of the way. The path up the Reek is slippery. Some of it is soft and muddy. The path was bad for nearly two parts of the way on account of too many people walking up and down. For the rest of the way, there were hard sharp stones and it got steeper. When I took a step, the stones were slipping down the slope from under my feet. I was nearly thrown two steps backwards at times. Nevertheless, I got to the top of the mountain. The first cairn where the people kneel is a short distance below the top. They say seven Hail Marys and the Apostles' Creed while on their knees. Then they go seven times around on their knees and say seven Hail Marys and the Apostles' Creed again. They will go from there to the top. There are four places for kneeling. Behind the chapel, there's the hollow where Saint Patrick used to sleep. The people, on their knees, say seven Our Fathers, seven Hail Marys, and the Apostles' Creed at this hollow, and they walk seven times on their bare knees around the hollow. They then walk in their bare feet around the other three hollows. The main pilgrimage is then to be made around the rim of all the various places seven times.

These seven times around are estimated to add up to a mile long, and on each of these seven rounds the cold blast of wind that comes up from Gleann na nDeamhan (demons' glen) can draw a tear from your eye with the cold on the warmest day of the year. Gleann na nDeamhan is the name of the glen stretching up from the lake to the east, where Saint Patrick banished all the devils and drove them into the lake.

If it's a fine day, when the white cap is lifted off the top of the Reek, there's a fine view to be had to the east and to the north. Achill Island is to be seen to the north, and Cliara (Clare Island), high and fairly wild, to the northwest. There's a fine view of green islands that would gladden your heart, smooth beaches, and sand dunes. When we have made the pilgrimage and are ready to go down, we like to look around us for fear we wouldn't ever come here again. We honor and thank God and Saint Patrick, and we go back down.

The sharp stones are again running down from under our feet, and we must have a big, long, strong stick to keep us on our feet going down the slope. We are coming onto muddy ground once more after having come down from the rough sharp stones. The path is soft and muddy. We try to jump from one hummock to another until we come down to the bottom. We bid farewell and a blessing to the Reek.

I saw people who went up and down barefooted. It was a painful pilgrimage for them. They were making a sacrifice, punishing the body.

SEÁN MAC CON RÍ (12) TELLING

ABOUT HIS NATIVE PLACE

I was born on the slope to the north of Dumhaigh Ithir (Dooye-her). The house was in the middle of the townland, and it was the highest house there when it was standing. It was a landmark for lobster fishermen, it was that high. I had a holding there, and I still have. The holding is sloping down to the border of Maíros, above the strand where the old cemetery is.

My mother's mother had a cousin, Micheál Ó Maoilchiaráin, who lived in Leitir Mealláin. He used to visit us in Dumhaigh Ithir and talk about Línseach Bhearna (Lynch of Barna) who had land in Leitir Mealláin. The Línseach had a book of prophecy, and he used to read it to Micheál Ó Maoilchiaráin. I never saw Micheál, but I heard the prophecy from people who heard it from him. It was Tióbóid de Búrca who taught it to me.

Sruth Sianach (Sianach stream) is in Maíros. Sianach was a bishop.[10] There was no particular day for making the pilgrimage at Sruth Sianach; you could go any Sunday you wanted. The (religious) brothers were in Maíros until the time of Elizabeth.

PÁDRAIC MAC DONNCHADHA (LIAM)

TELLING ABOUT SEÁN MAC CON RÍ

There was a good storyteller in Dumhaigh Ithir, a man they used to call Seán Veail Sheáin Mhic Eoin. He was of the Mac Con

Rí clan. He was an able young man, and he went to England to escape poverty and to earn his living sooner than fall in with the Protestant religion, as many people of the townland had done at the time. He was only a year in England when he began to lose his eyesight. He thought at the time that the heat of working in a furnace was the cause of it. He said to himself that he'd leave England and come home before he lost all his eyesight.

With a lively mind and good memory, he learned to be a fine speaker so that he could tell a story about the kingdoms of the world, how they lived and what they did. When the people of the townland saw how intelligent he was, they used to come to Seán whenever they had any spare time, for conversation and for his judgement on any matter they didn't already know about. In the end, they made him master of the whole townland. When many people from outside the townland heard Seán's stories, they came to him from near and far.

"Now," said Seán to them one day, "we'll never have a day's good fortune in this townland of ours until we find some way of driving out the Protestant religion, because it would only take a very small change in the weather for every man to lose the Catholic religion and to go over to the other side for the small gain they are getting for it."

They all spoke to one another, and they said that what Seán had said had the semblance of truth, and "we all may as well take his advice," they said. All the men came together to Seán and asked him what was the best way of driving them out.

"Now," said Seán, "sink their boats first, and they'll have no means of going to the town (i.e., Roundstone) or bringing anything home from there unless they go around by the road, and then we'll stop the cars being of any service to them." They did this, and the foreigners said to one another that they had no business staying there any longer. After that, only one man was left permanently to look after the church and the surrounding area. They continued to pay him for two years, hoping the people would convert and come back again, but in the end he too had to leave, and when the people got rid of him they knocked the roof off the church and off the minister's house and off the school-house and all. Only the ruins remain now, and never again will any man of that lot settle there. All of that happened on account of Seán Mac Con Rí and on account of the song he composed about the event.[11]

He (Seán Mac Con Rí) had a holding in Dumhaigh Ithir. His sisters married, and the place remained with Seán. He was living alone, and he was blind, and the local children were fetching cans of water for him and going to the shop. He wasn't able to do any work, and he spent every day walking from gable to gable outside. He had worn a path in the flagstone, walking from gable to gable. When a person would speak to him, he was able to recognize the voice immediately and welcome him, even if it was twenty years since he had heard it. I was living in Coillín. He had only seen me once. Ten years later when he heard my voice again, he recognized me immediately.

It is said that a Protestant bishop came over from England asking him to go over there to speak against the Catholic Church and that he'd be rich forever. Seán said that he wouldn't do such a thing.

TOMÁS MAC CON IOMAIRE (10)

It is very difficult to get Tomás Mac Con Iomaire to talk about himself. Long stories told by him are to be found in *Loinnir Mac Leabhair* as well as an account of himself. Here he tells of an adventure at sea:

We sailed out one evening. It was Thursday, the Feast of Corpus Christi. I never saw a warmer day. It was a very fine night until we had let out the net. It wasn't long until the sky closed in, and it looked like thunder and rain. It became very thundery and very wet. The wind went round to the northwest with the rain and strengthened into a strong gale. We began to set about lifting the net. The sea was so high and still rising in the gale that if we managed to pull in the net a fathom, it was sometimes swept out of our hands. It was as cold as a frosty morning, after such a warm day. When we had brought in the net, we set sail and we put the small sails to work instead of the big sails, the night was so wild.

The north wind had driven the boat so far south that it was ten o'clock before we got any sight of Aran, after sailing since four in the morning. The wind was coming straight from the north in the morning and a storm blowing, and we had to tack the boat as far as Aran. Each mountain of sea seemed as high as the mountains of Beanna Beola (Twelve Bens). When the water would recede from under the boat, she used to be down between two seas, and you'd think she'd never climb the mountain of sea that was coming down on top of her.

We came in between Árainn Mhór (more often called simply Árainn) and Inis Meáin. When we were past Oileán an Tuí (Straw Island, off Cill Rónáin), the sea was like a lake compared to the sea outside. We were inside in Cill Rónáin (Kilronan) at one o'clock. Some hookers weren't in until four in the afternoon.

When we were coming in, we saw the huge waves breaking on the cliffs of Aran. When you'd see that big wave coming, you'd think it would smother Aran, it was that high.

PARTHALÁN Ó GUAIRIM (BEAIRTLE RUA) (5)

In my grandmother's house is where I spent a great part of my life, said Beairtle Rua Ó Guairim to me while talking about his youth. I would rather have gone without food there than be with my own people. My grandfather used to work with boats. When he came home, he used to give me a penny. Tomás Ó hIarla used to come in, and he had a sally rod. I used to ask him for the rod.

"What will you give me for the rod?" he used to say.

"I'll give you a penny," I used to say, "when my grandfather comes home from Galway." He had a *gleoiteog* (a small sailing boat). He was drowned off Maínis.

I saw Máire Ní Cheallaigh who lived in Leitreach Ard Thoir (Letterard East). She was married to Pádraic Ó Domhnaill, and she used to spin flax. I used to be in her house when I was a child. She was a great woman for smoking tobacco, and I used to light the wisp of straw for her to light the pipe for fear she might stop spinning, because I used to have great fun with the spinning wheel. I saw the flax cut in fistfuls in Leitreach Ard. The linen would be dyed with oak bark and the roots of wild iris.

Long ago there was no lamp in the house, only rushes or *fíóga*. The rush was dipped in fish oil. A candlestick was made for the rush, an iron fork stuck in a block of wood with a broad base. Or maybe they would have a bog oak candle. The bog oak candle wouldn't be dipped; it had enough oil within itself. Or a cloth wick candle. They used to place the wick made of cloth in a scallop shell full of fish oil, with one end sticking out and aflame. It would soak up the fish oil from the scallop shell. They used to have a shell or iron melting pot too. (To melt animal grease in, before dipping the rushes in it.) At night the women used to be spinning or carding, or the men and women would be making nets out of linen thread for the fishing. Neighbors would have gathered in, to keep them awake and to tell stories. The story would be heard all over the house, and the child who was listening would be able to retell every story he had heard the following day.

SEOSAMH MAC DONNCHADHA (4)

Seosamh Mac Donnchadha from Aird Thiar is the greatest authority in Iorras Aithneach on the traditional history and lore of the Mac Donnchadha clan, and on the trading tradition that used to exist between Conamara and Guernsey. His people are around

here since the time of the O'Flahertys, and he can go back seven
generations, as far back as Aodh Buí Mac Donnchadha who was
drowned in Poll Aodha Bhuí near Oileán Mhic Dara. Drowning
has always been the fate of seagoing folk, and Seosamh's father
was drowned when Seosamh was only a youth. One day when
we were gathered in Maíros (Moyrus), telling stories and talking
about the old days, he told us about his father's drowning:

There's a dangerous foreshore on Fraoch-oileán (heather island). Many a boat was lost there. To the west of the island or to
the northwest is where my father was drowned, and the father of
this man beside me, Marcas Ó Maoilchiaráin, and two other men.
Four married men were going to pay rent. Robinson was collecting rent for Berridge. If you didn't have the rent on the appointed
day, you'd be served with a summons within a week, but if a tenant sent a bottle of poteen or a bribe to the summons server, you'd
be excused until you had the resource. There were people who
wouldn't give the bailiff a backhander, and they weren't given
any respite.

On March 28, 1892, my father Pádraic Mac Donnchadha,
Máirtín Ó Maoilchiaráin, Stiofán Mór Ó Maoilchiaráin, and
Seosamh Breathnach were going to Roundstone in a boat. Aircín
na hAirde (Ard creek) is where they sailed from on their way to
Roundstone. To the west of Fraoch-oileán there was another boat
going to Roundstone, and it was very near the boat the four men
were in. A whirlwind came up, and I suppose the boat was sunk
all at once. She lost the tack and she filled. The four men were
drowned. They were married. The bodies didn't come ashore,
nor did the boat.

The other boat that was near them didn't come to their rescue.
The wife of the man who was master of the boat had just had
a baby at home. When one of his crew told him the other boat
was lost and that they should turn back, he said he was more
concerned about his wife and child at home. His people had a
superstition that if they rescued someone from the sea, one of

themselves would be drowned. That superstition was current all over Conamara. The same man was drowned later, together with his two sons and four others, at the time of the Great War. A British vessel came alongside, and those on board threw a bomb into the boat in which the men were fishing. The boat was blown up, and all those aboard were drowned. There was never a word about it. 1917, in the month of May, was when the fishing boat was blown up.

Marcas Ó Maoilchiaráin was in the company in Maíros when Seosamh Mac Donnchadha was relating the above. The two men's fathers were drowned together, as has been told. Seosamh had a fit of anger as he was telling the story, anger at the cruelty of the rent collectors. There was a tremor in his voice as he remembered his father who was drowned when he himself was young. Marcas was as angry as Seosamh, but he didn't say a word. He was reared in Aird but moved up to Ros Rua twenty years ago. The sea is between him and Iorras Aithneach, and there are not many Irish speakers in his neighborhood. He was at the fair in Cashel and heard we were storytelling in Maíros. He didn't let the opportunity pass. He came here to us straight away, eleven miles, and stayed with us until after midnight. He is very correct in his Irish and has read a good deal of Irish literature.

PÁDRAIC Ó CLOCHARTAIGH (7)

I met Pádraic Ó Clochartaigh for the first time at Galway Docks. He definitely looked like a boatman and was dressed in island clothes—woolen homespun and flannel. He wasn't wearing a frock coat but a short *báinín* (a white homespun woollen jacket), and he wasn't wearing a tall or broad hat but a homespun tweed cap on top of his curly head of hair. His beard was short and curly, and there was a gleam of gold through the grey in it. He had a round keen face and small lively eyes. He was the epitome of a boatman above all I have ever seen, a boatman of the old style that hadn't changed from the time of Saint Peter. So well he should have the cut and appearance of a boatman. The sea has been the livelihood of his forbears since they first took possession of the shores of Conamara and the islands. They weren't reaping the benefit of the land until very recently, but the landlords were, who didn't love the land but coveted the rent. The Clohertys had to endure sea and strand, and had to plough the sea and produce its wealth. They cut the seaweed and shipped it. They hunted the basking shark, killed it, and sold its oil. They went to Guernsey off the coast of France and brought home a cargo unknown to the English fleet. They were great men in their day, and they are still great men.

Sailors are far more plentiful than boatmen at Galway docks at present, as the work of boats and the earnings of the boatmen have declined. As recently as fifty years ago and later, the Conamara boatmen were all over the bay. There used to be a hundred boats laden with seaweed in Kinvara, and they were more plentiful at the Galway moorings than anywhere else. Nowadays you wouldn't see one boatman against the hundred who used to be on the docks long ago. The seashore peat bogs have been depleted, and the selling of seaweed is nearly gone. The odd cargo still goes west from Galway to shopkeepers, and only for that very few boatmen would be seen on the quay wall, unlike the time when the butter used to come to Tadhg an Ime (Tadhg of the butter), fish to the fish market, seaweed to the farmers of East Galway, and turf from Roisín na Mainiach.

Pádraic Ó Clochartaigh is a man of the old style of living, and from the first day I met him at the docks, there was a bond of friendship between us. It wasn't long after that until he visited me. It was a very short visit as he only had a bit of a day, and he had a lot of *seanchas* to tell. It was obvious to me that he was a good witness of the sort of life the islanders lived when he was young and before that, and I promised myself I'd visit him in his own home when I could do so. His visit to me was in May 1933, and the following month I headed west to him one fine sweltering day. The heat was so great that you'd feel like doing as the Yank does and take off your coat. Pádraic Ó Gallchóir, who was in the car with me, knew the Ó Clochartaigh man too and had great regard for him. On our way west, a man asked us for a lift and we brought him with us. He was a man of sixty-five years or so, walked with a drag, and was heavy-footed from the heat. He wore heavy tweed clothes, without a coat or *báinín*, but a heavy woolen shirt and waistcoat. The men wear the same weight of clothes summer and winter for fear of catching a cold.

When he got his breath back and was sitting in the car with us, he was willing to talk, but he wasn't a *seanchaí* at all, and we soon found out why he was short of words. He was just three years back home from America where he spent twenty-six years paving streets in the city of Saint Paul. My interest grew when I heard the name of that city because it was in that same city that my father spent part of his life. The paving man never married, and when his working and earning days were over he came home. His manner of speech was as if he had never left Leitir Móir. He was slightly deaf, and you would think from his Irish that he spoke no other language over there. Many is the native Irish speaker like him that doesn't come home.

We stopped in front of Inis Léith, the bare island where the kelp-making went on when Sinéad Ní Sheachnasaigh was in this part of the country. The paving man went his way from us, and we reached Baile na Cille around four o'clock. The Ó Clochartaigh man's house is a half mile south of the road to Cuigéal Leitir Mealláin and about a mile from Cuigéal (narrow channel, between Leitir Mealláin and Gorumna). When we reached the house, we were told that Pádraic was on the sea, fishing, and that he would be coming ashore at the *cuainín* (little bay), and the little bay was a mile from the house. We headed for the little bay.

This side of Gorumna is flaggy and bare, with hardly even the scraw on the flagstone except in the hollows. Many of the hollows are under potatoes, and there are a few patches of oats to be seen. There are no houses between the storyteller's house and the shore. Between these islands and Aran is the great expanse of Galway Bay. The land of Gorumna is raised a little above the sea and is even more pleasant to the person who has his eyes open. The day was absolutely beautiful, and we could see Oileán Dá Bhruithneog and An tOileán Iarthach (western island, off the west end of Árainn), where the lighthouse is.

The storyteller had come ashore at the little bay before us and had moored his currach. It's a wooden currach he has that his brother's son made for him, and he's very proud of it because his brother was the first person in this country to make a wooden currach. We walked back to the house. On our way, the story-teller explained to us that all the land was covered with bog long ago and that the turf was cut down almost to the flagstone. The houses used to be between his own house and the sea until they moved inland one by one, and his own house is the nearest to the shore at present.

When we arrived back at the house, he hung the trawl line on the wall outside and laid the string of fish he had killed on the table. The house is on a height. It's a solid, spacious house, and there's a great view from the street. Cill Chiaráin Bay to the northwest and Cnoc Mordáin. Coillín hill to the west of us and Iorras Beag rising above it in the background. The Beanna Beola far off to the north and Caorán Aodha (Hugh's moorland hill) in Leitir Mealláin nearby. The house would need to be solid because there isn't a tree or a hedge around it or protection from any wind.

Pádraic's wife was in the chimney-corner. She's a kind, weak old woman. She had a cold, she said, but she didn't have much to say. The very moment we were seated, the storyteller was keen to begin, and his eyes were dancing in their sockets with the inter-est he showed in his speech and his story. There's a modesty in his manner of speaking, and he would never presume that there's anything in his memory you didn't already know yourself. But that doesn't diminish his desire to tell the story, quite the opposite. He began the story of "the smith who wasn't able to make anything but a colter for a plough." It's a long story, and I wrote it down because I took great pleasure in the fine speech, and Pádraic himself took even greater pleasure in the telling. We didn't leave a word behind us, and I was perspiring profusely before I had it all taken down. It wasn't the pen that I had difficulty with but the heat. The sun was intense outside, and I thought that we'd have shade and cool inside, but the kitchen was like an oven. There was a big, red fire on the hearth, as big as would be there on a winter's day. Neither Pádraic nor his wife in the chimney-corner showed the least sign of feeling the heat, but I was roasted myself. I had to ask the storyteller to come outside. We went outside and brought the chairs with us, and I was writing until seven o'clock.

Thirst is what put a stop to the work, and we went to the guest-house in Cuigéal. We weren't long there when the storytelling began again. Every storyteller has greater respect for the long stories than for the short ones, or for traditional lore based on reality, and it is difficult at times to lure them away from the long stories. It seems that the storyteller's reputation was based on the long stories in the old days. That's why the storytellers are so fond of them. I wouldn't like to say that the days of the long stories have come to an end; the speech in them is fine and eloquent, and their artistic turn of phrase doesn't ring false. They will be of benefit in the future to learners and writers. It wasn't too difficult, however, to lure Ó Clochartaigh onto the short stories, and we spent until ten o' clock listening to humorous little stories and writing them down, stories such as you would find in Aesop but with humor, the humor of the Irish language.

I was in Árainn a short time after that, and I met Ó Clochartaigh there. He was on a visit to the great Flaherty who made the film *Man of Aran*. It was Robin Flower who went to Cuigéal for him and brought him to Cill Mhuirbhigh (church of the sea plain).[12] I seized my opportunity that day, and I wrote down from Ó Clochartaigh's own mouth the lore about Cathal Óg Ó Flaithearta.

I was collecting traditional lore later in Iorras Aithneach. Cill Chiaráin Bay is between it and the islands, and the tellers of traditional lore there often mentioned them and the smugglers and notable people who lived in the islands. I wanted to get reliable information about them. I had an idea that Ó Clochartaigh would have that reliable information about them, and I left Carna one winter's day on my way to Gorumna. Pádraic was at a friend's house before me, and we spent the whole night in *seanchas*. When he got up to go home, the island was covered in snow and it was difficult to distinguish the road from the bog. But I had a knowledgable man beside me in the car, Seosamh Ó Mongáin, and we reached Baile na Cille without accident or mishap. We bade goodbye to the storyteller who had left us with a big bundle of stories. We had his own story and his people's story, Sinéad Ní Sheachnasaigh's story, the story of the bad days when there wasn't a chapel within seventeen miles of Baile na Cille, the story of the Gaelic priests, and the story of the poor scholars, and a great deal of the history of the islands for the past hundred years.

This man got a fine upbringing in the Irish language, and it is a source of great delight to himself to have such literature committed to memory. He knows a lot of poetry, and is able to recite his poems like music and do justice to the poet's words. Irish-language literature is a spoken literature, and its music and sweetness is lost unless it is given its due right in speech. Ó Clochartaigh would be a great master of learning if he had pupils around him and learning from him.

PÁDRAIC Ó CLOCHARTAIGH TELLING
ABOUT HIS PEOPLE AND HIS YOUTH

My own father's mother's father built the house I'm living in. Seán Ó Conghaile was his name. His mother was a Breathnach

(Walsh), Nuala Bhreathnach. Seán Nuala is what he was called. The Conghaile clan used to go to Guernsey.

My grandmother was born in this house. She married an Ó Clochartaigh man in Leitir Calaidh. That's where my father was born. A son of Seán Nuala was a boatwright in Baile na Cille (Ballynakill, village of the church, in Gorumna) in the old house. When my father was a young man, he came to that house to learn the trade from his uncle Peadar. Peadar married a *de Brún* woman in Eanach Mheáin. There was another uncle who never married, and my father settled in the place. The house was built over a hundred and fifty years ago.

Seán Nuala used to go to Guernsey as did Seán Óg, his son. They used to kill basking sharks to the west of Inis Bó Finne (Inishbofin). On May Day the boats used to sail from Leitir Mealláin (for the basking shark fishery).

My brother was a boatwright, and his son is a boatwright in Inis Ní. My brother was the first boatwright to make the wooden currachs, and there are many of them now.

Some of the Ó Clochartaigh men were poets. My grandfather's father was a first cousin of the Ó Clochartaigh man who composed *Cúirt an tSrutháin Bhuí*.[13] The Sruthán Buí is near Brandy Harbor, where Colm de Bhailís had his little house. Micil Dhiarmada Ó Clochartaigh was the poet's name.

When I was young, there were no bridges linking the islands between Béal an Daingin (Bealadangan, opening of the stronghold) and Ceann Gólaim (Golam Head, the westernmost point of Na hOileáin). The bridge between Leitir Mealláin and Gorumna was the first bridge to be built. Droichead an Daingin was the next bridge to be built between Béal an Daingin and Eanach Mheáin. Droichead na dTráchta (bridge of the crossings) between Eanach Mheáin and Leitir Móir was the next bridge, and after that Carraig an Logáin (rock of the hollow) bridge was built between Leitir Móir agus Gorumna. There's another small bridge going into Foirnis (outer island) between Leitir Mealláin and Foirnis.

Daighinis (ox island) is still without a bridge, as are Inis Airc (*orc*, sea monster, or *arc*, piglet), Inis Bearchain (St. Berchan's island), and An tOileán Iarthach (western island, off Ros Muc).

"In my father's time," said Pádraic, "there was no chapel in Gorumna; the nearest chapel to us was in Na Mine at An Tulaigh (the hillock; Tully), seventeen miles away. On the odd Sunday, the priest used to read Mass in a dwelling house. There wasn't a chapel in Leitir Mealláin, or Leitir Móir, or in An Cheathrú Rua, or in Ros Muc.

"Cnocán an Aifrinn (hillock of the Mass) is in Baile na Cille to the northwest of Baile na Cille lake. The Mass used to be read in the glen while people were on guard on the hillock. There's an old cemetery in old Baile na Cille and there's an old chapel still standing there. It is very old.

"I was born in 1862. I am seventy-four years old now. When I first learned to keep my ears wide open, there was no talk of Parnell or Davitt. Fishing, kelp-making, sowing potatoes, and raising pigs is what the people of the townland used to do when I was young. Weavers were plentiful. All they got was threepence a yard; they get eightpence now. We had cobblers in this part of the country, and they were able to make fine shoes. There was a tailor going around from house to house. I saw the flax being sown, threshed, and spun. My mother was able to make fishing nets and to weave the fishing line from linen thread. When a ball was made (of the thread), it was sent to Galway to be payed out into fishing lines by a man whose trade it was. The man who payed out the thread would make the fishing line fine or strong according to how you wanted it. There were three strands in every line, but some strands were stronger than others."

CRÍOCH / THE END

NOTES

1. The unsuccessful French invasion in Mayo in 1798. See Beiner 2007.
2. See Mac Giollarnáth, 1936b and 1941b.

3. *Mhúscraí:* from *múscraí,* dank, dark.

4. These places are on the inner reaches of Galway Bay, in both counties Galway and Clare.

5. *Cleithín (Cleheen):* ensiform cartilage, "fallen chestbone," treated by pulling back into position by hand or with a cup heated to form a vacuum.

6. *The Rose:* erysipelas.

7. *Fear Fábhairne:* a man fishing in another man's boat.

8. *Báinín:* a white (*bán*) jacket made of homespun woolen cloth.

9. *Reek: cruach,* from the shape of the mountain; *Cill an Ghaobhair:* church(yard) of proximity.

10. *Sianach:* Often identified with St. Mac Dara.

11. A local man who attended the Protestant Minister was punished by a group of neighbors one night by drowning his horse. The man's name was also Seán, and "Capall Sheáin" was the name of the song.

12. *Flaherty* stayed there while making his film in 1932–33.

13. *Cúirt an tSrutháin Bhuí:* "the court of the yellow stream," a famous comic and greatly exaggerated song of praise by Colm de Bhailís, praising his makeshift shelter as a "court." At de Bhailís's own request, Ó Clochartaigh composed the last few verses of the song.

—⚉—

MEET THE STORYTELLERS

LIAM MAC CON IOMAIRE

BRIEF NOTES AND SUMMARY DETAILS regarding the named contributors of this collection are provided below with references to secondary literature as appropriate.

MICHEÁL MAC DONNCHADHA (1864–1937),
ROISÍN NA MAINIACH, CARNA

The most complete account of Micheál Mac Donnchadha is to be found in an obituary written by Mac Giollarnáth and published in *Béaloideas* in 1941: "Sgéalaidhe Mór Ruisín na Maithnidheach." Mac Giollarnáth first met Micheál Mac Donnchadha in the company of Séamus Ó Duilearga on April 1, 1930 through the offices of Josie Mongan who arranged that Micheál would be present in his hotel when they had arrived from Galway. Legal affairs, court hearings presumably, made the first claim on Mac Giollarnáth's time, and Micheál Mac Donnchadha remained ensconced in a room with Séamus Ó Duilearga throughout the day, without even pausing for a meal, to ascertain the range and depth of his repertoire. Having compiled a preliminary list of one hundred stories as a result of their joint labors, the ediphone was then

Figure 15.1 Micheál Mac Donnchadha (1864–1937), Carna, April 1930. © National Folklore Collection, University College Dublin. Photographer: Séamus Ó Duilearga. Ref: M003.01.00299

produced that evening, and a queue of potential informants had assembled outside the room Ó Duilearga and Mac Donnchadha were working in. Mac Giollarnáth's entry to the inner sanctum precipitated an end to the recording, and after approximately ten continuous hours, both Mac Donnchadha and Ó Duilearga were exhausted. Following refreshments, Mac Donnchadha was driven home to Roisín na Mainiach at 1:30 a.m. or so. Funds were obtained from the Folklore Institute and the Rockefeller Institute to employ Peadar Ó Coincheanainn (1878–1957), a native of Inis Meáin, to transcribe Micheál Mac Donnchadha's material in his house on Bohermore in Galway city. Mac Giollarnáth expresses some doubts about Ó Coincheanainn's methodology as a faithful transcriber but acknowledges the extent of their work together. Aiming to collect any remaining material from Micheál Mac Donnchadha, a collaboration developed which saw the collection and compilation of a vast repertoire at Mongan's Hotel after court sittings and at Micheál's house in Roisín na Mainiach. Micheál's children—Sorcha and Marcas—also came into contact with Mac Giollarnáth and were considerable tradition bearers themselves. Micheál contributed to twenty-three of forty-five segments in "Tiachóg ó Iorrus Aintheach" (1932), two of ten stories in *Loinnir Mac Leabhair* (1936), thirty-one of seventy-two segments in "An Dara Tiachóg as Iorrus Aithneach" (1940), and seventy-four of two hundred fifty-one segments in *Annála Beaga ó Iorrus Aithneach* (1941). The information given in the introductory material to *Loinnir Mac Leabhair agus Sgéulta Gaisgidh Eile* (1936) also contextualises Micil Pháidín Shéamais Nábla Mac Donnchadha's extended contribution to Mac Giollarnáth's various collections throughout the 1930s and 1940s. Born in 1864, thin, small of stature, and lame due to childhood illness, Micheál apparently spent a good deal of time at the hearth listening to the lore of his father, his mother, and his maternal grandfather, Máirtín Réamoinn Mac Donnchadha. He attended the National School at Aird Mhór, and subsequently spent some fourteen years harvesting seaweed and kelp, locally in Iorras Aithneach and further away in north Co. Clare and along the inner reaches of Galway Bay. By 1936 he had more or less retired and was keeping sheep on commonage near his holding at Droim Shíodúch by Loch Caola, a half mile or so inland from the shoreline of

Roisín na Mainiach. Micheál Mac Donnchadha, 864MRM, is also referred to as Maidhcil 'ac Dhonncha in *The Irish of Iorras Aithneach*.[1]

PÁDRAIC MAC DONNCHADHA (LIAM),
AN COILLÍN, CARNA

Pádraic Mac Donnchadha (Liam) lived in An Coillín, but his father, Liam, originated in Roisín an tSamha, emigrated to America, placed some of his daughters in an orphanage in Clifden, and brought his wife, his son Pádraic, and a single daughter to Pittsburgh for two and half years before returning home to live with a brother of his. Following the death of his father, a house was built on common land in An Coillín by Pádraic and his mother. The local bailiff, Robinson, consented to the holding and struck rent of £1 on the property. Mac Giollarnáth reports that a slate roof was added to the house in 1933 and that Pádraic was cultivating potatoes on the holding and had acquired a field for stock nearby. An aunt of his mother was married to the poet Seán Bacach Ó Guairim. Pádraic Mac Donnchadha (Liam) contributed seventeen of forty-five segments in "Tiachóg ó Iorrus Aintheach" (1932), five of seventy-two segments in "An Dara Tiachóg as Iorrus Aithneach" (1940), and fifty-two of two hundred fifty-one segments in *Annála Beaga ó Iorrus Aithneach* (1941). In an account of Domhnall Ó Cearbhaill's folklore collection in Iorras Aithneach, Máire Uí Chuinneáin reports that Pádraic Mac Donnchadha (Liam), or Pat Bhilly, also supplied tales and lore to Ó Cearbhaill who published this material in the *Irish Weekly Independent* between 1934 and 1939. Séamus Ennis, working with Colm Ó Caodháin, also collected songs from Peait Bhillí Mac Donncha, who was related to Colm Ó Caodháin, on June 9, 1944. He died in 1955. Pádraic Mac Donnchadha (Liam), 875PCO, is also referred to as Pait Bhilí/Bhile 'ac Dhonncha in *The Irish of Iorras Aithneach*.[2]

PÁDRAIC MAC CON IOMAIRE (1869– 1962), AN COILLÍN, CARNA

Pádraic Mac Con Iomaire is described in *Conamara Chronicles* as a renowned storyteller and custodian of traditional lore. Considerable material was collected from him by Liam Mac Coisdeala and Séamus Ennis for the Folklore Commission. His paternal grandfather also named Pádraic Mac Con Iomaire was renowned for walking great distances. His maternal grandfather was Marcas Ó Laidhe, from Maínis originally. Pádraicín Mhacaí, as he was known locally, married Máirín Pháidín Choilm Nic Con Iomaire from Fínis Island in 1901, and they had eight children, one of whom, Ciarán, assisted his father as an informant for Heinrich Wagner's *Linguistic Atlas of Irish Dialects* at point forty-six. Nollaig Mac Congáil reports that Heinrich Wagner spent an entire month with Pádraic Mac Con Iomaire and collected a great deal of material from him. Although Wagner passed away in 1988, thirteen tales, songs, and stories were subsequently published in *Zeitscrift für celtische Philologie* in 1995. Over one hundred stories in the tradition of Aesop's fables were collected by Domhnall Ó Cearbhaill (1891–1963) from him and published weekly in the *Evening Herald* between November 1941 and December 1942. This material was brought together, edited and reissued in 2009 as *Aesop i gConamara*. Pádraic Mac Con Iomaire contributed three of forty-five segments in "Tiachóg ó Iorrus Aintheach" (1932), fifteen of seventy-two segments in "An Dara Tiachóg as Iorrus Aithneach" (1940), and twenty-four of two hundred fifty-one segments in *Annála Beaga ó Iorrus Aithneach* (1941). Pádraic Mac Con Iomaire, 869PCO, is also referred to as Pádraicín Mhacaí 'ac Con Iomaire in *The Irish of Iorras Aithneach*.[3]

SEOSAMH MAC DONNCHADHA (1880–1952), AN AIRD THIAR, CARNA

Seosamh Mac Donnchadha is described by Seán Mac Giollarnáth as being the knowledgeable authority on the origins of the Mac

Figure 15.2 Pádraic Mac Con Iomaire (1869–1962),
An Coillín, July 1942. © National Folklore
Collection, University College Dublin. Photog-
rapher: Séamus Ó Duilearga. Ref: M003.01.00187

Donnchadha family and the history of trade between Conamara
and Guernsey in the English Channel. He can claim descent from
Aodh Buí Mac Donnchadha. His father Pádraic Mac Donnchadha
(Peaitsín), along with three others, was drowned at sea on March
28, 1892 while sailing to Roundstone. Joe Pheaitsín or Joe Phádraig Sheáin Fhéilim (1880–1952) married Anna Phádraig Sheáin
Risteard Nic Dhonnchadha from An Aircín, An Aird Thiar, and
they had ten children, one of whom was renowned sean-nós singer
Seán 'ac Dhonncha or Johnny Joe Pheaitsín (1919–1996). Seosamh
Mac Donnchadha contributed three of seventy-two segments in
"An Dara Tiachóg as Iorrus Aithneach" (1940) and forty-three of
two hundred fifty-one segments in Annála Beaga ó Iorrus Aithneach (1941). Seosamh Mac Donnchadha, 876JAI, is also referred
to as Jó 'ac Dhonncha in The Irish of Iorras Aithneach.[4]

PARTHALÁN Ó GUAIRIM, LEITREACH ARD, CARNA

Mac Giollarnáth's edition of the tale "Artúr Mór Mac Rí i n-Éirinn" in *Béaloideas* records Beairtle Guairim's age as sixty-two in 1934, which would give 1872 as year of birth. Beairtle Rua was raised in his grandmother's house, by his own preference, and his grandfather was a boatman. Beairtle Ó Guairim contributes two of seventy-two segments in "An Dara Tiachóg as Iorrus Aithneach" (1940) and eleven of two hundred fifty-one segments in *Annála Beaga ó Iorrus Aithneach* (1941). Beairtle Ó Guairim's referential in *The Irish of Iorras Aithneach* is 870BLA.[5]

SÉAMAS Ó CONGHAILE, AN AIRD, CARNA

Although this contributor is recorded in the list of contributors at the beginning of *Conamara Chronicles*, no further reference is made to the contributor throughout the work.[6]

PÁDRAIC Ó CLOCHARTAIGH, BAILE NA CILLE, GORUMNA ISLAND

Seán Mac Giollarnáth first encountered Pádraic Ó Clochartaigh by Galway docks where his appearance as a boatman in a short flannel and tweed cap made a great impression on him. Sporting a short, curly, graying beard, Ó Clochartaigh had a round face and small, lively eyes. Ó Clochartaigh visited Mac Giollarnáth at his home in May 1933, but it appears that time was short and insufficient for the satisfactory collection of lore, and on a very warm day in June 1933, Mac Giollarnáth journeyed to Baile na Cille on Gorumna Island to meet with Pádraic Ó Clochartaigh who was out fishing. Nevertheless he entertained Mac Giollarnáth at his house later that evening and at Óst na nOileán—The Hotel of the Isles—in Cuigéal in Leitir Mealláin. Living on the other side of Cill Chiaráin Bay, Pádraic Ó Clochartaigh was able to provide a complementary perspective on the links between Iorras Aithneach and Ceantar na nOileán, the archipelago consisting of Eanach Mheáin, Leitir Móir, Garmna (Gorumna Island), and Leitir Mealláin. His great-grandfather was Seán Nuala Ó Conghaile (Conneely) who traded with Guernsey. Pádraic claims that his brother was the first boatwright to make a wooden currach. He was distantly related to the poet Micil Diarmada Ó Clochartaigh. Born in 1862, he was seventy-four when Mac Giollarnáth recorded tales from him in 1936. Pádraic Ó Clochartaigh was suggested to Séamus Ó Duilearga as a potential participant in Robert Flaherty's 1935 film, *Oidhche Sheanchais*, and appears to have spent two periods in June and July 1933 in Árainn as part of the preparations for the production. Seán Ó Briain was also considered (see 9 below), but Seáinín Tom Sheáin Ó Dioráin (c1870–1935) was eventually chosen. Pádraic Ó Clochartaigh contributes twelve of two hundred fifty-one segments in *Annála Beaga ó Iorrus Aithneach* (1941).[7]

PARTHALÁN MAC DONNCHADHA, AN AIRD THIAR, CARNA

Parthalán Mac Donnchadha contributes three of seventy-two segments in "An Dara Tiachóg as Iorrus Aithneach" (1940) and two of two hundred fifty-one segments in *Annála Beaga ó Iorrus Aithneach* (1941). Beairtle Mac Donnchadha, 879PAI, is also referred to in *The Irish of Iorras Aithneach*.[8]

SEÁN Ó BRIAIN (1852–1934), LOCH CONAORTHA, CILL CHIARÁIN

Seán Mac Giollarnáth provides an atmospheric portrait of Seán Ó Briain in the introductory material to *Loinnir Mac Leabhair agus Sgéulta Gaisgidh Eile* (1936) as a tall, broad eighty-year-old, possessing of a fine nose, long cheek, and kindly face with sharp, bright eyes. The situation of his house in Loch Conaortha is

Figure 15.3 Seán Ó Briain (1852–1934), Loch Conaortha, 1930. © National Folklore Collection, University College Dublin. Photographer: Séamus Ó Duilearga. Ref: M003.01.00101

described with his boat lying up at the gable end of his house, and his industry on land and at sea receives favorable comment. He apparently worked as a steward or bailiff at Gabhlán near Doire Iorrais. His father's ancestors hailed from Cill Bhríde, near Fionnaithe (Finny) by Loch Measca, but Ó Briain has lived on the easterly fringe of Iorras Aithneach since he was two years of age. He claims to have been confirmed in the Roman Catholic religion by Archbishop John MacHale (1789–1881) on the same day as fellow contributor Micheál Mac Donnchadha. In late December 1892, Seán Ó Briain encounters Alma and Jeremiah Curtin and apparently supplies four stories for the collection *Hero-tales of*

Ireland (1894) during a period of ten days or so, working through the parish clerk, Séamas Ó Laidhe, and a man of the surname Ó hUaithnín or Greene, apparently from Roisín na Mainiach. Seán Ó Briain contributed three of ten stories in *Loinnir Mac Leabhair* (1936) and six of seventy-two segments in "An Dara Tiachóg as Iorrus Aithneach" (1940) but strangely does not appear to have made a directly referenced contribution to any of the segments in *Annála Beaga ó Iorrus Aithneach* (1941) despite his presence on the Index of Contributors. It appears that Seán Ó Briain was amongst the preferred choices for the role of scéalaí in Robert Flaherty's film *Oidhche Sheanchais*. Travel to Árainn was not considered a difficulty, but traveling to London to facilitate sound recording and dubbing proved more of a challenge. However, Brian Ó Catháin has published an account compiled by a daughter of Seán Ó Briain's, Mary O'Brien, which indicates that tailoring and other preparations had been made for the trip to Árainn prior to Ó Briain's illness and death on January 1, 1934. Séamus Ó Duilearga describes Ó Briain as "the finest storyteller I ever encountered in my travels throughout the Gaeltacht of Ireland" in an edition of three tales told by Seán Ó Briain and published posthumously in 1962. Seán Éadbhaird Ó Briain's designation as informant is 852SbLC in *The Irish of Iorras Aithneach* (2007).[9]

TOMÁS MAC CON IOMAIRE, AN COILLÍN, CARNA

Tomás Mac Con Iomaire was a brother of Pádraic Mac Con Iomaire (3 above) and the youngest of four siblings. It is thought he was born c.1874. Writing in *Loinnir Mac Leabhair agus Sgéulta Gaisgidh Eile* (1936), Mac Giollarnáth reports that Tomás was healthy, robust, a skilled boatman, and an industrious worker of his holding. A calm man who had apparently read a book of fiannaíocht stories on Oileán Máisean (Mason Island), Tom Mhacaí contributed four of ten stories in *Loinnir Mac Leabhair* (1936), five of seventy-two segments in "An Dara Tiachóg as Iorrus

Aithneach" (1940), and three of two hundred fifty-one segments in *Annála Beaga ó Iorrus Aithneach* (1941). Tomás Mac Con Iomaire was one of the participants in an Irish government scheme to record Irish dialects. Under the direction of Dr. Wilhelm Doegen (1877–1967), his assistant Karl Tempel recorded Tomás Mac Con Iomaire and other informants from Connacht in September 1930 at University College, Galway, as it then was. Tomás Mac Con Iomaire, 875TCO, is also referred to as Team Mhacaí 'ac Con Iomaire in *The Irish of Iorras Aithneach*.[10]

SEOSAMH Ó MONGÁIN (1880–1951), TD, CARNA

Seosamh Ó Mongáin, Joseph William Mongan, or Josie Mongan, as he was known locally, was a Cumann na nGaedheal and later Fine Gael Teachta Dála (member of parliament) for Galway West between 1927 and 1951, with the exception of the term of the eighth Dáil between 1933–1938. Mongan was a grandson of Loideán Mór or Máirtín Ó Loideáin (Lydon) and owned and ran a hotel and a shop in Carna. He was first president of the Irish Hotel Federation 1937–47 and a founder member of the Connemara Pony Breeders' Society. A brother, James, ran a public house across the road from the hotel. Mongan's Hotel was frequented by a range of travelers such as Micheál Mac Liammóir, Hilton Edwards, Margaret Burke Sheridan, and John McCormack in addition to prominent members of the Cumann na nGaedheal party such as W. T. Cosgrave, Ernst Blythe, and James Dillon. Seán Mac Giollarnáth stayed regularly at the hotel and received and recorded his collaborators here. Josie Mongan contributed three of two hundred fifty-one segments in *Annála Beaga ó Iorrus Aithneach* (1941).[11]

SEÁN MAC CON RÍ, LEITIR DAIMH, ROUNDSTONE

Originally from Dumhaigh Ithir, Seán Mac Con Rí or Seán Veail Sheáin Mhic Eoin, is thought to have been born in 1852 and was

Figure 15.4 Seán Mac Con Rí, Leitir Daimh,
Roundstone, 1931. © National Folklore Collec-
tion, University College Dublin. Photographer:
Séamus Ó Duilearga. Ref: M003.01.00184

living in Leitir Daimh near Roundstone when Mac Giollarnáth
collected material from him. Seán Mac Con Rí emigrated to England and Scotland in his youth, worked in a coal mine, suffered
an accident, and was blinded at the age of twenty-four. On his
return home, he spent eleven years living alone until going to live
with a married sister. Seán Mac Con Rí was a sworn member of
the Irish Republican Brotherhood from his days in Scotland. It is
said that the Irish Church Mission School in Maíros was effect-
ively closed as a result of a satiric song composed by Seán Mac Con

Rí. Seán Mac Con Rí contributed a single segment of forty-five to "Tiachóg ó Iorrus Aintheach" (1932), a single story in *Loinnir Mac Leabhair* (1936), a single segment of seventy-two in "An Dara Tiachóg as Iorrus Aithneach" (1940), and eight segments of two hundred fifty-one in *Annála Beaga ó Iorrus Aithneach* (1941). Seán Mac Con Rí, 1852SDU, is also referred to as Seán Veail 'ac Con Raoi in the *The Irish of Iorras Aithneach*.[12]

MÁIRE NÍ DHOMHNAILL, CALADH AN CHNOIC, CARNA

The sole female contributor recorded by Séan Mac Giollarnáth in this collection. The single tale "Big Marcas Mac Cualáin" is attributed to her. In relation to gender and folklore collection in general, Mac Giollarnáth makes the following statement in his short monograph, *Conamara*: "I have not met many women who could tell any of the old tales, but women folk are gifted in conversation in their own little meetings at knitting or wool-carding, as you may judge from the frequent laughter of their exclusive gatherings."[13]

TOMÁS Ó MÁILLE, COILL MHÍOLCON

One short three-line segment is attributed to Tomás Ó Máille. The placename is originally rendered as Coill a' Méileacáin, which we take to signify Coill Mhíolcon or Kilmeelickin or more commonly known as Béal Átha na mBreac. This townland is adjacent to Muintir Eoin, the home of the distinguished Ó Máille family— Pádraic Ó Máille TD (1878–1946), Micheál Ó Máille (1879–1911), and Tomás Ó Máille (1880–1938) who was Professor of Modern Irish Language and Literature in University College, Galway from 1909 until his death. It is likely though that this Tomás Ó Máille refers to a first cousin of the Ó Máille brothers, Tommy Ó Máille, who introduced the accomplished storyteller Micheál Breathnach (1864–1943) from An Mám to Séamus Ó Duilearga.[14]

LIAM BAIRÉAD, AN COILLÍN, CARNA

Contributor of a single segment, "Ard Castle and Mad Tadhg," in *Annála Beaga ó Iorrus Aithneach* (1941).

MÁRTAN Ó MÁLÓID, COUNTY COUNCILLOR, CARNA

Máirtín Ó Málóid (Martin Mylotte) was originally from Cre-evagh, Neale, Co. Mayo and married Mary Kate Mongan, a sister of Josie Mongan (11). Mylotte served several terms on Galway County Council for Cumann na nGaedheal and Fine Gael, beginning in 1925. One of his sons, Máirtín (Meaic) Mylotte, acquired a public house from his uncle James Mongan, which came to be known as Tigh Mheaic. It appears that Ó Málóid contributes a single short segment, "Mac Donnchadha of the Four Penny Bit."[15]

PÁDRAIC MAC DONNCHADHA
(ÉAMOINN), AN AIRD, CARNA

Contributor of a single short segment regarding the exorbitant level of rent exacted by the Law Life Assurance Company in respect of their holdings at Más and Cnoc Buí.

ISAAC Ó CONAIRE (1886–1942),
SEANTALAMH, GALWAY

Born in Galway city, Isaac Ó Conaire (Conroy) was a son of Tomás Ó Conaire and Nóra Nic Dhonnchadha from Crapach in Leitir Mealláin (Lettermullen). He had two brothers, Micheál and the acclaimed writer Sean-Phádraic Ó Conaire (1882–1928). Isaac resided in Shantalla, Galway when the *Conamara Chronicles* were being compiled. His uncle, Peter Joseph (PJ) Conroy, owned a public house in Cill Chiaráin and was married to Mary

Mylotte, a sister of Máirtín Ó Málóid (16). Contributor of two segments concerning "Tobacco from America" and "O'Flaherty of Aghnanure."[16]

LMCI
April 2019

NOTES

1. See Mac Giollarnáth 1936b, xvii–xxi; Ó Súilleabháin 1952, 295, 300; Ó Súilleabháin and Caulfield 2011, 267, 273; Robinson 2011, 199, 242; and Ó Curnáin 2007, 13.

2. See Mac Giollarnáth 1941a, 319; uí Ógáin 2009, 449; Máire Uí Chuinneáin in Mac Congáil 2009, 20; Robinson 2011, 133, 291; and Ó Curnáin 2007, 13.

3. See Ó Súilleabháin 1952, 287–302; Ó Súilleabháin and Caulfield 2011, 257–270); uí Ógáin 2009, 439–40; McGonagle and Wagner 1995, 94; Máire Uí Chuinneáin in Mac Congáil 2009, 41–43; Robinson 2011, 155–56; Ó Curnáin 2007, 13.

4. See Mac Giollarnáth 1941a, 353; uí Ógáin 2009, 443–44; Robinson 2011, 118; Ó Curnáin 2007, 13.

5. See Mac Giollarnáth 1934a, 342; 1941a, 350; Ó Curnáin 2007, 13.

6. There are no references to this contributor in any of Mac Giollarnáth's collections.

7. See Mac Giollarnáth 1941a, 355–66; Ó hÍde 2019, 43–45, 243.

8. See Ó Curnáin 2007, 13, 22.

9. See Mac Giollarnáth 1936b, xiii–xvi; Bourke 2019, 25; Ó Duilearga 1962, 154; Ó hÍde 2019, 47; Ó Catháin 2004, 219–20; Ó Curnáin 2007, 13, 21.

10. See Doegen: https://www.doegen.ie/ga/node/2307; Mac Giollarnáth 1936b, xxi–xxiv; 1941a, 348.

11. See Mac Con Iomaire 2009, 91–94; Robinson 2011, 174, 176; uí Ógáin 2009, 553.

12. See Mac Giollarnáth 1936b, xxiv–xxvi; 1941a, 345; Robinson 2011, 137–38; Ó Curnáin 2007, 13.

13. See Mac Giollarnáth 1954, 50.

14. See Robinson 2011, 72–73; Nic Giolla Chomhaill 2018, 21; 2019, 7; Mac Giollarnáth 1934d, 432.

15. See Mac Con Iomaire 2007, 99.

16. See Mac Con Iomaire 2007, 98–99; Robinson 2011, 11.

BIBLIOGRAPHY

A Búrc, Éamon, Liam Mac Coisdeala, and Kevin O'Nolan. 1982. *Eochair, Mac Rí in Éirinn/Eochair, a king's son in Ireland*. Dublin: Comhairle Bhéaloideas Éireann, University College Dublin.

Almqvist, Bo. 1977–1979. "The Irish Folklore Commission: Folklore and Legacy." *Béaloideas* 45/47:6–26.

Andrews, Hilary. 2001. *The Lion of the West: A Biography of Archbishop John MacHale*. Dublin: Veritas Publications.

Becker, Heinrich. 1997. *I mBéal na Farraige: Scéalta agus Seanchas faoi Chúrsaí Feamainne ó Bhéal na nDaoine*. Indreabhan: Cló Iar-Chonnachta.

Beiner, Guy. 2007. *Remembering the Year of the French: Irish Folk History and Social Memory*. Madison: University of Wisconsin Press.

Blake, Henry. 1825. *Letters from the Irish Highlands*. London: J. Murray.

Bourke, Angela. 2003. "Legless in London: Pádraic Ó Conaire and Éamon a Búrc." *Éire-Ireland*, 38 (3&4): 54–67. [See also Partridge, Angela]

———. 2009. "The Myth Business: Jeremiah and Alma Curtin in Ireland, 1887–1893." *Éire-Ireland* 44 (3&4): 140–70.

———. 2016. *Voices Underfoot: Memory, Forgetting, and Oral Verbal Art*. Hamden, CT: Quinnipiac University Press.

———. 2019. "Alma agus Jeremiah Curtin i gConamara." In *Life, Lore and Song: Essays in Irish Tradition in Honour of Ríonach uí Ógáin*, edited by K. Fitzgerald, B. Ní Fhloinn, M. Ní Úrdail, and A. O'Connor, 19–27. Dublin: Four Courts Press.

Breathnach, Diarmuid, and Máire Ní Mhurchú. 2014. "Mac Giollarnáth, Seán (1880–1970)." *Beathaisnéis*. https://www.ainm.ie/Bio.aspx?ID=276. Accessed January 2019.

Breathnach, Micheál and Séamus Ó Duilearga. 1936. "Mac Dobharnáin, Mac Rí na Beinne Brice." *Béaloideas* 6 (2): 298–312.

Briody, Micheál. 2007. *The Irish Folklore Commission 1935–1970: History, Ideology, Methodology.* Helsinki: Finnish Literature Society/SKS.

———. 2010. "Ceapadh Chéad Choimisiún Béaloideasa Éireann." *Béaloideas* 78:168–86.

Brown, Charles R. 1900. "The Ethnography of Carna and Mweenish, in the Parish of Moyruss, Connemara." *Proceedings of the Royal Irish Academy,* no. 6 (1889–1901): 503–34.

Curtin, Jeremiah. 1894. *Hero-tales of Ireland.* Boston: Little, Brown and Company.

Dallas, Ann Biscoe. 1872. *Incidents in the Life and Ministry of the Rev. Alex. R.C. Dallas, A.M.* London: J. Nisbet.

de Bhaldraithe, Tomás. 1953. *Gaeilge Chois Fhairrge: an deilbhíocht.* Dublin: DIAS.

———. (editor) 1985. *Foirisiún Focal as Gaillimh: Deascán Foclóireachta 4.* Dublin: RIA.

de Bhaldraithe, Tomás, Hans Hartmann and Ruairí Ó hUiginn (eds.). 1996. *Airneán: Eine Sammlung von Texten aus Carna, Co. na Gaillimhe.* Tübingen: Niemeyer.

Delargy, James Hamilton. 1945. "The Gaelic Story-teller: With Some Notes on Gaelic Folk-tales." Sir John Rhys Memorial Lecture. *Proceedings of the British Academy* 31:177–221. [See also Ó Duilearga, Séamus]

Edgeworth, Maria. 1950. *Tour in Connemara and The Martins of Ballinahinch.* London: Constable.

First Report of the Commissioners of Inquiry into the State of Irish Fisheries. 1836. Dublin.

Gibbons, Erin. 1991. *Conamara Faoi Cheilt—Hidden Conamara.* Letterfrack, Co. Galway: Connemara West Press.

Hardiman, James. 1975. *The History of the Town and County of the Town of Galway: From the Earliest Period to the Present Time.* Galway: Kennys Bookshops and Art Galleries.

Lever, Charles. 1856. *The Martins of Cro' Martin.* London: Chapman and Hall.

Mac an Iomaire, Séamas. 1938. *Cladaí Chonamara.* Dublin: Oifig an tSoláthair.

Mac an Rí, Seosamh. 2000. "Carna". In *Pobal na Gaeltachta: a scéal agus a dhán,* edited by Gearóid Ó Tuathaigh, Liam Lillis Ó Laoire, and Seán Ua Súilleabháin, 409–26. Indreabhán: Cló Iar-Chonnacht.

Mac Coisdeala, Liam, ed. 1944. "Dhá Amhrán don Edifón." *Béaloideas* 14 (1/2): 271–73.

———. 1946. "Im' Bhailitheoir Béaloideasa." In *Béaloideas* 16, No. 1/2, 141–71.

Mac Congáil, Nollaig. 2003. "Man of Aran agus Scannán Gaeilge le Robert Flaherty." *Feasta* 56 (2): 19–21. [See also McGonagle, Noel]

———, ed. 2009. *Aesóp i gConamara.* Galway: Arlen House.

Mac Con Iomaire, Liam, trans. 1992. *Conamara Theas: Áit agus Ainm.* Dublin: Coiscéim.

———. 1997. *Conamara: An Tír Aineoil.* Indreabhán: Cló Iar-Chonnacht.

———, trans. 2002. *Camchuairt Chonamara Theas.* Dublin: Coiscéim.

———. 2007. *Seosamh Ó hÉanaí: Nár Fhágha Mé Bás Choíche.* Indreabhán: Cló Iar-Chonnacht.

Mac Giollarnáth, Seán, trans. 1925. *Saoghal Éanacha.* Dublin: Oifig Díolta Foillseacháin Rialtais.

———, ed. 1929. "Trí Sgéal ar an Sionnach." *Béaloideas* 2 (1): 90–94.

———. 1931. *Fí-fá-fum.* Dublin: Oifig Díolta Foillseacháin Rialtais.

———, ed. 1930a. "Cóitín Luachra." *Béaloideas* 2 (4): 333–38.

———. 1930b. "Peadar Mac Tuathaláin." *Béaloideas* 2 (3): 326–30.

———, ed. 1932a. "Sgéal Sméid." *Béaloideas* 3 (3): 342–49.

———, ed. 1932b. "Tiachóg ó Iorrus Aintheach." *Béaloideas* 3 (4): 467–501.

———, ed. 1934a. "Artúr Mór Mac Rí i n-Éirinn." *Béaloideas* 4 (3): 331–42.

———, trans. 1934b. *Éirghe na Gealaidhe.* Dublin: Oifig Díolta Foillseacháin Rialtais.

———, ed. 1934c. *Peadar Chois Fhairrge.* Dublin: Oifig Díolta Foillseacháin Rialtais.

———, ed. 1934d. "Seán a' Droma." *Béaloideas* 4 (4): 414–24.

———, trans. 1935. *Ríoghacht na nÉan.* Dublin: Oifig Díolta Foillseacháin Rialtais.

———, trans. 1936a. *Emil agus na lorgairí.* Dublin: Oifig Díolta Foillseacháin Rialtais.

———, ed. 1936b. *Loinnir Mac Leabhair agus Sgéalta Gaisgidh Eile.* Dublin: Oifig Díolta Foillseacháin Rialtais.

———, ed. 1940a. "An Dara Tiachóg as Iorras Aithneach." *Béaloideas* 10 (1/2): 3–100.

———, trans. 1940b. *Féilire na nÉan.* Dublin: Oifig Díolta Foillseacháin Rialtais.

———, ed. 1941a. *Annála Beaga ó Iorrus Aithneach.* Dublin: Oifig an tSoláthair.

———. 1941b. "Sgéalaidhe Mór Ruisín na Maithnidheach." *Béaloideas* 11 (1/2): 143–49.

———, ed. 1943. "Sliocht de Sheanchas Mhicheáil Bhreathnaigh." *Béaloideas* 13 (1/2): 102–29.

———, ed. 1946. "Seanchas Beag Thuama." *Béaloideas* 16 (1/2): 72–90.

———, trans. 1947a. *Cladach na Fairrge*. Dublin: Oifig an tSoláthair.

———, ed. 1947b. "Seanchas Fola." *Béaloideas* 17 (1/2): 113–30.

———. 1949a. *Cúdar agus Scéalta Eile*. Dublin: Brún agus Ó Nualláin.

———. 1949b. *Mo Dhúthaigh Fhiáin*. Dublin: Brún agus Ó Nualláin.

———. 1954. *Conamara*. Dublin: Cultural Relations Committee of Ireland at the Three Candles.

Mac Giollarnáth, Seán, and Diarmuid Ó Cearbhaill. 2001. "Pádraic Ó Conaire." *Journal of the Galway Archaeological and Historical Society* 53:187–89.

———. 2005. "Patrick H. Pearse: A Sketch of His Life." *Journal of the Galway Archaeological and Historical Society* 57:139–50.

———. 2006. "James Connolly: A Study of His Work and Worth." *Journal of the Galway Archaeological and Historical Society* 58:136–55.

———. 2012. "Seanchas Fola: Folklore from East Galway." *Journal of the Galway Archaeological and Historical Society* 64:106–27.

MacKillop, James. 2004. *A Dictionary of Celtic Mythology*. Oxford: Oxford University Press.

Mac Murchaidh, Ciarán. 2012. "*Seanmóirí* an Easpaig Séamas Ó Gallchóir: eagráin, aistriúcháin agus aidhmeanna." In *Féilscríbhinn do Chathal Ó Háinle*, edited by Eoin Mac Cárthaigh and Jürgen Uhlich, 417–44. Indreabhán: Cló Iar-Chonnacht.

Mahon, William J., ed. 1991. *Doctor Kirwan's Irish Catechism by Thomas Hughes*. Cambridge, Mass.: Pangur Publications.

McGonagle, Noel and Heinrich Wagner. 1995. "Téacsanna as Carna." *Zeitschrift für celtische Philologie* 47:93–175. [See also Mac Congáil, Nollaig]

Morley, Vincent. 2009. "Mac Giollarnáth (Mac Giolla An Átha; Forde), Seán." In *Dictionary of Irish Biography*, edited by J. McGuire and J. Quinn. Cambridge, UK: Cambridge University Press.

Nagy, Joseph Falaky. 2001. "Observations on the Ossianesque in Medieval Irish Literature and Modern Irish Folklore." *Journal of American Folklore* 114 (454): 436–46.

Nic Dhonncha, Róisín. 2004. "An tOireachtas agus an Amhránaíocht ar an Sean-nós: Cruthú agus Sealbhú Traidisiúin." *Bliainiris* 5:28–84.

Nic Giolla Chomhaill, Ailbhe. 2018. *Solas i nDorchadas: Staidéar sochchultúrtha ar scéalta draíochta as Dúiche Sheoigheach*. PhD Thesis, NUI Galway. http://hdl.handle.net/10379/7168.

———. 2019. "An saol i scáthán an scéil: léamh soch-chultúrtha ar scéal iontais a d'inis Mícheál Breathnach ón Mhám, Contae na Gaillimhe." *ComharTaighde* 5:1–17. https://doi.org/10.18669/ct.2019.02.

Ní Fhlathartaigh, Ríonach. 1976. *Clár Amhrán Bhaile na hInse.* Dublin: An Clóchomhar. [See also uí Ógáin, Ríonach]

Ó Catháin, Brian. 2004. "Oidhche Sheanchais le Robert J. Flaherty: An Chéad Scannán Gaeilge dá nDearnadh." In *Bliainiris 2004*, Ráth Chairn: Carbad, 151–234.

Ó Catháin, Séamus. 2008. *Formation of a Folklorist: Sources relating to the visit of James Hamilton Delargy (Séamus Ó Duilearga) to Scandanavia, Finland, Estonia and Germany 1 April – 29 September 1928.* Dublin: The Folkore of Ireland Council.

Ó Ceannabháin, Peadar, ed. 1983. *Éamon a' Búrc: scéalta.* Dublin: An Clóchomhar.

Ó Cearbhaill, Diarmuid. 2007. "Full of the Old Galway Spirit: The O'Kellys of Creeraun and Cooloo." *Journal of the Galway Archaeological and Historical Society* 59:72–95.

Ó Colchúin, Dónall. 1995. "Seán Mac Giollarnáth 1880–1970." In *Iris an Phléaráca 1995*, Conamara: Coiste an Phléaráca, 12–13.

Ó Con Cheanainn, Tomás. 2002. "Seanchas ar Mhuintir Laidhe." *Éigse* 33:179–225.

Ó Crualaoich, Gearóid. 2017. "Folkloristic and Ethnological Studies in Ireland." In *Irish Ethnologies*, edited by Diarmuid Ó Giolláin. Indiana: University of Notre Dame Press.

Ó Crualaoich, Gearóid and Diarmuid Ó Giolláin. 1988. "Folklore in Irish Studies." *The Irish Review* 5:68–74.

Ó Curnáin, Brian. 1999. "Observations on a Recent Edition of Recorded Speech from Conamara." *Éigse* 31:135–58.

———. 2007. *The Irish of Iorras Aithneach, Co. Galway.* 4 vols. Dublin: DIAS.

———. 2016. "Amhrán faoin bportach as Carna." *Éigse* 39:226–30.

Ó Duilearga, Séamus. 1932. "Editorial Notes." *Béaloideas* 3: 500–01.

———. 1960. "Sir Slanders, Mac Rí i n-Éirinn." *Béaloideas* 28:65–78. [See also Delargy, James Hamilton]

———. 1962. "Trí Shean-Scéal." *Béaloideas* 30:121–55.

Ó Fotharta, Domhnall. 1892. *Siamsa an gheimhridh.* Dublin: Patrick O'Brien.

O'Flaherty, Roderic, and James Hardiman. 1978. *A Chorographical Description of West or H-Iar Connaught : Written A.D. 1684.* Galway, Ireland: Kenny's Bookshops and Art Galleries.

Ó Giolláin, Diarmuid. 2000. *Locating Irish Folklore: Tradition, Modernity, Identity*. Cork: Cork University Press.

Ó Glaisne, Risteard. 1974. *Ceannródaithe*. Westport: Foilseacháin Náisiúnta Teoranta.

Ó Héalaí, Pádraig. 1996–7. "Liam Mac Coisdeala." *Béaloideas* 64/65:356–61.

Ó hÍde, Tomás. 2019. *Seáinín Tom Sheáin: From Árainn to the Silver Screen*. Dublin: Comhairle Bhéaloideas Éireann.

Ó hÓgáin, Daithí. 1999. "The Mystical Island in Irish Folklore." In *Islanders and Water-Dwellers: Proceedings of the Celtic-Nordic-Baltic Folklore Symposium held at University College Dublin 16–19 June 1996*, edited by P. Lysaght, S. Ó Catháin, and D. Ó hÓgáin. Dublin: DBA Publications Ltd. for the Department of Irish Folklore, UCD, 247–60.

Ó hUiginn, Ruairí. 1992–1993. "Tomás S. Ó Máille, 1904–1990." *Nomina* 16:134–35.

———. 1994. "Gaeilge Chonnacht." In *Stair na Gaeilge: in ómós do Phádraig Ó Fiannachta*, edited by Kim McCone et al. Maigh Nuad: An Sagart, 539–609.

———. 1997. "Tomás Ó Máille." In *Léachtaí Cholm Cille 27: Scoláirí Gaeilge*, Maigh Nuad: An Sagart, 83–122.

O'Leary, Philip. 1994. *The Prose Literature of the Gaelic Revival, 1881–1921: Ideology and Innovation*. Pennsylvania: Pennsylvania State University Press.

———. 2004. *Gaelic Prose in the Irish Free State 1922–1939*. Dublin: University College Dublin Press.

———. 2011. *Writing beyond the Revival: Facing the Future in Gaelic Prose, 1940–1951*. Dublin: University College Dublin Press.

Ó Máille, Tomás. 1934. *Micheál Mac Suibhne agus Filidh an tSléibhe*. Dublin: Oifig an tSoláthair.

Ó Murchadha, Gearóid. 1934. Review of *Peadar Chois Fhairrge*. *Béaloideas* 4, no. 4 (1934): 462–63.

Ó Murchú, Séamas. 1998. *Gaeilge Chonamara*. Dublin: Institiúid Teangeolaíochta Éireann.

Ó Súilleabháin, Seán. 1952. *Scéalta Cráibhtheacha*. Dublin: An Cumann le Béalóideas Éireann.

———. 1970. *A Handbook of Irish Folklore*. Detroit: Singing Tree Press.

———. 1973. *Storytelling in Irish Tradition*. Cork: Mercier Press.

Ó Súilleabháin, Seán, and William Caulfield. 2011. *Miraculous Plenty: Irish Religious Folktales and Legends*. Dublin: Comhairle Bhéaloideas Éireann, An Cumann le Béaloideas Éireann.

Partridge, Angela. 1980–1981. "Ortha an triúr bráithre: traidisiún meánao-iseach i mbéaloideas na Gaeilge." *Béaloideas* 48–49:188–203. [See also Bourke, Angela]

———. 1983. *Caoineadh na dTrí Muire: téama na Páise i bhfilíocht bhéil na Gaeilge*. Dublin: An Clóchomhar.

Rees, Alwyn, and Brinley Rees. 1961. *Celtic Heritage*. London: Thames & Hudson.

Robinson, Tim. 1990. *Connemara. Part 1: Introduction and Gazetteer*. Roundstone: Folding Landscapes.

———. 1997. *Setting Foot on the Shores of Connemara and Other Writings*. Dublin: The Lilliput Press.

———. 2006. *Connemara: Listening to the Wind*. Dublin: Penguin Ireland.

———. 2008. *Connemara: The Last Pool of Darkness*. Dublin: Penguin Ireland.

———. 2011. *Connemara: A Little Gaelic Kingdom*. Dublin: Penguin Ireland.

Stenson, Nancy, ed. 2003. *An Haicléara Mánas: A Nineteenth-Century Text from Clifden, Co. Galway*. Dublin: DIAS.

Uí Chollatáin, Regina. 2004. *An Claidheamh Soluis agus Fáinne an Lae 1899–1932: Anailís ar phríomhnuachtán Gaeilge ré na hAthbheochana*. Dublin: Cois Life Teoranta.

———. 2016. "Ó Chéitinn go Conradh: The Revivalists and the 1916 Rising." *Studies in Arts and Humanities* 2 (1): 52–66.

Uí Laighléis, Gearóidín. 2017. *Gallán an Ghúim: Caidreamh an Stáit le Scríbhneoirí na Gaeilge: Máirtín Ó Cadhain, Seosamh Mac Grianna agus Seán Tóibín*. Dublin: Coiscéim.

uí Ógáin, Ríonach. 1996–1997a. "Colm Ó Caodháin and Séamus Ennis: a Conamara Singer and His Collector." *Béaloideas* 64/65:279–338. [See also Ní Fhlathartaigh, Ríonach]

———. 1996–1997b. "Proinnsias de Búrca (1904–1996)." *Béaloideas* 64/65:353–55.

———. 2009. *Going to the Well for Water: The Séamus Ennis Field Diary 1942–1946*. Cork: Cork University Press.

———. 2017. "Séamus Ó Duilearga's *Leabhar Sheáin Í Chonaill* (1948), translated as *Seán Ó Conaill's Book* (1981)." *Journal of Folklore Research* 54 (3): 285–91.

———. 2021. *Colm Ó Caodháin*. Cork: Cork University Press.

Vendryes, Joseph. 1953–54. "Manannán mac Lir." *Études Celtiques* 6:239–54.

Wagner, Heinrich. 1958–69. *Linguistic Atlas and Survey of Irish Dialects.* 4 vols. Dublin: DIAS.

Wakeman, W. F. 1852. *A Week in the West of Ireland.* Dublin: Hodges and Smith.

Wigger, Arndt. 2004. *Caint Ros Muc.* 2 vols. Dublin: DIAS.

Williams, Sean and Lillis Ó Laoire. 2011. *Bright Star of the West: Joe Heaney, Irish Song Man.* Oxford: OUP.

MAPS

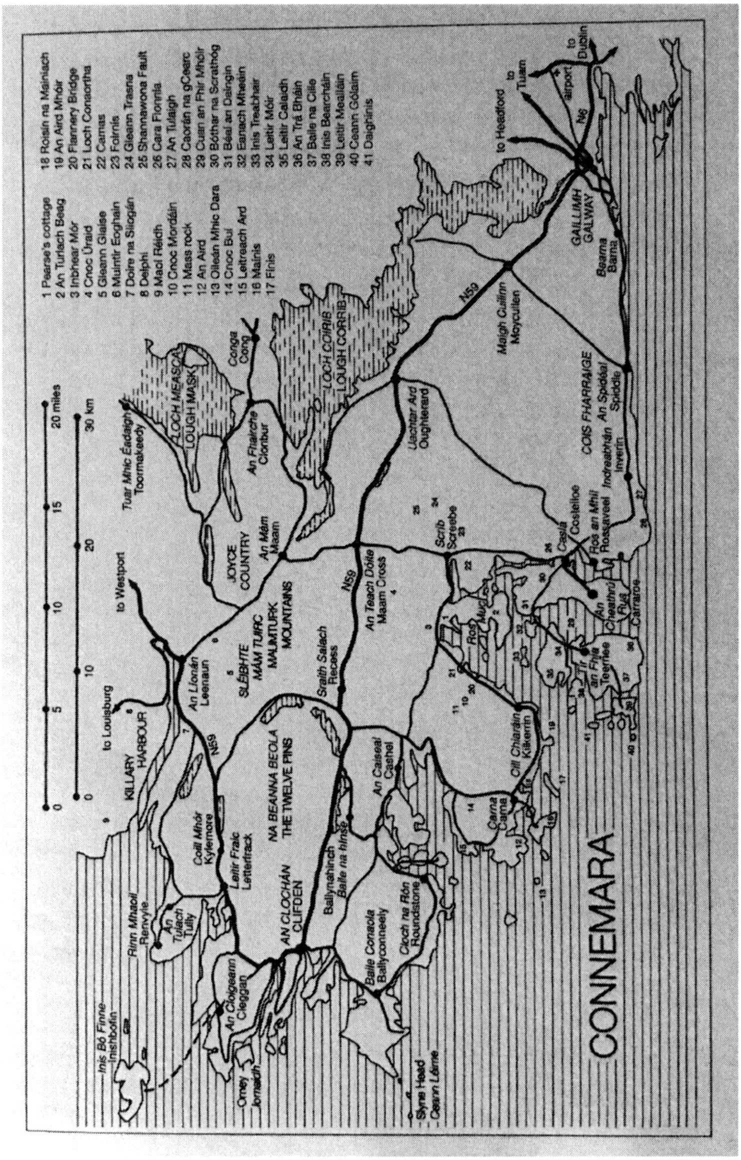

Map 1 Small scale map of Connemara, based on the cartography of Tim Robinson, Folding Landscapes, 1990.

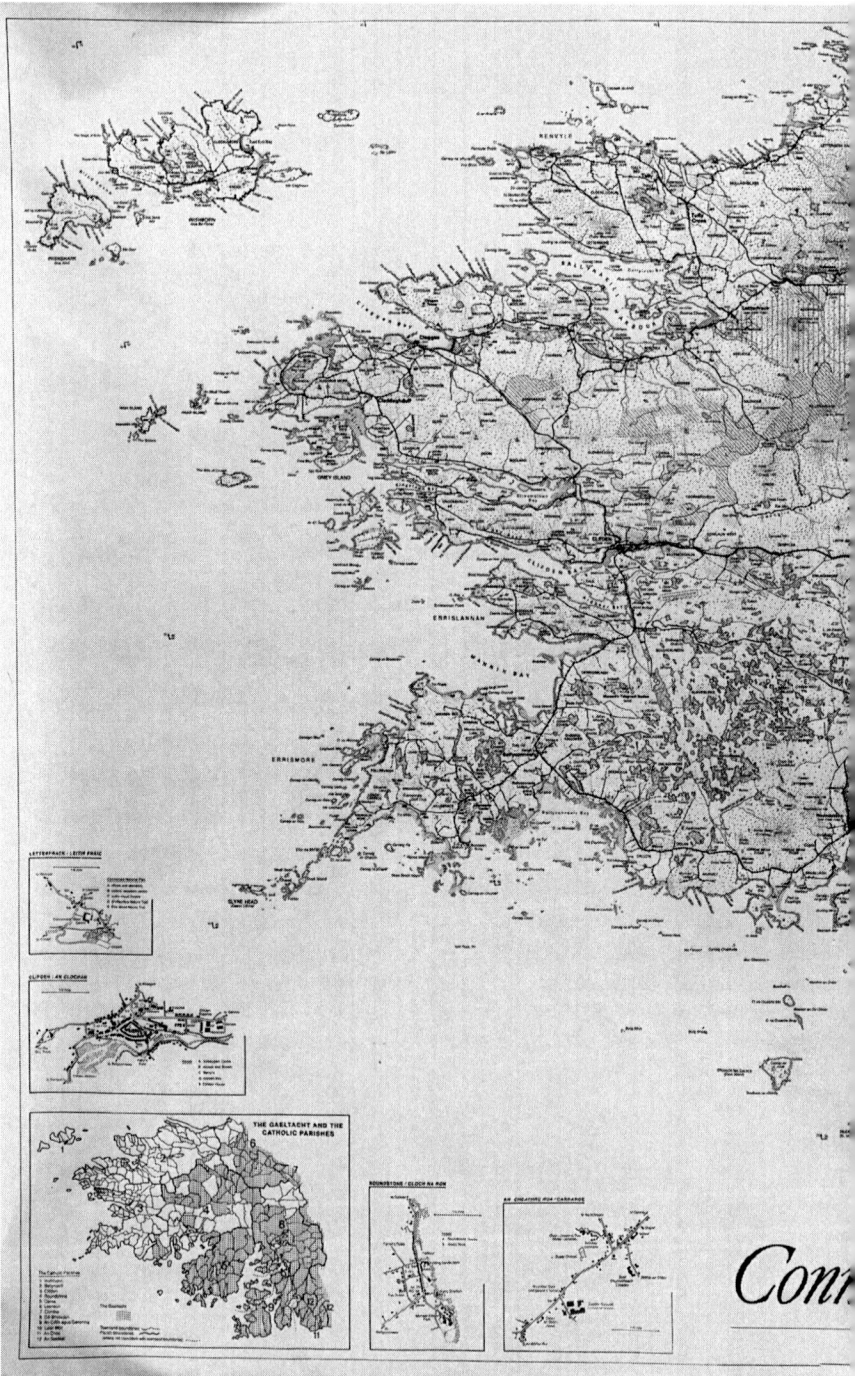

Map 2 Map of Iorras Aithneach (1:63, 360), based on the cartography of
Tim Robinson, Folding Landscapes, 1990.

CONNEMARA
Part 2 a one-inch map
reraitructed and drawn by Tim Robinson
published by Folding Landscapes
Roundstone Co. Galway, Éire

NA SOILEÁIN

AUTHOR BIOGRAPHIES

SEÁN MAC GIOLLARNÁTH (1880–1970) was a writer, judge, and folklore collector in his native Co. Galway. A key figure in the Irish cultural revival, he combined a long career as a District Justice with the compilation of folktales and traditional lore from collaborators in Conamara and beyond. Originally published in 1941, *Conamara Chronicles* is a treasury of traditional lore and folk history.

LIAM MAC CON IOMAIRE (1937–2019) was a teacher, journalist, and writer from Casla, Co. Galway. Major publications include biographies of Breandán Ó hEithir and Seosamh Ó hÉanaí, and, in collaboration with Tim Robinson, *Graveyard Clay* (Yale, 2016), the translation of Máirtín Ó Cadhain's novel *Cré na Cille* (1949). He was an acknowledged authority on Irish language usage and traditional singing in Irish.

TIM ROBINSON (1935–2020) was born in Yorkshire in 1935, studied maths at Cambridge, and worked as a visual artist in Istanbul, Vienna, and London. He moved to the Aran Islands in 1972 and commenced a multi-decade project of mapping and writing about Aran, the Burren, and Connemara. He was the author of the two-volume *Stones of Aran* and the Connemara trilogy. The translation of *Conamara Chronicles* was his final collaboration with Liam Mac Con Iomaire.

PLACENAME INDEX